THE BURIAL

OF THE

COUNT OF ORGAZ

& OTHER POEMS

THE
BURIAL
OF THE
COUNT OF ORGAZ
& OTHER POEMS
BY
PABLO PICASSO

EDITED WITH TRANSLATIONS BY
JEROME ROTHENBERG & PIERRE JORIS

WITH THE ASSISTANCE OF
DAVID BALL, PAUL BLACKBURN, MANUEL BRITO,
ANSELM HOLLO, ROBERT KELLY,
SUZANNE JILL LEVINE, RICARDO NIRENBERG,
DIANE ROTHENBERG, COLE SWENSON, ANNE WALDMAN,
JASON WEISS, MARK WEISS, & LAURA WRIGHT

AFTERWORD BY MICHEL LEIRIS

EXACT CHANGE ∗ CAMBRIDGE ∗ 2004

Originally published in French as *Écrits*
© 1989 Éditions Gallimard and Pablo Picasso
© 1989 Spadem Paris

Ouvrage publié avec le soutien du Ministère Français de la Culture
Grateful acknowledgment is made to the French Ministry of Culture
for financial assistance in the preparation of this translation

Cover photograph by Pablo Picasso: "Self-Portrait in the Studio at Villa Voiliers"
© Estate of Pablo Picasso / Artist Rights Society (ARS), New York
Courtesy Réunion des Musées Nationaux / Art Resource, New York
Inside cover: manuscript pages from "The Parchment Notebook"

Exact Change books are edited by Damon Krukowski and designed by Naomi Yang

Exact Change
5 Brewster Street, Cambridge, MA 02138
www.exactchange.com

Distributed by D.A.P. / Distributed Art Publishers
155 Sixth Avenue, 2nd floor, New York, NY 10013
www.artbook.com

Printed in Canada on acid-free paper

CONTENTS

PRE-FACE

*I abandon sculpture engraving and painting to dedicate
myself entirely to song.*
PICASSO TO JAIME SABARTÉS, APRIL 1936

When we were compiling *Poems for the Millennium* we sensed
that Picasso, if he wasn't *fully* a poet, was incredibly close to the
neighboring poets of his time, and when he brought language
into his cubist works, the words collaged from newspapers were
there as something really to be read. What only appeared to us
later was the body of work that emerged from 1935 on and that
showed him to have been a poet *in the fullest sense* and possibly,
as Michel Leiris points out, "an insatiable player with words...
[who, like] James Joyce... in his *Finnegans Wake*,... displayed an
equal capacity to promote language as a real thing (one might
say)... and to use it with as much dazzling liberty."

It was in early 1935, then, that Picasso (then fifty-four years
old) began to write what we will present here as his poetry — a
writing that continued, sometimes as a daily offering, until the
summer of 1959. In the now standard Picasso myth, the onset of
the poetry is said to have coincided with a devastating marital
crisis (a financially risky divorce, to be more exact), because of
which his output as a painter halted for the first time in his life.
Writing — as a form of poetry using, largely, the medium of
prose — became his alternative outlet. The flow of words begins

abruptly ("privately" his biographer Patrick O'Brian tells us) on
April 18, 1935, while in retreat at Boisgeloup. (He would lose the
country place the next year in a legal settlement.) The pace is
rapid, violent, pushing and twisting from one image to another,
not bothering with punctuation, often defying syntax, expressive
of a way of writing/languaging that he had never tried before:

> *if I should go outside the wolves would come to eat out*
> *of my hand just as my room would seem to be outside of*
> *me my other earnings would go off around the world*
> *smashed into smithereens*

as one of us has tried to phrase it in translation.

Yet if the poems begin with a sense of personal discomfort
and malaise, there is a world beyond the personal that enters
soon thereafter. For Picasso, like any poet of consequence, is a
man fully into his time and into the terrors that his time pres-
ents. Read in that way, "the world smashed into smithereens" is
a reflection also of the state of things between the two world
wars — the first one still fresh in mind and the rumblings of the
second starting up. *That's the way the world goes at this time or
any other*, Picasso writes a little further on, not as the stricken
husband or the discombobulated lover merely, but as a man, like
the aforementioned Joyce, caught in the "nightmare of history"
from which he tries repeatedly to waken.* It is the time and
place where poetry becomes — for him as for us — the only lan-
guage that makes sense.

---

*Or Picasso himself: *"history's bottom of the heart which has us by the throat neither
more nor less."* (10.2.37) And again: *"That death could fall from heaven on so many,
right in the middle of rushed life, had a great meaning for me."* (Interview with Simone
Gauthier, 1967)

That anyway is where we position Picasso and how we read him.

As with his work as a painter, such a reading can take off in multiple directions. The poetry is centered, first and foremost, on this person writing day by day — no titles as such for most poems but dates only and occasional markers of the times and places where the poems are being written (Paris, Juan-les-Pins, Cannes, Boisgeloup, Mougins, or, still more specifically: the Café de la Régence or the Antibes train). But the field of the present is further expanded by a sense of history and of events unravelling around him. It is our contention in fact that the writings throughout are set against a ground of present terror — implicit always but sometimes wholly foregrounded as in his *Dream and Lie of Franco*. Written in the same year as his memorialization of the bombing of Guernica and accompanied by an extraordinary suite of images in comic strip mode (the personal/political theme of the "weeping woman" is also first introduced here), this poem ends with a catalogue of people, animals, and things in dissolution:

> *cries of children cries of women cries of birds cries of flowers cries of wood and stone cries of bricks cries of furniture of beds of chairs of curtains of casseroles of cats and papers cries of smells that claw themselves of smoke that gnaws the neck of cries that boil in cauldron and the rain of birds that floods the sea that eats into the bone and breaks the teeth biting the cotton that the sun wipes on its plate that bourse and bank hide in the footprint left imbedded in the rock.*

If this is the shadow voice of great events, there are also the smaller ones gleaned from reports he reads or hears: *in the papers everyday misleading pictures of the families who beat their kids so that they can be copied by the likes of me who paint and sing.* And finally, in recollection of the pasted papers of his early cubist days, collages from the newspapers themselves:

> *Paris 14-12-35 ("Le Journal" 8-12-35 page 2)*
> *Maxima : on the ground — under shelter — minima — under shelter — maxima under shelter 755 millimeters (1.007) maximum + 5*
>
> . . . .
>
> *— Salon d'Automne, Grand Palais — French association for the Defense of Animals — Pasteur's precursors — martyrized or kidnapped children ... and the Christmas message — A.C. of 35 and 285 R.A.L. artistic matinée at 2 p.m. — after the call of the war dead and the minute of silence*

Since we are dealing here with what Robert Duncan liked to call a "multiphasic" poetry, the private and public worlds within the poems play off against deep images imbedded in the mind or, still more likely, in the seedbed of a culture. The tauromachian [bull fighting] symbols — as in the paintings also — are obvious and persistent, but along with them comes a range of other images drawn from folk memories and recollections* (Spanish, Catalan) or echoing a still more distant or occulted past. The tone throughout is raw, *transgressive* — a concept and mode later explored in the fiction and poetics of his acquaintance Georges Bataille. If it is sometimes (but rarely) sentimental and often (comically or tragically) self-disparaging, it strikes us with a Rabelaisian — or, maybe better yet,

---

*"*Critics have said that I was affected by Surrealist poetry as well as by family problems. Absolute nonsense! Basically I've always written the same way.... Poems about the postman or the priest.*" (Picasso to Roberto Otero, circa 1970, in Richardson, I.107)

Artaudian — ferocity; with secrets of the body: food and sex and all the lower human drives. And, like others in the French tradition he adopts, the work hums with new inversions (invocations, blasphemies) of catholic images and dogmas:

> *the festival of wheat there on the altar cloth the sepulchre the joyjoy portrait pissing the whole globe away with smells of fat cigars or playing ball beneath black curtains dribbling out its clear white egg wax daubing the glass windows of the wondrous reliquary's chest of drawers the lacy porker liquefied between the almond sheets* [6.7.40]

These intensities and densities come into the poetry before — at the time of Guernica and into "the war years" — they inform the paintings. They are in fact the markers of a transition in his work in general. And they enter there with a fullness and kaleidoscopic richness that language now allows him. As with other poets, there is a sense in which language is itself a part of the work he makes — the ways in which it can be made to reveal and equally to mask the life from which it issues. And as with other poets also, the thoughts on language and poesis aren't his alone but are shared visions. For Picasso, since his first entry to Paris and the larger art world, was in close contact with poets who were exploring language's limits in a way that paralleled his own workings with pictorial form and image. (He was also — it is now quite evident — a heavily engaged reader.*) His

---

*"There were many books in his home... detective or adventure novels side by side with our best poets: Sherlock Holmes and the publications of Nick Carter or Buffalo Bill with Verlaine, Rimbaud, and Mallarmé. The French eighteenth century, which he liked very much, was represented by Diderot, Rousseau, and Rétif de la Bretonne.... Thanks to Rimbaud and Mallarmé, it is certain that Picasso's work owes something to literature." (Maurice Reynal, 1922) And Christine Piot, citing this and much else adds: "As we see, his literary culture was most eclectic."

relations with Stein, Apollinaire, Jacob, and Reverdy remain a part of the Cubist myth a hundred or so years after the events themselves. The chalked sign over his studio door read AU RENDEZ-VOUS DES POÈTES, and the exchanges with poet friends would have been not only about the new painting but the new poetry as well. (The "new spirit" or "new mind," Apollinaire would call it in a famous essay.) Writes his principal biographer John Richardson about the ambience of what he calls Picasso's "think tank": "It enabled the artist to become vicariously a poet — a poet in paint, not yet a poet in words." And even so the verbally dense newspaper collages and isolated stencilled words that marked his Cubist canvases give us a measure of how far he had already gone in opening his art to language.

Through all his work in fact there was a "need for poetry"* (the phrase here is John Cage's, in relation to his own writings), and that need brought Picasso to an alignment — in the 1920s and 30s — with the younger poets who made up the core of Paris-based Surrealism. Prior to the 1924 *Manifesto of Surrealism* and the founding that December of *La Révolution Surréaliste*, members of the about-to-be Surrealist group countersigned Breton's essay "Hommage à Picasso," which appeared in the June 20th issue of *Paris-Journal*. From 1924 to 1929 works by Picasso were reproduced in eight of the eleven issues of *La Révolution Surréaliste*, and he was often cited by Breton and other poets as an exemplary Surrealist figure — "their prophet," Patrick O'Brian writes, with sufficient quotations to back it up. Or Breton, who had "claim[ed] him" as "one of us": "If

---

*"Picasso, after reading from a sketchbook containing poems in Spanish, says to me: *'Poetry — but everything you find in these poems one can also find in my paintings. So many painters today have forgotten poetry in their paintings — and it's the most important thing: poetry.'"* (Daniel-Henry Kahnweiler, 1959)

Surrealism is to adopt a line of conduct, it has only to pass where Picasso has already passed and where he will pass again."

In all of this — from Apollinaire and Stein to Breton and Paul Eluard — Picasso must have been fully into, fully aware of the poetry around him, and when he let it rip in April 1935, it wasn't as an isolated or naive voice but as a participant in what was then a verbal art in transformation. The poetry through much of 1936 was probably his dominant activity (the painting by most accounts had then been put aside), and he would often pursue it on an almost daily basis. It is hard to guess how much stock he put in it; Roland Penrose, who was close to him, speaks about "[his] reticence in showing his poems" and his "[lack of] pretensions about the quality of his poetry."* And yet when Stein dismissed the poems he read to her (and those of *all* other painters and Breton's as well), it probably marked the low point of a friendship which by then was almost over. "The egotism of a painter," she wrote and lectured him in explanation, "is an entirely different egotism than the egotism of a writer." And again: "This was his life for two years, of course he who could write, write so well with drawings and with colours, knew very well that to write with words was, for him, not to write at all."

By contrast the response of the younger French poets was immediate and strongly in Picasso's favor. Like Stein they recognized in Picasso's art a mode akin to writing, but where she would draw a line between the genres, they were open — enthusiastic even — to his crossing over into poetry as such. Because of

---

*But another account, decades later: "Picasso once told a friend that long after his death his writing would gain recognition and encyclopedias would say: 'Picasso, Pablo Ruiz — Spanish poet who dabbled in painting, drawing and sculpture.'" (Miguel Acoca, "Picasso Turns a Busy 90 Today," *International Herald Tribune*, 25 October 1971)

that the first publication of the poems came shortly after he started writing — a curiosity since, for all his reputation, he published only rarely after that. By the end of 1935, then, Breton had arranged a special issue of *Cahiers d'art*, with a number of Picasso's poems translated into French or shown in Spanish typescript, accompanied by Breton's own introduction ("Picasso poète") and shorter pieces by Eluard and Georges Hugnet. Of the poems' impact (bright, mysterious), Breton writes:

> The play of light and shadow has never been observed more tenderly or interpreted more subtly and lucidly; it keeps the poem within the bounds of the present moment, of the breath of eternity which that moment at its most fugitive contains within itself. Nothing is more characteristic of this than the care Picasso has taken to indicate in the text of several of these verse or prose poems the place, day and hour in which they were composed. We have the impression of being in the presence of an intimate journal, both of the feelings and of the senses, such as has never been kept before.

In writing this, Breton was aware as well — or seems to have been — that the actual process of the poems wasn't linear — all moving in the same direction — but that the written — the handwritten — works were circular or else, like palimpsests, were reaching out in all directions. If we're unable to show that hand-play, that concrete writing, in these pages, we would direct the reader of Picasso to those handwritten poems that consist — at least in part — "of words that appear to have been thrown onto the page without any preconceived links and that Picasso has joined together by red, yellow and blue lines in such a way

that they can be read in various directions [so] that the hand-
written page looks like a dew-laden spider's web under the first
rays of the morning sun."*

Poetry in this sense remains a fiercely formal undertaking, or
else an interplay, forever shifting, of form *and* content. In admit-
ting Picasso to his company of poets, Breton, whose 1924
Manifesto had announced a new surrealist poetry that would be
"psychic" at its core ("psychic automatism in its pure state"),
still could not evade its other, "formal" features. For Picasso, as
for Breton in his actual practice as a poet, the work of poetry
wasn't restricted to unmediated psychic acts or automatic writ-
ing, but subject, in its workings — however rapid — to a flux of
changes, scratch marks, and erasures. "*I am intent on resem-
blance*," he said, "*and resemblance more real than the real.... For
me surreality is nothing else, never has been anything else, than
that deep likeness far beyond the shapes and colors of immediate
appearance.*" (Picasso to the photographer Brassai) For this, from
Picasso's perspective, the issue was not "pure" automatism, but
something more impure, more unapologetically deliberate and
artful:

> "*Poems?*" he said to me, "*...when I began to write them I
> wanted to prepare myself a palette of words, as if I were
> dealing with colors. All these words were weighed, filtered
> and appraised. I don't put much stock in spontaneous*

---

*"After a swim, on the beach at Golfe-Juan, we are talking about Chinese characters
(*écriture*). A Chinese friend is drawing Chinese characters on the sand. Picasso had
amused himself before by drawing his own ideograms in the sand: bulls, goats, faces of
peace. He is fascinated by the interplay of Chinese characters, the strengths and econ-
omy of their construction. '*If I were born Chinese,*' says he, '*I would not be a painter but
a writer. I'd write my pictures.*'" (Claude Roy, 1956)

*expressions of the unconscious and it would be stupid to think that one can provoke them at will."** (Picasso to Louis Parrot, 1948)

If this represents a kind of *faux*-surrealism — and it does — it puts him closer to later practitioners, not unrelated to their Surrealist or Dada forerunners but clearly divergent as well. He is willing also, like poets of all persuasions, to sometimes move the oral or the auditory into the central position — *"not to tell stories or describe sensations, but to suggest them by the sounds of words."* (Picasso to Sabartés, 1946) It is clear too — here as elsewhere — that *Picasso poète*, like other poets worth a backward glance, makes his own moves, the total configuration of which marks the achievement of his writing and, thereby, his vision. And if we trust him here — or trust those others who report his words — we must look to the music of his poems, both in their *melos* and in what Pound otherwise spoke of as "the dance of the intellect among words." With Picasso, suggests his French editor Marie-Laure Bernadac, that dance is "in the incantatory and monotone manner of flamenco or in the staccato rhythm of *taconeo*... the deep and disturbing chant of *cante hondo*."

His way is persistent — both sound and meaning — from its onset in 1935 to the culminating work (*The Burial of the Count of Orgaz*) in 1959. As with some other — but surely not all — early avant-gardists, punctuation is set aside, allowing thereby a

---

*And further: *"'The work of madmen,'* he told me, *'is always based on a law that has ceased to operate. Madmen are men who have lost their imagination. Their manual memory belongs to a realm of rigid mechanism. It is an infernal machine that breaks down and not an intelligence that progresses and constantly creates in order to progress. One cannot compare poems resulting from automatic writing with those of the insane. The work of a madman is a dead work; the poetry it contains is like the ghost which refuses to give up its corpse.'*

play between the apparent rush of writing and the ways that meaning comes into the works when read. Such unpunctuated prose blocks — coming at the time they do — are almost uniquely his and bring with them a number of other moves, exploring the varied possibilities of what Bernadac calls "this new 'plastic material' [of language]... chipping, pulverizing, modeling this 'verbal clay,' varying combinations of phrases, combining words, either by phonic opposition, repetition, or by an audacious metaphorical system, the seeming absurdity of which corresponds in fact to an internal and personal logic.... Lawless writing, disregardful of syntax or rationality, but which follows the incessant string of images and sensations that passed through his head." (The lack of titles and their replacement by the dates of composition is another marker of his work, as are various rearrangements of words and phrases from one text to another, "as if he were moving paper cutouts in a painting or drawing." [C. Piot])

In all of this there are two languages through which he writes — the Spanish of his childhood and the French to which he came by incremental stages — and possibly a third, unwritten one as well, the Catalan he spoke with friends and that may be a hidden stream beneath the others. It is however the Spanish that dominates the early poems, that never leaves him, and that emerges again in the final poem. But most of the work in between — including the two full-length plays, *Desire Caught By the Tail* and *The Four Little Girls*, not included in these pages — is written in his characteristic and idiosyncratic French. (Sometimes also he translates himself from one language into the other.) Picasso's writing is — in that sense, and in others as well — what one of us has called a rhizomatic or nomadic art, that is a writing not at home (i.e. settled and at rest in some

convention or other) but always *"unterwegs,"* — on the way —
as Paul Celan put it.*

It is curious now — having moved out of Picasso's own cen-
tury — to find how close the written work is to what would later
become a postmodernism working through and struggling with
the more "experimental" and "lawless" sides of modernism. For
this Picasso's poetry stands without further comment on his part.
It is at points prolific — when he seems to work it as a day-by-
day endeavor — and it plays out as a denser and often more
intimate complement to his even more prolific art. (It has a
resemblance in this sense to the Minotaur engravings
[*Minotauromachy*] — in which the painter/sculptor also plays a
role — first issued like the poems in 1935 and carried forward
like them in the later work.) There are also the two plays among
his writings, one of which, *Desire Caught by the Tail* (1941),
became his best known written work, translated often (including
a venture into German by Paul Celan) and performed by experi-
mental groups throughout the world.** Still there's very little
publication over all and virtually no poetics or written state-
ments about poetry (or art — his own or others' — for that
matter). This leaves us dependent for such statements on his
biographers or on the numerous witneses reporting "conversa-
tions with Picasso." Some of those we've presented here as
footnotes — radical insights sometimes and always with that

---

*A fuller exploration of the nomadics theme in Picasso's poetry follows this pre-face.

**The initial perfromance/reading took place (March 19, 1944) at Michel Leiris's
place in Paris, with "actors" who included the Leirises (Michel and Louise), Jean-Paul
Sartre, Simone de Beauvoir, Raymond Queneau, Jean Aubier, and Dora Maar. The
director was Albert Camus and the musical accompaniment was by Georges Hugnet.

sense of poetry's centrality and presence* that was a given for
the artists and the poets (even the "antipoets") of his time.

Our own work here is derived from *Picasso: Ecrits*, a massive
and heavily illustrated volume (some three hundred and forty
dated texts in all) published by Gallimard in 1989. (The identi-
cal volume was published by Aurum Press in London, with only
the introductory essay by Leiris and essays on Picasso's poetry
and written work by Bernadac and her co-editor Christine Piot
translated into English.) We have accordingly been dependent
on the *Ecrits* for transcriptions of the work, which retain many
— but certainly not all — of the manuscripts' particularities.
While we have made do with what we were given, we might
have preferred to work with the poems in their more rough and
ready forms or, of still more interest, to attempt translations that
would show the way Picasso positioned his words in the act of
composition. At the same time, however, we recognize that too
visual a representation — at least at this juncture — would like-
ly detract from our contention that Picasso as a poet of words —
even a "language poet," if we can use that term — is a force and
a presence not to be ignored.

For the time being, then, it's worth noting Picasso's own com-
ments about the irregularities of grammar and spelling in his
written work: "If I begin correcting the mistakes you speak of
according to rules with no relation to me, I will lose my individ-
uality to grammar I have not incorporated. I prefer to create
myself as I see fit than to bend my words to rules that don't
belong to me." (Picasso quoted by Sabartés, 1946) There is an
assertiveness here, a playfulness reminiscent of Fluxus artists

---

*"*Painting is never prose*," he declared to Françoise Gilot, "*it is poetry, it is written in
verse with plastic rhymes [...] Painting is poetry*."

and Beat poets of a later generation — even more so in the
account (again by Sabartés) of Picasso's truly innovative projec-
tion of a work — like William Blake's perhaps, or Mallarmé's —
that broke new and outrageous ground for the presentation of
language:

> The book Picasso would like to create would be a perfect
> reflection of his personality and the most faithful por-
> trait of the artist. In its spontaneity, we would see his
> own disorder. Each page would be a true "potpourri,"
> without the slightest hint of organization or composi-
> tion. There would be letters and numbers, aligned and
> non-aligned, sometimes parallel, sometimes perfectly
> horizontal, now ascending, now descending, as if written
> by one unaccustomed to script, or driven by enthusiasm
> or impatience. There would be notes, scribbles and
> splotches, additions between the lines, arrows pointing to
> sentences in the margins, figures and objects, sometimes
> entirely comprehensible, sometimes less easy and read-
> able.* Simplicity and complexity would be united as in
> his paintings, his drawings or his texts, as in a room in
> his apartment or his studio, as in himself.... Picasso
> confided this layout to me, or better, this image of his
> dream book, one morning in the month of July (1939).

Unrealized as most such schemes have been, this brings us to the
boundaries none the less of what Maurice Blanchot would later
call "the book to come."

In the actual books, then — the writings left behind —
something similar prevails. Some of the writing was in a little

---

*"A few attempts at illegible writing or writings with 'unknown words' appeared in
1938 and 1949." (Christine Piot) See page 154.

notebook that he carried with him;* also, we're told, "[on] draw-
ing paper, letter paper, backs of envelopes, backs of invitations,
pieces of newspaper and even sheets of toilet paper." (M.-L.
Bernadac and C. Piot) His instruments were "black or colored
pencils [...], blue-black ink (in 1939-1940), ballpoint pens or
markers (in 1951 and 1959)." From 1935 to 1939 poems (in
highly calligraphic, highly visual form) "were directly written
or recopied in India ink on sheets of Arches paper" and were
then gathered together in portfolios. Others were written in
larger notebooks, a couple of which give titles to the poem cycles
in our book. In addition some of the manuscripts — most of
those on Arches paper, for example — were typed by Sabartés,
the visual elements stripped away, as if in preparation for read-
ing and/or publication of the texts as such.

As editors of the present work we have been constrained —
as stated above — to work with such typed versions and with the
texts transposed further into the uniform typography of print-
ers' fonts. In the resultant Gallimard edition the poems appear
in their original Spanish or French (the French outnumbering
the Spanish by some two hundred to one hundred forty texts)
and with the Spanish ones further translated, usually by the edi-
tors, into French. For our own division of labor, Joris has
concentrated on the French writings and Rothenberg on the
Spanish, and we have invited contributions by a range of con-
temporary poets/translators as a mark of Picasso's entry into
our own time. Of these the most radical translator is Paul
Blackburn, who shifts Picasso's medium from prose to verse. (He
was also of course the first important American poet to bring

---

* *"writing in his small notebook — elbows sticking out one more than the other over the
table's edge — the left hand holding the already written page the other on the paper —
the point of the pencil here — where I press it"* (Picasso, 3 november XXXV)

Picasso into English.) With the others who have joined us here, the invitation was to translate a small selection each and otherwise to make their own decisions as to form and voice. In both our own work and in theirs, the choice has been to stay with the text while creating, in various ways, a work that speaks in a demotic, largely American English and that stresses exuberance over a probably futile "literalism." We have remembered too that in this kind of writing — as in much of our own — meaning is slippery and has, like our desires, to be caught (again and again) by the tail.

The result is a reflection of the past that is also, we would urge, a beacon for our workings in the present.*

— JEROME ROTHENBERG, WITH PIERRE JORIS
NOVEMBER 2003, ENCINITAS, CALIFORNIA

PRINCIPAL WORKS CITED

Dore Ashton (ed.), *Picasso on Art: A Selection of Views*. New York: Da Capo Press, Inc., 1972.

Marie-Laure Bernadac and Christine Piot (eds.), *Picasso: Ecrits*. Paris: Editions Gallimard, 1989.

Paul Blackburn (translator), *Hunk of Skin* by Pablo Picasso. San Francisco: City Lights Books, 1968.

Patricia Leighten, *Re-Ordering the Universe: Picasso and Anarchism, 1897-1914*. Princeton, New Jersey: Princeton University Press, 1989.

Marilyn McCully (ed.), *A Picasso Anthology*. Princeton, New Jersey: Princeton University Press, 1981.

---

*In my own case, a special acknowledgement must be made to Manuel Brito, who looked over all my translations from the Spanish and kept me more on the mark than I might otherwise have been. (J.R.)

Steven A. Nash (ed.), *Picasso and the War Years 1937-1945*. New York and London: Thames and Hudson, 1998.

Patrick O'Brian, *Pablo Ruiz Picasso: A Biography*. New York: W.W. Norton & Company, 1976.

John Richardson, *A Life of Picasso*, volumes one and two. New York: Random House, 1991, 1996.

Gertrude Stein, *Picasso*. London: B.T. Batsford Ltd., 1938.

THE
NOMADISM
OF
PICASSO

Superficially one could argue that Picasso's nomadism is most visible in his switching of languages, leaving the Spanish mother tongue to write in French (both languages, as already indicated, probably ghosted by Catalan at some level). And yet the question of a nomadic writing is not necessarily rooted in the writer giving up the mother tongue — as, indeed, Picasso never completely does. Rather, the matter of a nomadic writing is anchored elsewhere, specifically in the syntactic and grammatical manipulations the given language is subjected to, in order to free it from a range of traditional constraints. Picasso's writing is thus nomadic in terms of its free flows, unhampered by the sedentarizing effects of normative grammar, syntax and discursive forms. To use the terms of Deleuze & Guattari, the lines of flight of a Picasso poem (and they *are* lines "of flight" also in the more traditional poetic definition) are never reterritorialized, are never re-inscribed onto the grid of just "literature." One need only compare his writing to that of, say, Breton to see the absolute difference: despite Breton's call for a "pure psychic automatism" that would break social and literary norms & barriers by the very speed of the writing (*vitesse v.v.v.,* etc.), few

writers — be it in poetry or prose — compose in a more tradi-
tionally rhetorical, not to say high classical, French *style* than
Breton himself.

Picasso, the non-French artist and poet, has the considerable
advantage of not being burdened by built-in or acquired stylistic
grids that would contain or modulate his explorations. He *raids*
this foreign language (raids that he has already practiced on
the mother tongue, i.e. the language of the country he has by
now long left behind) — and the core principles or rather the
practical engines are a nonstop process of connectivity and het-
erogeneity along the entire semiotic chains of the writing, the
characteristics of a rhizomatic and nomadic writing. The way
this plays itself out in Picasso's poems can be traced not only in
the heterogeneity of the objects, affects, phenomena, concepts,
sensations, vocabularies etcetera that can and do enter the writ-
ing at any given point, but mainly at the level of the assembling
of these heterogeneities: eschewing syntax and its hierarchical
clausal structures, the writing proceeds nomadically by paratac-
tic relations between terms on a "plane of consistency" that
produce concatenations held together (& simultaneously separat-
ed) either by pure spatial metonymical juxtapositions or by the
play of the two conjunctions "and" or "of." One could of course
claim parataxis as a category of syntaxis, though it seems to me
that in Picasso's writing the very exorbitant use made of the
paratactic process suggests that one may better see this process
— in Giorgio Agamben's word — as "atactic." How traditional
conjunctions and prepositions function in such nomadic atactic
semantic chains is worth a closer look.

Because of their repetitive omnipresence — they seem to be
evenly distributed or, rather, used with equal ferocity, joy and
energy throughout the writing from 1935 to 1959, with the pos-
sible exception of the plays — these conjunctions lose any causal

or subordinating effects they have in traditional syntactical con-
structions. The conjunction "and," maybe the most basic
ligature in our languages, is in Picasso — just as it is in chil-
dren's telling and, at times, in epic narrative — a pure
accelerator of action, a way of getting from one thing to the
next; its multiplicity immediately overcomes the (mis)use (as
brake) of this accelerator when present singly and made to func-
tion as a divider, separator, creator of dialectical or ontological
differentiations between two terms, and thus as the originator of
all dualisms (the good and the bad, the beautiful and the ugly).
Thus never just one "and," but always "and...and...and..." In
that sense the multiple "ands" do not set up one-to-one relations
between the terms they align, but function vectorially, pointing
to nomadic spaces outside and beyond those terms. As Deleuze
writes: "The AND is not even a specific relation or conjunction,
it is that which subtends all relations, the path of all relations,
which makes relations shoot outside their terms and outside the
set of their terms, and outside everything which could be deter-
mined as Being."* Or, to draw on Picasso's other art: his "ands"
are gestures: they resemble the arm movements of the painter,
picking up his brush, putting paint to canvas, dropping his arm,
picking the brush up again, and so forth. "And," then, as a mus-
cle contracting/extending, an action, a speed that makes visible
a multiplicity of events.

   "Of" is, at first look, a different kind of conjunctive particle,
as grammatically it is considered a preposition, i.e. a word placed
before a substantive and indicating the relationship of that sub-
stantive to a verb, an adjective or another substantive. The
opening dictionary definition of "of" in the American Heritage

---

*Gilles Deleuze & Claire Parnet, *Dialogues*, New York, Columbia University Press
1987, page 57.

Dictionary reads: "Derived or coming from, originating at or from." And indeed, Picasso's "de" or "of," taken singly, can be read in that fashion. But, again, the concatenation of "of's," the rhizomatic *agencement* of this particle linking wildly heterogeneous series of terms, subverts any of its single or double genitive functions, forcing the reader to eventually relinquish causal/grammatical readings — something the translator, to his or her initial chagrin and frustration, experiences at first hand when approaching the poems. But this relinquishing of the desire to locate the specific semantic unit(s) from which a given term is supposed to be derived, leads the reader/translator to experience this endless chain of derivations as an ongoing forward drive or as what the Situationists called a *dérive* — lines of flight through language that empty any desire for origin, for an original, singular term a single "of" may point back to.

Finally, I would propose that the nomadicity of Picasso's language is further enhanced (syntactically as well as visually) by the radical lack of punctuation marks — those "traffic signals," as Theodor Adorno called them. As already suggested in the Preface, Picasso is the most radical of his era's practitioners of such a complete obliteration of punctuation marks. This gives his poems the feel of a wide open field, a smooth, non-striated space, or blocks of space, through or along which one can travel unchecked, free to chose one's own moment of rest, free to create one's own rhythms of reading — an exhilarating and liberating, dizzying and breathtaking *dérive.*

— Pierre Joris

On the Translators

Unless otherwise noted, all of Jerome Rothenberg's translations are from Picasso's Spanish and all of Pierre Joris's translations are from the French. Translators throughout are identified by their initials at the end of individual poems or of poems in series, with the breakdown between Spanish and French as follows:

SPANISH TRANSLATORS
[PB]   Paul Blackburn
[SJL] Suzanne Jill Levine
[RN]   Ricardo Nierenberg
[JR]   Jerome Rothenberg
[JW]   Jason Weiss
[MW]   Mark Weiss

FRENCH TRANSLATORS
[DB]   David Ball
[AH]   Anselm Hollo
[PJ]   Pierre Joris
[RK]   Robert Kelly
[DR]   Diane Rothenberg
[CS]   Cole Swenson
[AW]   Anne Waldman
[LW]   Laura Wright

Since both the titles and subtitles mostly take the form of dates, we are using the translators' initials [in brackets] to indicate the completion of an individual poem or of a poem series.

COLLECTED POEMS

PABLO PICASSO

if I should go outside the wolves would come to eat out of my hand just as my room would seem to be outside of me my other earnings would go off around the world smashed into smithereens but what is there to do today it's thursday everything is closed it's cold the sun is whipping anybody I could be and there's no helping it so many things come up so that they throw the roots down by their hairs out in the bull ring stenciled into portraits not to make a big deal of the day's allotments but today has been a winner and the hunter back with his accounts askew how great this year has been for putting in preserves like these and thus and so and always things are being left behind some tears are laughing without telling tales again except around the picture frame the news arrived that this time we would only see the spring at night and that a spider crawls across the paper where I'm writing that the gift is here the others putting ties on for the holidays that we've already had it for the nonce and that it's just the start this time around if they don't want a centipede then it's the horse and bull that sticks it into him so that the lights will come on afterwards and in the papers everyday misleading pictures of the families who beat their kids so that they can be copied by the likes of me who paint and sing again because the blackbirds at this time of year have always been like that they straighten themselves out if they can manage one more time and so the world goes on and if it wasn't for their own self interest none of them would leave his house without first taking it apart as well they can and this time it's my turn that makes it worthwhile clobbering this worthwhile man who doesn't strut his stuff day after day and if he hits the jackpot this time it's not his to win but goes to those dumb boobs ahead of him and one more time he'll end up in the small boat like you know and see ya later cuz today's a holiday and they've cut out like they were looking one more time to yank the stick back from the man who made it so the chestnuts would be roasted and if not for that to pull them out again the partridges would all return on their own steam because it's all a mess already and if not just have them say how many times what's true has been a lie and if it's still not they should count from one to two and three to seven the result would always come out wrong albeit of pure gold and if it doesn't pass this time around he simply swallows which is good stuff for the navel as it always has been in his house and in his neighbor's who is there inside and afterwards they're fried up and we have to take the plunge so that we may be always friends like always and that once for always not just for today to make your mind up just a little if they ask and let them pick the thread up seeing afterwards the fans they're holding fade away

and it's raining all the green is wet but feels like it was made of fire and on their hands turned over tiles are jumping for pure joy

and wringing hands with pinky missing on the one who made
me — sorceress — and after let them come to me to say they
have no time that we can save it for another day and it's now late
and that again and then already well the soup is nearly ready
and the spoonful that I have to take an hour before is loving me
because it's certain also that they'll tell me then that I forgot it
but this glassy air the raindrops on the window have their shad-
ows upside down so that you have to paint them from the bottom
up and if it wasn't so nobody would have made a single thing
forever

so let's go to see what's happening if someone has wheat spilling
from their hands it's only to blow hot and then blow cold so
when it's over there's no memory of what was said and seems
like an illusion that the wolves are no more righteous than the
turtledoves up in the olives that's the way the world goes at this
time or any other and contrariwise the waves are growing almost
tender and are crying out that it makes them believe in some-
thing other than themselves and later on they're banished and
are beaten down as if it wasn't any more than sticking on a
stamp and mailing them that even if they don't arrive there
with intentions clearly spelled out they can still be gussied up
with hats and sexy talk but things have always been like that and
someone's always telling me we should be careful that we
shouldn't do what others do not want that pears are good and so
chorizos are and grilled steaks with a frozen lemon squash and
even so in spite of everything you have to see what peoples when
it's nearly night are hiding inbetween their fingers as they gath-
er up the rain that later on will be their nest and if it were the
custom here to say I'll tell it all to you tomorrow no it's not the
same to do some little thing then jump into the lake because to
have to spin it out is not the siren's song I mean and get a move

on so that all we have to do is ring them bells and not to chop
wood in a single mortar when the tail end of the spindle is
enough. And afterwards if you don't see the sidewalk when it
throws the book at him and if he doesn't fall another woman can
be made his just because it's paid for and the only smells around
are from the beehive if some evening she gets lost she still will
fail to say that what is good isn't the hangman but the valencian
nights of fire that for the bullfights in the summer it's a small
thing in the kitchen and if you don't think so let them tell it to
you with your ears over their lips

and afterwards getting accustomed bit by bit and no one notic-
ing and carrying their destinies one behind the other no I don't
believe what folks are always saying unperturbed and tasteless
just the opposite of children and without your making them go
up and down so they can learn what they should want that
they're the teachers and some other time they'll come in with a
discount that they're ringing up because it's all a well known fact
that's what they are they're giving orders and they're talking
just the opposite of plants that are the most and least that's
what's been said and what's said now in all the school books

nothing more than that my little darling

so unknot your veil and tell your teacher that you're jealous that
it's all the same to me and if we trace a line from A to C and K to
T bypassing X and Y and subdividing D x H it's just the same as
what a parrot has so let them give it all to me I've seen it all a
thousand times and more I've got it clinched because it's neces-
sary to believe in mathematics and art is really something else

with the *curas* and their *culos* it's olé no way josé and the chick I

want to lay with a porkchop in her porgy and the swallows with
a switchblade clean and mean a little sky comes in between with
feet to prop the table up and some of those you know already
have packed whole armadas full of stuff their racks of yester-
year stacked up by nuns who are no more than the reflection of a
mirror in another mirror yes they have said it all before how
they climb up so high they gather up their skirts to make their
way under the bridge the stuff just isn't there nor do you brush it
with a knife not now and not until it's over that you have to see
what they are saying that they'll have to eat crow that I have said
it all before what shines no more is than the nose and has it and I
should not say that head for everyone is coming underneath the
covers the processions down there in your barrio I do no more
than lend an ear to what they're singing in the greenness keep-
ing quiet while the stones are cracking open dare I say it clearly
then the silence is a straw a curtain tell me all of you if some-
place else in place of doing what she has to do the california
nymph should not sit down in the reflection that she has to take
siesta hidden in her memory and as is natural why don't you all
stop hoarding signatures for making later into toothpicks or rein
in the disemboweled horse the flowers twist the bullring shoot-
ing sparks off from the sand in clocks with desiccated horn
batons all knotted up in their forgetful pockets softening them-
selves with them and taking off their stockings that are spread
out on the bull's horns so the blood rolls over them atop his cage
and turns a quart of saffron to two swords like ocean waves what
all the others would go out to gather in the secretary's flutes his
term left incomplete so you can see already that there is no rem-
edy in this small town of toads for so much shaking it with
fiddles in a game of chess of leather soles then growing into
silence they will stroke a nest for every one of them if they
should make it the reverse of all the others and the velvet coat

be strangled that way so it's better just to leave it so that when he
shows it in his portraits they can't tell him if he doesn't have the
right proportions they will get them from his neighbor seeing
it's unique and that what rubs against him is a beak that nips his
armpit and it's all a lie a mesh that's covering the back wall of
his rice house as he squats down in the corner underneath the
doorbell and the anguish of a branch tears through his heart he
takes a drink and senses in the heat of his horchata smells of
chocolate and coffee sprawled out on his bed in the valencian air
and throwing ice onto his hand before the window that which
india ink alone will not conceal and doing what his leg does dan-
gling outside has no remedy but to unpack the family jewels and
to build himself a boat and win in the regattas tempest tosst in
novice sugar ready now to set it up whatever comes on top of it
a hundred fires flames unmoving have expired from exhaustion
from the cries of chinese women from beyond the ice athwart
his foot while printed measurements are born from them
fatigued with waiting on the pile of spangles of the tuna fishes
also waiting that their secret be revealed that the toreros brought
about them in an auto without brakes unmuzzled also in some
other place as they themselves said not to recognize in them as if
the fault was in the sword to skewer the bouquet the bottle also
offer succor for his naked love of his own arm and it is true that
once the price they gave him rises then their hands will wring
the yellow from it and the thunder will conceal their shoes
inside his breast without a sense of shame one hundred and one
more besides are born again out in the hills and turning the dogs
loose the hunt files past in his receiving room just when the pot-
au-feu comes forth like sunrise on his table and it's afterwards
with curling-iron hairdos where the fleas nip at the bottles so
they make their contributions seem like sugar to the blind man
under sentence catapulting without rails offspring of canvases to

make the wheels endure sans stoppage cod fish that he sets into
his finger ring in profile and he makes a grill work out of all that
falls down from the tree transforms himself into a sergeant of
the peace for all of which may he be blesst now and forever on
the wall that no way imitates his shadow's raised relief the river
that divides him from it now the winesoaked buns the honey
plums and marinades of sausages and castanets so walk with her
the summer well nigh over tell her that they're giving you strict
orders old saws mussels nuts dates figs monks cold cuts lindens
socks snails wires pillars pigeons olives radishes and fathers
now step forward to the music elsewhere in the middle making
exercises with your thoughts on higher things and scrambled
eggs I had forgotten in my need for writing it the toenail of
the monkey in Anise del Mono I have always had recourse to
putting things aside until tomorrow letting off a yawn in
friendly conversation any christmas eve not making a big deal of
squeamishness and gypsy-style fandangos and recalling faces
that they made with smells of tar and silk of blisst-out moles
without applause but held back for hours sitting in first class
without an apron you yourself become a mutton stew without a
new pipe and it's clear all clear clear blue clear green clear pink
pale blue pale blue clear pink clear yellow pale clear clear pale
clear blue clear pale blue green clear clear pale clear pale blue
pale blue pale blue boneless thick skinned burns the prison of
his body without twist of ancient knot without a taste of
curtains making gnarly face of captive lily upon sleeves of
streetlamp tender hopes of nest in august or september thread
that twists its beak that counts on fingers with respite of snow
in summer on metallic table under trees the blood from turnips
isn't mortar soup for making garlic white which is hard diamond
without faith with clams on beach with ink of calamares the
diageneses gnaw the inner fruit of apples on a point of pin

oysters are born mad with love with orient and silence on the
back of soundless breasts the olive trees are all around them they
drive off their friends without a second number to the stirrup of
the hairless ape who shaves the mirror that the birds have
trimmed down and alone there with their fringes hauling wheat
stalks off with daggers and without the shadows of the twisted
paths of moon clocks blown apart a handkerchief that holds
some form of light the blond trunk of his honeyed sword the
cold bees are uncorking in his quilts and that his breath's enfold-
ing in his book and in the copper plates that reach the tower's
height of someone who has left his mark there and on track sets
his zambomba* on his table's floor mid waves and all the while
beats down his hatred as the other woman brought his voice
back to beginnings of the scale he fishes for it in his temple and
disrupts the peace he sways his hips the razor that befuddles
expectations underneath the stone the fissures crackle in the
mute shield that his sealed lips feel so bitter does the oil boil in
his mouth giddup giddap my garden maid put on your cap throw
down your spade and guess what square the disc runs o'er what
blind man's mouth insanely climbing always quickly in his duds
he scoops the weather cock the colored pencil up oh do melt
down your pleasure there in she-wolf's presence gobbling down
the safety pin tucked in between the folds of veil a little girl a
root a parchment strip and two stripes cutting the diagonal from
where it leaves the bedroom and pours forth the cluster the sum
total in the room that fronts the stroke of midday zanzibar elec-
tric booth who paddles his elastic life turned inside out his myths
intact discs perfect so his virtue's bunched up in the copper

---

*A drum used in southern Spain, the head of which is pierced by a small hole through
which a string is threaded. The string is scraped against the drum-head, producing a
continuous drone.

creases of his chair a little boy who rushes blue- and crosseyed
fragment of Trafalgar map we hear him in among reed curtains
shot of sherry twisty mouth who croons in Barcelona seated
betwixt pinewood hands amid the noise the silence of the ball-
room two o'clock at night with friends who fondle you poor
cricket we will see each other here again so if you can just tell it
to me just one letter at a time up on the wall the strip of hemp
hung up the sausage paring down his knife he lays out the atten-
dant gears who from his bed assists the bull in its deceptions and
kicks up a fuss the wine jug wakes the double spouted pitcher oil
lamp that the deaf man snuffs the brown skinned girl who
chews her finger pointing to his randy open fly and thus with
aches and pains the blueness of his prison taken up already by
all those who make their augusts boreal while shaking nuts and
cutting cards jack knight and king he's strutting the fandango
jump my pretty tell your mother that I'm dynamite and get your
big butt out of here today's the day there's nothing more than
once back of the rapid shadow where he twists the neck of all
his letters of exchange and for some other day I'll pay her for a
glance the cape transfixed with needles stains the tablecloth pro-
vided that it not be more than just a test of what to do what can
be done this morning beehive hair stained glass mid afternoon
in circus as in house of filthy folk there where they always wash
their hand which rips night's papers makes his tablecloth spill
blood on maytime flowers hiding in the earth his living secret
lightning rods and underneath his arm he holds the rainbow fast
asleep between the creases centipedes the carpet drawing stripes
across his finger weaves around her tit his spikenard origin so
that his reason fades in capuchin obstruction from his guard
receipts come without rhyme or reason and he grasps the brush-
work underneath the arrow makes the voice gallbitter to reflect
around the eye of paintbrush there atop the flute and doesn't

have the chimes that in the morning blind the well today in
the small bit of canvas and crisscrossed once more the iron nut
rebounds midst branches gathering the plaudits down to bottom
of the sea in stews more than a hundred years old once more hits
the target the spinal bone ceded to hatred and wound round the
spider's thread and your voice growing tender receiving the
smile that the mailman has brought you the concierge new born
her flag is unfurled the grenade going off in her hands like one
hundred fingers that lessen the years thus to bring in her voice a
glove if six ten and fourteen make two and a half at least if they
tell me it's ready that there is no more to do than I've written
already then there is no way to leave from here in any other way
with still more grace olé olé olé go way go way go way good as it
goes it goes it goes olé olé what joy that this is good and gets here
straightaway olé olé with castanets olé and with a sun that cracks
exploding seeds and making bells ring that already rang with
stings and kisses and so olé and so olé so that now it's all okay the
past is nothing more now than the coolness of an afternoon in
summer and the table laid out for a holiday with flowers and
with fruits and little fishes and with peppers and tomatoes
cucumbers and egg plants lettuces and olives green and black
and violets on top and gold below in hot pursuit of pink and
raining blows on blue between the red of streamers melting
down with happiness so that it sings now in its pretty lingo the
festoons of cries of pleasure absolutely true and stars that start to
drive nails in his skin what they will have to wait for stretched
out on the station platform so that now we'll get to see that it's
enough already just to push for what's impossible so as to keep it
from arriving

and just you tell me why the heifer's eye is melting in his hands
the same way that the day again seems laced with the clear

water in the night of what lies hidden in the turn his life takes
and the stimulus kills in the bullring when the little girl has
flown the nest that's nothing more than memories thrown into
brine ground into crumbs the birds have come to scribble in his
hand too bad for you that you can still believe in peace that this
is not a day to sit outside and bear the burden on your shoulders
of payments in advance a thousand times you have collected
every moment opposite of all the others and how good the
weather is to make folks see just what you have to teach them so
that afterwards they won't say that you took it to extremes and
that you left the fishbones over but it's something that you have
to do today when the bright face of his jackknife hides behind it
up against your breast and it unhooks the river and inflames his
loves until it leaves him stretched out in the middle of the grass
which is enough to steal away the filament and pluck the colors
one by one until you have the well run over blind just like they
did it in his house and let them tell it to the linden's shadow see
the coins are falling in between the leaves that they're awaiting
the eclipse and maybe they will pocket all the change without a
word to anyone but soldering his hair and gathering the sun up
in his hands while seated at the window this May afternoon out
in the country looking at the cows and gobbling up the grammar
without having learned it and the dogs pursuing butterflies the
flowers snowing down on meadows so the roses start emerging
from their breaths the way they rearrange each other's skirts and
jealousies and spit between them in somebody's face in silence
how they hate themselves and scratch each other's eyes so that
the cocks accuse them of imposture and crack the silence open
without knowing what to say about the treats the lady of the
house will give them on the table and the swallows mowing
down the sky will take communion with mosquito wafers in this
country which is everybody's where they can they remove me bit

by bit but as for me I have already given all I have for them to gnaw on as they can for what I have invented is a parachute for heaven and if there is no point in saying it I have already said it this and otherwise and right away and later on and now and not tomorrow one way or the other wanting not to say a single thing more than I damn well know and say that makes it all seem pointless and you never know what's there to be explained I stole it and will give it as a gift some other day to anyone who wants it to dress up in for the holiday in gold and let him break a beak on it

A JOTA DANCE

fire fly fire fly
fire fly fire life
fire fly fire fly
fly fire of my life
fire fly fire fly
fire fly fire fly

and just you tell me that you know it tell me if it's possible this afternoon that it's still raining in my heart moist recollection of her face and let the greyness of the heavens be undone in green of tree and tell me furthermore if one day I will have to grasp the fingers that the sun slips through the blinds some morning waking up down by the sea the mediterranean and with the smells of toast and coffee and because although I come from far away I'm still a child and have a yen to eat and swim in salty waters there atop the picture painted on transparent canvas and exposed to perils in the middle of the living room up on the ceiling moving in a mesh of light just as the boat floats past it's drawn in living color in expanding tenderness it's murdering the drape atop the carpet that a wave of bed sheets brings to knee

down on the ground the mirror takes as prisoner the angle of the
room seen from the open door and hidden in the blackness of
the hallway and the fan smashed into smithereens legs spread
open on a silken chaise that hides its heat beneath the bed the
forearm covering the face and once more setting everything in
place to rhythm of their pulsebeats in the silence of the bedroom
and the singing of the bells the blackbirds scratching now this
afternoon at six so I'm already worn down by the miracle of
knowing nothing in this world not having ever learned a thing
but loving lots of things to eat them up alive and listen to their
faretheewells the hours sounding from afar as they run off to
play on the horizon midst the many reasons that they have for
not revealing how or why they came to light and shaking off the
prism that they're cloaked in carrying their wings up to the nest
that hides the bamboo flute in a vocabulary of raisins and dried
figs of hazelnuts and toasted almonds so that the chestnuts die of
laughter just to see themselves so plump that they would think
they were already dried and measured out in meters and the
cadence of the past still worse in that the day got there so fast for
them that now it's night and with its coldness they will burn
them in the fire of the treacherous snail's spiral captive of his
crisscross staircase in between the drops of rain that chastise love
that makes the night a target lighting up his stogie in the forest
calling forth his smile and searching deeply and by ear along the
street that I do not forget nor the collision that brings down the
level turns her undergarments smelly and asleep inside her
body's warmth the nest between her legs convulsing and the
hand of memory *Recuerdo* sparkling in the bathroom one more
time she soaks and shaves it putting off the freshness for another
holiday so that they tingaling caresses and prepare a dish of
nards with garlics and with twisted beans around the olé peek-
ing through the lock's eye when his key slips in and gathers up

the light of melted wax inside her ring and now that I have won
the lottery and hit the jackpot the penalty is that they mustn't
shut the prison down and cast the prisoners aside and pick the
blue road from among a hundred in the world of money of her
bosom looking for the wall and for the nail for hope that leaves a
taste of broken branches where to hang the pole to fish the
future and to pass the cable slung between her tits with eyes in
blindfolds and with hands that twist a lightbeam raising the
reflection from the lake and searching hard in empty space a
summer town with mercury in motion on the silken paper sur-
face and her nakedness recovered on the street a rainbow of
plain-chant and cante hondo sings its sorrow iris in between the
sands of life it burns her skin and hides the laundry woman's
bluing when she shuts her eyes in orange and a branch the shad-
ow of her arm that shakes the oceanside into a powder in her
powder box then calms down for a day sucks up the boat's oars
and the net is raised and hung up in the clouds a sail that's melt-
ing drop by drop and that ignites the fire from this ballad
gathering an air of fish and more and more a fountain with a
lemon so the escabeche tells its lie the bread grows soggy on her
fingertips the mandragora nibbles on the floating cork her hips
bob up and down and she escapes it running between tales and
proverbs cannot figure what to do about a day that's painted in
canary yellow and the white that gushes from below and that the
dagger pierces and subdues it leaving her a place without a
memory a hand that moves a needle back and forth while wait-
ing for the hour with a barely faithful pair of scales her
labyrinth

the battle began at two that afternoon the roses started shooting
rounds and yanked out their gunpowder nails in little dandruff
filings which did open fire on the snares and cut the words to

pieces hanging from the olive tree when hands were twisting
waves and threw themselves down on the ground and naked pol-
ished off the stone enchantment blinding their delights up in
the bough the song will rockabye a cricket feeling that the oval
in the park couldn't be waiting for the coolness just because the
heat the sun is bringing rubs its nose into the mud and moving
its desires through the silk of her left arm collecting the aromas
that have spent the night there with his hand tucked in an
armpit of warm grass erected on the hydrophilic rock walk that
the chasm of his luminescent sword has polished off refuting all
his lies a body mirrored where the listing boat drifts by atop his
griefs and leaking anise from his magic flask while working out
the rage around his necktie out there where the chorus takes its
seats and where oblivion is born anew with neither form nor
witness but fatigued with waiting for his looming destiny close
by the killer rose deserving of the punishment its legs contracted
by necessity receiving a lost smile the tribute of the rose bush as
it kills itself beneath a grey sky and the blow that ever present
moment when the bicycle produces tears along the road seen
from the window and the rain pins down the hour which has got
to be the lie the wheat inside the oven proves untrue by calling
everything into the corn cob cannon sopping wet and still does
not refute his honest anger if one wants it but is lost between the
clinches of his days and days and days while transporting the
nuance of an anchor as a vest and overcoat that moves around in
crystal with his idea gushing forth festoons it in the time that
burns afar and through the trees comes face to face with me in
spite of how it rains but look here buster just because you have
to check what's happening that it's no more than just a summer
shower and if you believe it then you're ready and already you
will have to see how much things cost when everything goes sky
high while economizing mirrors get inflated and the bees are

sleeping peacefully nailed down by trucks in history museum halls they say are natural but I refute them $37 - 47 - 10 - 347 - 60 + 10 + 25 - 0 - 1 - 2 - 3 - 5 - 40 - 100 + 20 - 2$ and no use in looking for it all because already I will give the bunch of you my secret for a pittance and you'll say a melon slice is natural a history of guillotines that cuts through terror and makes french fries out of peace there in its frying pan of credos where the proofs of the fiesta are already on the table

so that lettuces with bacalao sorrows cry from plates where vinegar is growing taking an accounting of a blackboard fish that's swimming in oblivion the intellect obscured in love's blind light in midst of sighs and tender chocolate is breathing out its joys unhappy baby bird who draws his cage of eyelashes and paints his cheeks with morning's aura hidden underneath his body as desire sleepyheaded moves a hand and strokes the painted paper that the years have splattered in the shadows wanting an ingathering of grapes the color of its smell inside his iris free of reason but retaining voice and screaming out a silence that the cotton bell repeats beneath the water where it asks the well's support atop the castle so his hands may touch the portion of the bull's brow that retains pink flowers from his scream a lance that digs hard into his past delighting that handful of air now that he threads his fate and wears it as a collar his own thought a catapult that hurls and cracks the distance in a thousand pieces terrifying in his hand the stone that makes the clock diminish drop by drop $3 . 4 . 5 . 10 - 14 . 50 . 10 . 24 . 0 . 2 . 3 . 1 . 2 . 5 . 1 . 2 . 24 . 22 . 34 . 1 . 2 . 23 . 1 . 2 . 2 . 0 . 1 . 10 . 1 . 1000 . 2 . 1 . 0.$ I give a thousand proofs of this in what I say and factor the results between the curved horns and the smells now settling in among the gold hairs taking seconds of adobo on tip toe down by the oceanside so they can string the doves up as they fall down from

the sky the printers proofs of arguments sewn by machine that
doesn't cry its saffron in the middle of the bull ring cadence that
his courage brings tied to that chair the toad weaves in its nut in
jet and does he shake his ass he does and stands before the
chitlins sets his countenance to trembling lined in blue that car-
ries his reflection and that tramples on his words valencian
horchata hidden in the bell between the leaves afire in the fero-
cious book of his palm sunday or his hand that casts an arm
behind the garden wall and pins down rumbles among school-
girls' laughter soaring among sheep tied to their rhymes and
pissing feather duster magic that descends a car stripped of its
wheels there in the course of night and laying flat the rabbit that
escapes face down and fucks the dog atop a labile labyrinth who
gnaws his nails uncorks the inkwell so it explicates his ashtray
smile the fashion of his garments gives a nippon look to and the
fundament of cloth the butcher carrying his burlap hour wet
with benzene of repeated pleasure chews with prudent wisdom
on the twisted hairpin as it sleeps between the table legs stripped
naked and he thinks he recognizes in his breath his sojourn the
tenth part of what puts spice into the wolf's heart sent from else-
where on this very date and dancing the fandango in the
moonlight sealed into a granite envelope atop the counter dis-
combobulates desire draws a handkerchief across the nose of the
defendant pecking at the chicken the bull fiddle that the arrow
has turned foul all that his work was and he cruises down the
street by car a third time drawing in his breath and trampling
out the vintage solid as a rock with hammer blows not bad the
way the light engulfs his glance the mirror that can pull a fast
one crackles with a curtained anger that upsets the way he tells
his secret come what may oh calm yourself my heart and then
repaint in blue the hours all around you and refresh the lines
inside your hand of your love's juice pour forth your tenderness

caress the summer afternoon and rock her in your arms until she
falls asleep today a day of spines a shoeshine boy who hauls his
third palanquin hoping for a southwest wind a carpet made of
abalone shells and ledgers in arrears the copper balance puts his
love to sleep a metamorphosis a virgin free and clear a stirrup
scatterbrained with corn cakes and a slice of watermelon it's her
veil that tears her happiness to shreds a necessary baggage
bound with froth that draws the motor from her parasol in green
the itchiness of silence of a haven for misogynists the fireworks
disintegrate it in its progress simplifying how the clock atop the
cornice strikes forgotten in the tale that rapidly and silently has
set the time ahead inside the square wheel that bombards the
vessel that has packed the railing polished and repolished by the
prisoner with so much show it carries off the shawl between its
fringes so they punctuate the whistles from the locomotive out
behind the river that the hand extracts and draws conclusions
with the cardinal point ejected and in no time getting plastered
on the wall the lime resuscitated in the nard that shaves his pas-
sion singing in the railyard sentry box completing his capricious
saeta stone on stone and brick and goes on climbing up the wall
and so exposes his desire for a little of his life at every instant
and he sucks the damask pit up with his mouth on horseback
through the salt and chanting gloomy *soleares* hauls the land-
scape on his chain the *calamares en su tinta* blazing in the
casserole and soaking up its fiery sauce with supple daily bread
inscribes it with his finger on the supple copper plate his secret
sweet upon the palate while again far off eleven hours strike at
night flesh of my flesh and sleepless eyes the gaze of heifers and
fried blood the best in town a paradise of canvas and the brooms
of chambermaids and modern household gadgets hard work
never ending recognized as useful and essential to the progress

and the order of the precincts standing halfway open and recov-
ered from the knockout blow the nasty hideaway in sewers line
of sight and body of an owl photographs in darkness on the
muddy plate that operates the bell jar that the air of his harp
measures in minute detail the oil that spreads across his drawing
for eternity upon the bloody mantelpiece tapdancing on the floor
and flings a cup right at the bull that stretches out the bull ring
by a half castillian league asleep in ash of chicken soup the
trumpeter contorts dressed as torero melancholy sun that spits
into the hole his track his albacete jackknife taste of sugar on the
mouth of jug still stuck and stopped up in the gutter reminiscent
of the gold that mends the hempen pipe and tans the color of his
hair the captain of a gang of bandits silence silence silence let
nobody move nobody take off *mira mira* further out behind the
leaf draw and withdraw your bulk so they don't see you running
off and save yourself still not too late still you can cut their shad-
ow down and sing a — a — a — a — a — a — a — a — a — a — i — a — i —
a- i - a — a — a — a — a — a — a — a — a — a — a — a — a — a — a in
the dark green there's another lighter green and another darker
sort of blue another blacker and one still greener than the
browner green one and still another lighter than the black dark
green another one still greener than the dark green and another
greener still than all the battling greens so green that bells ring
green and you applaud and plug them up and stomp down on
the list of them a — a — a — a — a — a — a — i — a — a — a — i — i — a —
i - a — a — a — a — a — a — a — a — a — a — i — a — i — i — i — i — i — a — i
that plug and unplug the jug a bird that crosses from the side the
hands that stroke him in his flight which lets a smell of violets
fall from the cup there at the tree's mouth as that receives the
gift in recognition of so much graciousness and hoping to
respond in kind and with a million thanks and fond farewells

your faithful servant who does lick your boot straps and who squashes in his hand the fattest and most smelly bedbug of them all

[JR]

[MAY-JUNE] XXXV

nothing more to do than careful not to have the thread that stitches up the fates which stain the crystal robbery with mud thus shaking up the hours shrunken into memories and roasted on the grill with mint and azure summer that hides wings that pins up ads for cables on the branches of a silence frozen in the shade of words too lightly spoken and reduces the amnesia of his life no salt strewn on his friendship's shoulders cast down on the thistles made into a soup of lamentations popping in the frying pan a soup of spikenards splattering his body with a rain of peace the hour that devours sand inserted in his pocket as it screws the moment into place the moment caught between the white dove's teeth the dove that beats the sky resounding on the drum that distances the bell to leave it wilted wet with pleasure and vibrant with terror caught in the heat with eyes tight and mouth wide little girl see the bogeyman coming and snatching the children who just sleep a little I know it already that you are the best of the best in this world a dress set with lentils a cask filled with wine a circular staircase a sunray so silent it crosses her hand reflecting a kiss on an apple a table of limestone fond hope that burns in a corner the noise of a fish in the mouth of a jug sounding forth a cloud that waits in the quadrant to twist a beak back on the notebook with plaudits unplugging the prism's devotion that sings from the wall the profile of his or her face and that hides from its light the sphere that bursts into stars falling onto the ground the words that fly off and return to the dovecote to make their nest there in that bracelet of copper and iron silk cloth that the sun skein does scratch by the thousands and his the kilometer balanced offensive arms placed at the top of his art which gale force does rattle the system and shirtless in back of the glance that exposes his lusts through a curtain of reeds never quiet and laughing at everything all the while summer is passing a melon slice that the grasshopper torches and drags through his wounds the sword in the bullfighter's cape up and down the silence uncovers a shadow an angle that stretches his voice out that nails a window of light to a handkerchief mouse-like is climbing a rope in a well the abyss of the street and the runt who goes off with his doll to sensible all-night wild parties who fluffs up the stars on the bullfigher's jacket and tosses them down on the beach right on top of the fish net and perfumes his verses who stumbles and fractures his skull in the void who pours his blood out like violets red stripes that slice through blue skirts that float somewhere over the sky words rocking on seesaws of promises checking the paint brushes jumping with feet bound together the fences of cries that these branches have torn from the earth who turns in his bed a hundred times over then enters his dream and drop after drop checks the filters illuminates every last one with all colors and there on the inside installs his workshop of illusions the table of weights that measures the air of his intellect over against his new garments seed of the lily a stud horse he mounts free willing and prances in front of the bull he sticks him with darts with grace and with graciousness wraps him up with his laughter and presses a dove to his breast the bells loud and clear and his hands spouting waves rolling down in their courses a prisoner circling the sun chews the bitter reward of his virtue turning his life into wine while a flea bites the heart of a rooster pure heehaws and squeezes indifference out of a lemon his black fate illuminates

table set up for lunch shreds of lobster and lettuce leaves loaf of
fresh bread and the wine and the air debonaire tapping drum-
sticks the spa-side cabanas lift masses of grasses and teach him
some nastiness later replayed in the shade to some turtledove
those who could listen in back of the clusters of grapes of the
most and the least that was said between bills for the granules of
pepper and salt where they dance on oiled bye bye floors and
caramel caramel heating up caramel burning caramel cutting
and pasting caramel bursting caramel pricking and piercing col-
ored in pink and in green caramel evenings and sundays locked
in a room with no bullfights with nothing and wrapped up in
paper so one must do everything ragged old rags sheets enfold-
ing insomnia wild for caresses and science with flags in the free
port their manner of fashioning silks that the wind can shake
loose and keep cool walking by on the water his life as a little
man edgy awaiting the hour for seeing the sun and so happy the
good times are starting right now and someone is raising the
curtain afire and bearing the past in its folds in dusty bottles in
blue gold that sucks up the bluest of blues and it's plenty for now
and we have to go easy and count 1 . 2 - 3 . 4 . 5 . 6 - 7 . 8 - 9 . 10 -
11 . 12 . 13 . 14 . 15 . 16 - 17 . 18 . 19 . 20 . 21 - 22 . 23 . 25 - 26 . 27
- 28 . 29 . 30 - 31 . 32 . 33 . 34 . 35 . 36 . 37 . 38 . 40 - 50 . 21 . 32 .
17 - 34 . 60 . 70 . 80 . 110 - 120 . 0 . 0 . 0 . 0 . 0 . 0 . and let the sun
burn them and bake them until they sing sad songs at nightfall
alone and so lonely in loneliness waiting to find just a breath of
fresh air 1 . 2 . 3 . 4 . 5 . 6 - 1 . 2 . 3 . 4 - 4 . 5 . 6 - 1 . 2 . 3 . 4 . 5 . 6 .
7 - 1 . 2 . 3 . 4 . 5 . 6 . 7

[JR]

Paris 28 July XXXV

go ahead and let him rage on — because today is sunday and there aren't any bullfights here — and the music is like lead — and the tooth that's biting her has laid her flat and twisted her arm back — and he only wears a shirt to make a buck and grab a car and keep an eye out for the exit — because the worst fate has in store is for the afternoon to turn grey and to get hot for hire and for the noise outside to turn to cotton — such a pain to bring the wheat to someone just to give him bread to dunk into a soup made from his blood — and with all the good will in the world they'll kill him — with such a lot of song and music underneath his shoes — so that the bells for just a little more will fit him with half-soles and heels — and all the while the goldfinch in his cashbox yaps away — and little sparrows peck at him while sticking banderillas in the sand that's growing old — among the hammer blows from the carnations' odors — scorching in his cup — who draws the needle forth that wins the race — and carries it in tatters past the open window — and pastes it on a sky of turtledoves — that bleed into his blue eyes in the mirror — the while she combs the honey in advance of memory — wrapped as she is inside her nacre shawl — the lilac colored arm

[JR]

1st August XXXV

[1]   and what about the silence stinking in your bed a dream at night — if not dawn's profile — what soaks its feet down by the shore — shakes out a flaming curtain in the woods

the tread mill will soon break its shears against the diamond — will erect its scaffold in the bull ring

[II] that rats may make their feasts where'ere they want — but shall not eat the pigeon in its nest — nor drape a flag or lantern over the open wounds — and later in the morning there will only be lamenting — that all that's left is to unleash the dogs to kill them — so when the hour arrives for buying furniture it's useless if no happiness accrues that very moment — if they don't intertwine their castanets with laughter — and festive colors with guitar airs — because what counts is being crowned with roses — being happy to see ugly things turn lovely — to trick them out with sweet talk and your cape thrown down before them — then to bring forth a meal the table set already prettied up with flowers — and to sing and shout that it's already here — to lay the bed out so it hides a rainbow in between its sheets

[JR]

Paris Sunday 7 August XXXV

[I] scooping up the handout in his golden plate — in garden garb — here comes the bullfighter — his joys are bleeding through his pleated cape — and with his pinking shears he cuts out stars — his body shaking out the sand from clocks — inside a square that dumps a rainbow on the bull ring — that fans an afternoon of painless birth — a bull is being born — a pin cushion that cries out loud — that whistles as the race track whizzes by — a round of handclaps ink aflame in cazuela — his hands that draw the air out of the melted glass — the crown of mouths — and eyes like "birds of paradise" — the flags in hand go sailing off — at roof's edge — he climbs down a ladder hanging from the sky — cloaked in desire — love — behind the fence he

soaks his feet — he swims around the bleachers like a
champ

[II] *this venus pricked by pin point disappears — and leaves her*
lover staring after her only the imprint of her body on the
sand — and that the wave erases in its haste

[JR]

italicized section translated from French

PARIS 9 AUGUST XXXV

I don't want any more
today
than just to tame the wolf
deep in the goggles of the eskimo
and in the lambkin's eye
so hot to play it plays its final card
to straighten out the blade that skews the fountain

to drink its blood
and rock it in my clouds
the memory of a july afternoon
this summer
in the garden where the birds
were bathing in the gold dust of
time past
when the shadows of this very hour

are knives that slit cravats
the latest wrinkle
for the unhanged man

the hanged man carrying a ladder
broken   on his shoulder

swallow that stops an arrow in midair

and gives him a first class burial in
the box of raisins bulging with toreros

in the hand that lies across the kerchief
nailed down with donkey ears
on the points of the rose compass
the hours dropped down wells to stay asleep
forever
every clock that rings its bells
already knows what's up
builds no illusions
crows foot that sews things up beside the void

cuts down the sorrows rose of daybreak
dawning
star in his hand that flashes its disgust
hides fingernail inside the cup
a shake of shoulders that awakens silence
spills its color in the spoon
and wipes its day out the illusion of its body
little lamb that swims
responds from this side of the wall to that
and to the signal that the hand is making

[JR]

Paris 10 August XXXV

without taste or trumpets — making water from every parch-
ment — stretched out beside the rigid sea — like a blind
watchman — his palate lies — licking its mystery from the
string — which in haste and silence — tramples on the embroi-
dery that sings in its fortune — the flute's anger — that the
blackbird pierces — now that the bells ring 11 pm around me —
and at a distance the train fixes in place — the tape that
inscribes its heat in August — this night the moon says nothing
more — not yes or no — and the sky of the zambomba — faint
lies down — and is covered by the continuous drone of the drum
— filled with water tempered in the sword — that shields its
life — and pays no mind to the rain of flowers — while — choir
that burns — and explodes on the paper — its light blocked by
the hand — the shadow falling from the window — and softens
the tapestry with its flame — carries bleeding between its
fingers — the little horse that shakes its tremulous wings —
opens its eyes and shouts — here's the bouquet — composed of
all the words of all the tongues — which mad with joy and
drunk with happiness — loose — flying — free — swift —
passing each other in every direction — kissing each other each
time they collide in their swift flight — with their bellow's
breath — that love ignites with his flames — but it's nothing —
and the wings — love — bouquet — horse — tongues — happi-
ness — loose — joy — words — mad — swift — freedom —
collide — flight — bellow's breath — in all directions — with
his flames — ignite — bouquet — joy — words — swift —
flight — breath — wings — mad — collide — tongues — love
— horse — and more and a hundred and a hundred who will

fall in drops of mercury in rule and measure once dead — and
then the dance begins

[MW]

Paris 11 August XXXV [i] [ii] [iii]

[i]   I can't get along with castanets unless they bring me the
      mirror hidden among the skirts and its warmth wrapped in
      a grape leaf but what do you expect the world's like that
      and sorrows kill poets with pleasure because one has to lis-
      ten to that which paints within the hawk's eye the light
      that's nothing more than a guitar string regardless of its
      excuses but listen don't hide my harvest beneath your veil
      because even now the trapped dove sings his lover's lament
      who from one Sunday to another the whole week dances he
      holds it in his hands the drum has laid an egg the chimney
      hangs from the blue the swifts scratch it and the hour that
      arrives doesn't want to wake the drunk asleep in the ivy
      placed a slice of bread on top of the houses opposite that the
      brush caresses blots out in blue and rings out the answers to
      stupid questions night's bottle will soon be filled

[ii] tell me why it rains on Sunday if it's not the bugle killing
      the promise asleep on the white leaf — wave which after
      breakfast the pen scratching its lice longs for — only the
      chain devoured by the watch and dragged off by small
      mules — how sad this is

[iii] it merely shines despite the hundreds of candles in the
      room where I stand by the open window that the precise
      beginning of this August night which holds back the bell
      with its breath — the blows of the bull's forehead on the

blue velvet drum — at the edge of the foam that the tapes-
try stains with blood — around the deep box overflowing
full of seawater placed upright today carried singing on the
ten shoulders of the hour that the clock sounds this very
moment and that other clocks challenge arranging a later
meeting tough guys knives in hand until there only remains
the hour that gives itself entirely without saying what it
gives which is already a lot to the pimp philosopher poet
canticle beggar and flirt who looks for the fair and carries it
off in a coach

tough guys the hours knives in hand fight and until there
only remains that which is given without saying what it
gives which is already a lot to the pimp who looks for it and
carries it off to the fair in a coach and who is philosopher —
poet — canticle — wolf and beggar and flirt and feudal
castle — chime of bells on the fire and a patched and
mended strait-jacket become a flag — forest of lances —
the itch of mange — ear of hare and fox piss — lamplight
— rope of a well with a drowned man in it — paella valen-
ciana left on the fire longer than it should be and a suit of
lights bought second-hand from a bullfighter who died in a
boardinghouse and here is the washerwoman's list 4 shirts
three pairs of socks and two handkerchiefs 2 pairs of under-
pants and a tie a set of sheets and a pillowcase and a sword
which ironically passes through the garden and cools the
mid-night that it is at this hour

[MW]

Paris 13 August 1935

sugar in the street brushes violet behind
shutters — barking at the cat — smell
of lilies and roasting coffee — scratching she runs
her fingers

[SJL]

14 August 1935

i will no longer paint the arrow
we see in the drop of water
trembling in the morning
as the inscribed hour hisses
in the wind swept away by the swing
laughing

written on the train to Dieppe on August 14 MCMXXXV

[SJL]

15 August XXXV

i am now here in the nest where the lamb and the bear — the
lion and the zebra — the wolf and the panther — the fox, the
winter and the summer weasel — the mole and the chinchilla
— the rabbit and the sable weave in silence above an abandoned
staircase after the party has washed the week and wrung out the
handkerchief raining a perfume that wanders in search of its
shape in a sad afternoon that has so many reasons to stretch into
the oil blue of a silk duvet the corner of his eye rips drowning in
shreds the landscape he sighed in the place where the beehive
yearns to form its ice

[SJL]

17 August XXXV

a cup of coffee courts the aroma everlasting
that corrupts the wing shaking a harmonium
caressing her timid white flesh as
kisses breeze through the window
fill the room with goldfinch words fluttering
in the ear soundless and singing
and laughing crazy trills through his veins

[SJL]

19 August XXXV [I] [II]

[I] sweet Andalusian road why won't you
let them see you follow me
and how you hide behind the little gentians?

today Sunday 18*th of August* XXXV

[II] the wing that twists seduces and perpetuates the coffee cup
so tenderly caressed by the harmonium of her timidity —
the window covers up the rear end of his quarters with a
plash of finches dying in the air — that kisses the aroma in
his veins but soundless to the ear — and how the little
grains of sand run sing and laugh atwitter

[JR]

20 August XXXV [I] [II] [III]

[I] venetian blinds the air shakes kills off finches in midflight
and sends them plashing staining with their blood the rear
end of his quarters where he hears the whiteness of a

silence passing by that death hides in his mouth aroma of
harmonium whose wing does pull a rope up from the well

[II] the finches here are the aroma plashing her wing's coffee
that reflects the blinds down at the bottom of the well and
hears the air in passing that the silence of the whiteness of
the cup

the silence hears in passing the reflection that the finch is
plashing down the well and in the coffee's silence wiping
out the whiteness of a wing

[III] shake the twisted curtain
do the garrotin dance
when the pigeon squeezed between your fingers
sacrifices
snow that's flying in the furnace
its perpetual flag

[JR]

22 August XXXV

rat face crook and shameless hussy scrapes away and mislaid cat's
eye tints it sepia and poor boy's bat wing sharpened razor talon
and a handkerchief with fringe a hand that takes a watch from
pocket air goes exiting from down below the sidewalk's curb
edge singing out his sorrows with their teentsy city smells with
papers letters crumpled no replies to social clubs with hours split
into a thousand bits car wheels and juiceless oranges with skele-
tons of fishes broken chains cries pasted onto envelopes for
streets with no address or name — dark eyes that look athwart

the rising moon — a watermelon — night burns up from sun-
day — but why *should* we tire out the candle with our eyes shut
tight at noon if the venetian blind does what it has to do to with
claws to tear it into shreds the nest you wove with multicol-
ored feathers and perfumed it with the loves of flowers — roses
jasmines violets carnations spikenards lilies mignonette and
heliotrope a black sun spins in the machineworks singing out its
judgments in the trumpet now you sit down after lunch and start
to write

a noise so very far off stuck into his pocket armpit on st johns
night bonfire and fingernails that scrape the sweat off pull the
hairs out and the sighs emergent from his chest he marinates
where you are satisfactions in the smell of anchovies on beaches
they who dance the dance of fire on the grill the dishes at his
head are being thrown the sea as escort from the shore that you
already should have pulled the sheets off of the bed and should
have gone to sleep already it is getting late

[JR]

24 August XXXV [i] [ii]

[i] paint brush does burn and scoots in hot pursuit
     of thunderbolts his foot heel-first gets off
     a crack to smack his head against the rocks
     such languid satisfaction of an afternoon at end of
     this month august the commedia dell'arte
     & the rain does fan itself the rain

     waylays a faggot who portrays a fruitcake
     that his act subtracts and nothing more
     but whatta BORE

[II] silence is quicklime as it burns my dim inquietude the
lightbeam from his cigarette can't makes its way through
and he plugs his ear up screws it in the ice the weather drips
its lead onto this evening this

[JR]

5 SEPTEMBER XXXV

today is fifth day of the month september 35 when the redou-
bled pace of sword in quince pulp opens up his hand and lets the
secret in his loincloth get away prepares the emerald to let itself
be eaten undercover in the watercress with bits of whoopdeedoo
a whisper in his ear there at the back end of the road condemned
beforehand but content to go onto the pyre just too smart for his
own good and picks a pack of peanuts and a basket of hard
knocks for any sailor whom the cotton chafes undoes the weft
that scratches up his mask and measures with his rod the sultri-
ness that graces with its wheat the noggin of the wounded man
that gnaws the hopes to whom... kaboomboom chin chin lawdy
lawdy

[JR]

17 SEPTEMBER XXXV

I give and uproot twist kill pierce torch burn — fondle lick kiss
gawk — bang on bells in full flight till they bleed — frighten
pigeons make them fly around the dovecote till they drop down
to the ground dead from fatigue — I will plug up all the win-
dows and the doors with earth and with your hair will strangle
all the singing birds — and cut down all the flowers — I will
rock the lambkin in my arms and offer him my breast to gorge
on — bathe him with my tears of pain and pleasure — and will

lull him with my song of solitude my song of sorrows — will
engrave an etching of the fields of wheat and barley and will
watch them die there lying face up to the sun — will wrap the
rivers up in newspapers and throw them through the window
into an arroyo that's repentant but with all its sins still on its
shoulders goes off happy laughing still in spite of everything to
make its nest down in the sewers — I will break the forest's
music on the cliffs of waves and sea — and I will bite the lion on
his cheek — and make the wolf weep tenderly before a portrait
of the water in a bathtub where he lets his arm drop down

[JR]

21 OCTOBER XXXV

so the silence gnaws the flowerlets stuck in the little vase atop
the triangle that's wrapped around the onions and the candle
and the apples made with iron wires in the kitchen corner where
the coffee pot its neck raised toward the ceiling lost its voice
from too much squawking and incapable of bearing the offenses
that the gas inflicted on its freshness that the memory of origins
would weep and scratch the wall the smallest fleck of sunlight
passing between fingers so that it's sufficient that the weather
soaks his charming body in the faucet squeezing blood out drop
by drop without awareness of the time astir in the blue eggshell
of his destiny and burning at the bottom of so many facts that
sear and torch so many things already set aside and wrapped in
read and re-read papers prayer beads made by collars and by
wives who bound him to the mainmast of his boat and lost with
neither reefs nor waves above or hanging over saw the sea two
fingers off unable to change places with the sky his pocket knife
would cut the rope that binds up his ideas and shedding light
while making a clean sweep of every object changing how they

look and cooking dove on plate and partridge over bowl of fruit
and grape leaf over cheese and sword on spoon and languid
longing for sweet love in cup where lump of sugar crumbles
under darky's kiss and every item in its place the hand at throat
to squeeze out anguish and to make the tongue a flower sprout-
ing from her mouth and in the sauce pan to cook up the gifts
bound up with ribbons of all colors red ones bound with serpent
feathers yellow greens with turkey bristles pinks that bind up
pinks and lilacs that bind thistles black ones bound up with gui-
tar strings yellows bound with moving vans jampacked with
keepsakes and white ribbons binding up my lips that ever more
shall only tell me just how much I love her now that she's asleep
and I can see no more than just her honey from afar and out
across the rooms that separate us poor as I am now writing it
down

[JR]

28 OCTOBER XXXV

if I think in a language and write "the dog chases the hare
through the woods" and want to translate this into another lan-
guage I have to say "the table of white wood sinks its paws into
the sand and nearly dies of fright knowing itself to be so silly"

[PJ]

30 OCTOBER XXXV

[I] squeezes so hard the elephant comes forth with trainloads
and spits out its deep song from amidst the smells of stew
pots that deliciously in tunnels oft regurgitate a picture
frame around the image of a bullfighter as painted by the
bull

[II] it's chicken soup the hour selected by the leaf that from its
tree is rocking to and fro so daintily betwen so many little
kisses till it drops down on the grass and then remains there
fast asleep

[JR]

31 OCTOBER XXXV

in the nuptial chamber set precautiously at the edge of the win-
dow among the basket of vegetables the bottle of bleach and the
sprig of parsley the hand which squeezes a tear from every bread
crumb burns its lips at the flame of the paintbrush that effaces
the color clinging to the objects night kills with each bite and
continues its road between the screams and barks of each corner
of the kitchen that doesn't want to be recognized despite the
desire each evening brings to the shadow which in spite of the
orange's opinion which reveals the bottom of her thought when
getting undressed just to see her shaking her butt baring her
teeth and fixing the four corners of the *los toros* poster unearths
with her hands 2 plus 2 spell desire never again to say anything
do the dishes be a mouse that snows and fry the escaping word
while sleeping straightjacketed nest of accounts held by the
parisian illuminating gas company etcetera seated at the corner
of the white wood table dressed in blue the salmon imposes its
will on the carnations which hitting with the red of the foot of
reflectionless dictator gets excited and has to account to no one
despite her timid air protecting her neck with her hand in its
well-known lilac color separates at the edge of her breasts the
whiteness of the shirt hiding her fingers among the mass of
things that for some months now have been nesting in the sun-
light reflected in the yard by the window panes of the kitchen

across the yard with such politeness yet despite all if the happiness the smell of leaks gives me and the remaining scraps of cauliflower lingering in the folds of her skirt and under the feet of the chair isn't it better to suffer her caressing looks than to slowly climb up the fragile scaffolding of so many dinner rolls straight as a poker and sopping wet from tears all of literature promenading along the thread lying on the floor brings up from the distant source a flute song which through each hole waters a live speech but sleeping stretched out on the table and which the smallest noise without the air overflowing the cup order and measure a single word could wake them but that behind the door and held by its oath which keeps it in chains the rooster sings his wing his thighs his rump and the love of his sweethearts and despite all it's not so sad I find this story rather funny the only thing which right now saddens me is not to be able to be with her and tell her let's go out take a walk in the garden like this morning let's go buy cheese and bread let's eat them seated on the bench facing the large tree

[PJ]

1ST NOVEMBER XXXV

this morning the sun rose covered with snow

199	199
one hundred ninety-nine	ciento noventa y nueve
17	17
seventeen	diecisiete
34	34
thirty-four	treinticuatro
22	22
twenty-two	veintidós

0	0
zero	cero
1	1
one	uno

camisa de dormir removiendo su culo*

[PJ]

3 NOVEMBER XXXV

this Sunday stamps its feet all its courage bites the corner of the
table cloth with rage and whistles into the ear getting warmed
by — a little bit of sun left at the bottom of the staircase —
which runs away — cannot scream — nor weep from laughing
so much — nor cut out the profile of the smell filling the room
— otherwise than by folding into forty-six pieces — the hope
that doesn't leave him — to dance and to sing — to swim naked
in the sun — at noon — and to make a fat winged horse with
the big noise of a thousand thunders — though while seated —
writing in his small notebook — elbows sticking out one more
than the other over the table's edge — the left hand holding the
already written page the other on the paper — the point of the
pencil here — where I press it — festoon enervated by the louse
bites — that tell me time as it passes — and act as if they were
reading — and think of nothing else — than to have fun among
themselves and to make fun of me — who am a veil — tonight
at 10 to five — which alights so carefully on all the furniture —
and moves from one chair to the other and embraces them and
dries their tears and whispers sweet and caressing words and

---

*nightshirt shaking its ass.

lowers the table's feet and licks the dresser — but the lamp exasperated by his pride at the sound of the measure the alarm-clock dictates — melts from love — only if the hour — can hold itself back one little moment more — and pirouette through the window — and alight on my shoulder — for this so cavalier way — of presenting one's body — devoid of all willed lightning effect — wouldn't stand the inquisition any longer — to turn the shadow cast by his profile — into the sacrificial victim of his authoritarian desire — to change the position — of the angle — which the circumference burns — seen at the bottom of the water in the vase — where the flowers of the tuberoses fade — and the leaves of the branch of [   ] have dried — their little fists so tight — so unhappy — and let's not mention the violets for the poor things have given their all and are in distress — and the odor — coming on horseback from the kitchen — only adds to their hell — in the way they have of hiding the holes in their dress — so rumpled on top of it all — but what doesn't one have to say at this hour — to hide — the true drawbridge in my heart — and to shake the whole of this afternoon like a flag — so that the storm — will tear it — and to be able to play a game of cards — where one loses one's life with every hand — without having paid the bill — not to tell one's secret to anybody — who is not — persona grata — I know well that it's nobody's business — but what do you want — me — I'm having fun — and play frankly every forbidden game — up to and including death and am so happy to be yours so much yours — whom I love so much — my friend

[PJ]

4 NOVEMBER XXXV [I] [II]

[I]   tonight
      I saw
      the last
      person
      leaving the concert
      at the salle Gaveau

      and then I went to get some matches in the tobacco shop a
      bit further along the same street

[II]   mirror in its cork frame — thrown upon the waves at high
      sea — you see only the lightning — sky — and clouds —
      your open mouth is ready — to swallow the sun — but
      should the bird pass by — and live but for a moment in
      your gaze — and it will lose its eyes — dropped in the water
      — blind — and what laughter then — at that precise
      moment — won't they make the waves

                                                              [PJ]

5 NOVEMBER XXXV

but the spirit of salt doesn't count its wounds on the almond's
back which laughs at the crowd's angry stares and keeps its rea-
son on a leash only the better to mock in front of the mirror the
money bag formed in his hand by the coins paid back to the
enemy and that his long journey around the carp's somersaults
applauded by the butter in the pan know the path of the truncat-
ed tower covered with posters taking no account of the screams
and tears but always so cuddly so soft with lips pronouncing a
word only to caress it hug it against her heart looking at the sky

only when lying on the bed she lets her arms drift on the song broken by the raindrop which to follow the flight of the fly that alone in the world does not know her name nor is embarrassed by her sins lets out a big scream and raises the curtain and masticates the hour that will mathematically abolish the staircase who breaks her spine as long as her extraordinarily perilous position can't change her hand's hold on the window sill the smell of forests so wounded and dying he'll arrive tonight will never change the sweetness which at this hour knocks at the shutters comes in and sits down close by and reads over the shoulder the true and concrete history of a love without equal fresh like a rose still attached to the rosebush smiling in the sun

[PJ]

7 November XXXV

as long as the chair doesn't come to tap me on the shoulder with its usual familiarity and the kitchen table doesn't snuggle up in my arms and the hot-water bottle doesn't kiss my lips and smile laugh and whisper into my ears a thousand things I barely understand and the towel and dishrags don't start to applaud and beat their head against the line separates the little sun coming in the window from the marble's sulky pout despite the thousand ribbons of different colors that adorn it just to see them dance on the plate asleep in a corner the peas cheer up because the dialogue of the toro and the horse despite the evident drama playing itself out repeating itself in a thousand different ways and which I'll have to go tear from the bottom of each spectator's gaze with my finest needle though I'd prefer to let them enjoy themselves as they wish and cut the thread only at the end of the race to wake them only once dead and dragged by the mules leaving all the spent blood for others and X-raying my

portrait the prepared plate with a hundred sorcery ointments
enveloping me completely and the apparatus at the center inside
the deepest place of my body readied for all the most disagree-
able surprises capable of making you die with the laughter of
greatest happiness because in the toro's eye everything is
explained by numbers and nothing is clear at the bottom of the
taurine lake and only the odor that sings the wound can mathe-
matically tell the road traveled serpentined by the sword all of a
sudden more distressed to see the heat hiding beneath the skirts
break out in sighs than to see pain imprinted in capital letters all
around the arena feeling it vanish drop by drop despite the
ready-made idea of space and time and enveloping every inten-
tion in the garden without children some playing with hoops the
others the little girls playing hopscotch spreading the smell the
stink and the horror of the burst intestines in murderous hands
of blood escapes the horse's belly and begins the mass of the race
and each cry nails its carnation to the vase and each mouth sings
cut into four divided by two double mirrors set crosswise and
attached with a tenuous thread its end held by the inflamed
hearts of thirty thousand men and women forming but one flag
continuously perforated by bullets which the precise moment
forges with its fist attached to the incandescent handle held by
the amorous desires of the community of a whole people scour-
ing the entrails searching with its hands for the heart that
escapes with the life of the toro whose eyes the horse closes with
its hoofs weeping and with all its tears gathering alms for the
end of this afternoon that already touches on the age limit fore-
seen for mounting one's wings — leaps outside breaking the
shutters and rings all the bells in his ear and brings the veil's
color to the lilac blooming under its white armor which on the
ground tears the blunderbuss's hole in the toro's hide that
already a neapolitan slice spreads through the arena a bitter cold

of déjà vu and held in his chest exasperated by the music's silence and accentuated by the swift's cry piercing the canopy unable to completely lose its illusions despite the smell of grilled sardines and to have the actual time to sit down next to the lie that brutally explains its truth to the lines of the hand that it numbers and throws overboard into the cloaca and each to his own fate

[PJ]

8 November XXXV

no lies and hands raised doesn't one have to say more something else at this precise and solemn moment rather comic when the table stands up and presents its larded chest to the enemy overcome by laughing so much laughter and freaks the bloody rotgut blood of turnips and carrots cold and content in front of all the dangers of the knives escaping and lying in wait and without even thinking about it makes the onion tears turn tail and disregards the supplications and prayers of a whole mass of reasons that go get bloody noses blinded by the already so tired sun spot that is cooking his soup when the brilliant table cloth pours its yellow walking in lock step and marks the blue of the plates and dives into the green of the boughs only to make niches for the clockmaker and for the dog licking with its blade the biting wound that already at that instant appears in the fire like an image two sort of dove wings lilac colored that raise the pot into the air and discover speech coming to drink fresh water from the hand and climbs down and goes to lie down to write its history on the waves' crest

[PJ]

8 – 9 November XXXV

bullfighter's
jacket of
electric light bulbs
sewn with finest
needle
mist
invented
by the bull

[JR]

10 November XXXV

on the dining room table above a colossal carpet color of dry
blood the ashtray packed with butt-ends looked just like a little
death's head that stuck out its tongue at me today this very night
november tenth a quarter after ten by now which with three
more should make eleven by the clock which then will strike the
hour

[JR]

12 November XXXV

young girl correctly dressed in a beige coat with violet facings
150.000 – 300 – 22 – 95 centimes a madapolam combination
checked and adjusted with an allusion to ermine fur 143 – 60 –
32 a brassiere the open edges of the wound held separated by
hand pulleys making the sign of the cross perfumed with cheese
(Reblochon) 1300 – 75 – 03 – 49 – 317.000 – 25 centimes open-
ings up to date added on every second day set into the skin by
shivers kept awake by the mortal silence of the color lure genre

Lola of Valence 103 plus the languorous looks 310 – 313 plus
300.000 – 80 francs – 15 centimes for a forgotten glance on the
dresser — penalties incurred during the game — throw of the
discus between the legs by a succession of facts which for no rea-
son at all succeeded in making themselves a nest and in some
cases transforming themselves into the reasoned image of the
cup 380 – 11 plus expenses but the so academic drawing model
for all of history from his birth until this morning doesn't cry
even if one steps on the finger that points to the exit but spits out
his nosegay with the drinking glass only the smell organized in
regiments and parading by flag up front only if the tickling of
desire doesn't discover the auspicious place to transform the sar-
dine into a shark the shopping list gets longer only from that
moment on without the inevitable stop at the table at lunch time
to be able to write while sitting in the middle of so many mixed
hyperboles with the cheese and the tomato

[PJ]

14 NOVEMBER XXXV

Eugenia fragrant
little chapel of
guitar
strings
clothed in
poppy
black
carbuncles

[JR]

15 NOVEMBER XXXV

when the bull — opens the gateway of the horse's belly — with
his horn — and sticks his snout out to the edge — listen in the
deepest of all deepest holds — and with saint lucy's eyes — to
the sounds of moving vans — tight packed with picadors on
ponies — cast off by a black horse — and escaping now and ris-
ing like a butterfly — the mangled belly of the mare — a little
white horse — sees inside the conduit which sings as the blood
dances *trickling from a faucet in her breast* — a circus horse —
stands upright on his feet rear end decked out with blue and sil-
ver — white and blue feathers set on top atop his head —
between his two ears — and a pair of hands applauding —
plucks his eyes out from in front — the team of mules that block
his sight — that bounce and drag — his guts along the sand —
and screws the eye of the photographer — somewhere above the
banquet table — and pulls the wire out — a little at a time —
into the out of doors — and winds it in a ball — then draws a
likeness of his face so beautiful — onto a silver plaque — that
spatters — clenched fist — clean — the sun

[JR]

18 NOVEMBER XXXV

this stupid old age fuck and phantom shoved between her skirts
the farts that gnaw her nose with so much bullshit blissed out
rights to left the truth distorted from the years of bending under
the shameful weight of all you've known and learned by way of
enemas from all those cook books that boil down the praises of
their blackest sauces that have made the toilet overflow with just
a single stroke of magic marker slowly growing silent and then
shooting at the postman who takes a whiff of every letter and

then holds it captive nothing more than looking underneath her
skirts her spring night fragrance nothing more than bliss under
her arm enough for dog to howl and eat a plastic bone and gob-
ble up the night remembrance of a visit made to say that that's
the least of all my worries with those two now that it's nearly
one a.m. today the 19th of this month november in the year of
XXXV I'm going to unscrew this rotten light bulb teeth have
closed around here on my bed so I can sleep a while and get up
early and can send it flying with a well-placed kick with a bou-
quet of fuck it all skyscrapers

$$\text{[JR]}$$

20 NOVEMBER XXXV [I] [II]

[I] what rage salutes you so correctly bestriding its hate if not
the flower that burns its languor stretched out on the boat
that glides through these veins and suddenly opens the win-
dow of its cheek and for fun throws seeds of perfume down
into the street.

[II] Flower sweeter than honey $\bar{M}$ * you are my bonfire

$$\text{[PJ]}$$

24 NOVEMBER XXXV

the rat builds its nest in the eye a hundred times mended of fall-
en venetian blinds legs spread eagled legs up in the air there
over a fatuous bed made of fire of silences fallen asleep reduced
to a tattered old ragbag a corpse without redness that shouts up

---

* $\bar{M}$ refers to Marie-Thérèse Walter (1905-1977), female companion of Picasso from
1925 to the late 1930s.

its dance fork and knife made of ice laid out with most scurvy
intention in range of the bell that tolls forth holy wafer the bash
of the hour to each wound splits open that laughs

[JR]

24 – 28 NOVEMBER XXXV

tongue of fire fans the face inside the flute the cup
that singing nibbles the blue knife wound
lightly lightly
seated in the toro's eye
inscribed inside its head adorned with jasmines
waiting for the veil to swell
the crystal fragment
wind wrapped in fold of cape two-handled sword
caresses gushing
handing bread out to the blind man and the lilac colored dove
its wickedness crammed tight against the burning lemon's lips
with horn contorted
spooking the cathedral with its farewell gestures
swooning in his arms without an olé
a glance that blows apart the morning radio
that in its kisses photographs a bedbug sun
sucks out the fragrance from the dying hour
and moves across a page in flight
it tears the flowers into shreds and carries them away tucked in
between a sighing wing
and fear that still can smile
a knife that jumps for joy
right now this very day left floating in whatever way it wants to
this exact and necessary moment
at the summit of the well

a cry rose-colored
for the hand that casts it down
a little act of christian love

[JR]

SUNDAY 1ST DECEMBER XXXV

young girl has chewed the fingers off the frozen paint brush and
ailing and dressed up in rags resuscitates the leafage of a single
word that's spoken without fish or dream that coats with caramel
the fragment of an outcry she who breaks her fingernails against
the mirror so it opens up her mouth and swallows it at first crack
she receives across her shoulders what a memory it leaves her in
her eye the mote itself become so small and darling that they do
not see her there already naked and her face like new

[JR]

4 DECEMBER XXXV [I] [II]

[I]   when the street soaks bread in the blood the lamb pisses
away on the bullfighter's dress and the bull ends up wearing
the wings of a horse and they sweep up the rain that the
mules left behind and forgot when they gave a last tug on
the rope in the well and as only seems natural tangled it up
with thread from a spider that hangs from the tip of one tit
to the other the acrobat lady traverses it butterfly wings
opened wide and with thousands of blindfolded eyes minus
one that's reading what's written with light bulbs high up
in the sky and the tambourine tapping the name of the rose
that makes his hands shake and that casts them over the
eyes of the prisoner just when the firing squad shoots a

volley that lights up the night and excites it bespangled
with many small flags

$$[\text{JR}]$$

[II] the straw in the beam sees the eye laugh and kick the
speaking cloud obviously in white stitches while waiting for
the flute to notice the theft of the lantern buried in the sand

$$[\text{PJ}]$$

5 DECEMBER XXXV [I] [II]

[I] just for today the wheat winds its chimera round the mast
without a sail alone in middle of the cloth atop the table
and will wander through the streets linked arm in arm
down to the cockscomb's all night dances

[II] tongue that makes his bed when it's no longer worth a
damn the dew that slams against the mare while cooking
his arroz con pollo in the frying pan and getting ready for a
night of love with giggly gloves around the line of fire more
offensive and so pallid to the eye like ham that doesn't smell
and cheese that's all aquiver and the bird that sings and
wrings the curtain so it fans his face and rakes it in the snow
that bakes his particolored ribbons in the flute the cup and
sings to him as if the skull could sing that bites his hand
and carries it away suspended by a ring wrapped in the
sound of fly wings so the note the violin sustains doesn't
stop breathing squeezing on his throat with claws it gnaws
the knife wound as it swells in the balloon strung up with
wieners from estremadura urgent logic of the sky so blue so
lightly lightly seated on his curial chair and tucking up his

skirts each time the arrow whizzes by so fast it gives off salt
and pepper reads the future in the toro's eye a broken pot-
au-feu a spoon made out of boxwood and a wrist watch
laurel and oregano a silver basin a silk shoe and memory of
how a hand slides up along a knee and written on his head a
portrait on a poster with his resplendent name and that of
his own strain of fighting bulls adorned with jasmines and
a thousand reasons to be deaf and dumb this for the flea
that pisses such a downpour of café con leche that it shakes
the head hair waiting there behind the iron door and swells
the sail the classy education he received stretched out all
day in bed the crystal shard so that the wind wrapped in the
flap of cape over the two-edged sword gushing caresses
should do no more than run and curse the shriveled chest-
nuts and the thistle and should not inform him when he
hands out bread that he forgets the blind man and the lilac
colored dove but now that it's already evening and the
night's already falling he hauls out his hat and looks around
for his umbrella counting out his cards from 2 to 4 and 50
to 28 if he goes in for the kill his wickedness crams tight
against the lemon's lips the mirror burning like a mad
man and enflames the pitcher's fluted mouth and asks the
blind man for the shortest way to craze its colors in the cape
the horn contorted bent by you know who already and for
whom the light that falls and sprinkles stars over his face
bangs on a bell whose farewell grimaces are spooking the
cathedral that the air pursues and whips the lion mas-
querading as torero fainting in his arms without an olé and
already now as if exploding in his gaze the morning radio
so many late reports flat on his back he holds his breath
and on a neatly balanced plate they carry in a slice of moon
the shadow that the silence eats away that makes the guilty

man keep photographing in his kiss a sol si la fa re si mi fa do si la do fa bedbug sucking up the fragrance of the hour that falls and moves across the page in flight and if when he has packed his bundle he should tear the flowers into shreds and carry them away tucked in between a wing I know already why he's sighing and the fear that gives him back his image seen there in the lake and if the high point of the poem comes to him smiling he pulls down the curtain and pulls out the knife that jumps for joy and has no way out but to die from pleasure when right now this very day it leaves him floating in whatever way it wants to this exact and necessary moment not for me no more than when a ray of light comes through into the bottom of the well the color of the rose cries out against the hand that casts it down a little act of christian love

[JR]

6 December XXXV

never have you seen a tongue more vicious than the loving friend's who licks the little bitch with woolies twisted on the palette of the painter ashen faced and dressed in colors of a hard boiled egg and fortified with gunk that makes a thousand monkey shines down on his bed when the tomato warms him up no longer and no longer worth a damn now that the dew that doesn't know the winning number in the raffle pins a posy on the mare while cooking his arroz con pollo in the frying pan so it can tell the truth to him and extricate him from a jam while the zambomba sings to him and gets him ready for a night of carnal love with giggly gloves yet if around the line of fire still more raunchy than it seems and pallid set in motion in the eye like ham that doesn't smell and cheese that's all aquiver and is

coveting the bird that sings and wrings the curtain he does not
stand up or shout except for when the mortar tired out lies down
to sleep and dreams and fans his face and rakes it in the snow so
that the swallows tired out from reading grow so nervous when
they hear the casserole made of aluminum and baking its goat
melon ribbons of all colors in the flute the cup it sings to him as
if the skull could sing in horror of the ham that jerks and throbs
out on the griddle cognizant of bird smells in the wine it pulls
his leg and bites his hand and if the weather doesn't clear up
soon it just stays cold and there's no wit nor grit if he should
carry her away suspended in between the saw's teeth by a ring
wrapped in the sound of fly wings full of caramels so that
the note that holds the roof in equilibrium and that the violin
does not allow to breathe while squeezing on his throat a dough-
nut paper kite with claws in canvas shoes it gnaws the knife
wound as it swells in the balloon strung up with wieners from
estremadura urgent logic of the sky so blue so graceful seated on
his curule chair and tucking up his skirts each time the arrow
whizzes by so fast it sprinkles him with salt and pepper reads the
future in the bull's eye broken pot-au-feu a spoon made out of
boxwood and a wrist watch laurel and oregano a silver basin a
silk shoe and memory of a redoubled step a gloved hand in
among the flowers slides along a knee that bends beneath the
slogan written on his head from where the bees convey their
honey portrait on a poster pasted on the whore house wall with
his resplendent name drawn in carnations and that of his own
strain of Andalusian fighting bulls adorned with jasmines onion
smells a thousand reasons to be deaf and dumb before the flea
that pisses rain so fed up drinking milk and coffee that it shakes
her head hair waiting and despairing blond behind the iron door
to play the fool who hides her shame under the table cloth and
swells the sail the classy education he received stretched out all

day in bed directs the crystal shard that digs its nails into his chest so that the wind wrapped in the flap of cape over the two-edged sword gushing caresses should do no more than run and curse the shrivelled chestnuts and the thistle now a captive and should not inform him when he hands out bread among the wolves that he forgets the blind man in cheap clothing and the lilac colored dove but now that it's already late and that the night is falling he hauls out his hat and looks around for his umbrella counting out the cards from 2 to 4 and 28 to 50 if he goes in for the kill and crams his wickedness in tight against the lemon's lips the mirror his memento burning like a mad man tempering his blade and who enflames the pitcher's fluted mouth and in his monk's gown asks the blind man for the shortest way to craze its color in the cape the horn contorted bent by you know who already and for whom the light that falls and sprinkles stars over his face bangs on a bell whose farewell grimaces are spooking the cathedral with their blood and liver puddings that the air pursues and naked whips the lion masquerading as torero passing himself off as what he isn't fainting in his arms without an olé and already now how nice it is not to be making lost illusions clever though they be as if exploding he destroys them all the mighty captains the commanders the battalions rife with images and jammed after so long a time with barley chaff and in his gaze already the fandango so flamenco on the morning radio comes forth so many late reports flat on his back he holds his breath and on a neatly balanced plate they carry in a slice of moon the shadow that the silence eats away that makes the guilty man a blindfold on his eyes keep photographing in his kiss a sol si la fa re si mi fa do si la do fa bedbug sucking up the fragrance of the hour that falls and moves across the page in flight the way the leaf falls down as do the wings the horse abandons when it goes off bleeding circling the arena

dragging guts along and if when he has packed his bundle
quickly he should tear the flowers into shreds and carry them
away tucked in between a wing I know already why he's sighing
and the fear that gives him back his image seen there in the lake
the slice of watermelon makes and if the high point of the poem
comes to him smiling he pulls down the curtain and puts out the
millions of miscounted footlights and the knife that jumps for
joy and has no way out but to die from pleasure when right now
this very day it leaves him floating in whatever way it wants to
this exact and necessary necessary moment meant for me and
nothing more than when he sees a ray of light come through
into the summit of the well the color of a rose cries out against
the hand that casts it down a little act of christian love

[JR]

7 December XXXV

so little shame that crystal has for whom they make the rabbit's
    lying voice run on
whether or not his cape would float tied to his sailboat's broken
    mast
nor will the strutting prick now ever or again be able to be
    laughing from the rope that's hanging from the lamp post
whether it wasn't chance that made it happen
and the shadow's arbitrary form drawn finely by his kiss's
    silkiness the stirrup
and still and all in spite of which already he's locked in between
    the four walls of that grape seed
his urge to sing unto himself in rhythm with the trickling of the
    light onto the casserole
who's being all day on his knees before the rag so dirty as it
    dribbles down

love seated in a corner of the kitchen to amuse herself she cuts
   her nails

[JR]

8 December XXXV

if the drum boomboom consumes itself in flames free willing in
the sky and spikes it with a thousand thousand banderillas — if
the ink be hidden so it scrapes its scabies at its pleasure showing
naught of nose betwixt the flanges of the scissor in quick motion
— it is not that he is scared to climb the ladder to the paper light
athwart the little palm tree — nor to the reflection so distorted
that it causes grief and that the hand does falsely show him
underneath the table thus to fool him when the clock is stuck on
seven of this evening that may never end — if not the wish to
complicate the business of the painting — and to have no peace
and quiet even for a moment — nor to deck himself out from a
wish for silence — but the naked cup afloat atop the reddish
slabber on the tablecloth — an icy venus in his mouth — so like
an open knife — nor does he yet cry out — only the seesaw at
the deep end of the garden keeps up with the measure of his
grief

at twenty before one at night my grandmother's big balls are like
potatoes with tomatoes whistle jerk off up your ass
today december 9th of this year which is 1.935

[JR]

9 December XXXV

The round wing of the smallest alm the color is satisfied the
hand that gnaws let's not play then the flower that screams I

don't want to I don't want to the hopeless smell you don't want if
you its reason delousing itself but not for long floats the light it
has its hiding place in the sun two meters more with the length
of a head sticking out above the window sill is false absolutely
false he but if he lacks courage the color is satisfied it is false
absolutely false so sticking out one head with two meters more if
you the light it floats but not for long floats its reason delousing
itself if you do not want to with the hopeless smell I don't want
to he the flower that screams so let's not play but yes courage the
hand that gnaws the color is satisfied with the smallest alm one
head-length higher than the round wing

[PJ]

11 December XXXV
[portrait of sabartés]

glowing the ember of this friendship
clock that always strikes the hour
flag that flaps so happily
moved by the breath of kiss against a hand
heart's wingd caresses
rising up and flying from the highest limb
of tree in garden filled with fruit
if vantage point spreads velvet nigh the window
armchair replete with vest stripped off goose crying
covered with all the patience of a worm
and dyed by ribbons of a mediterranean color
table set with so much grace
over the beggar's hand
only adorned with blossoms
alms collected through those worlds

he pulls along   a trencher
with its ropes rose-colored
braided in some kind of way
to write down words that by themselves
have to sing out their names

[JR]

14 DECEMBER XXXV [I] [II]

[I]   Paris 14 – 12 – 35 ("Le Journal" 8 – 12 – 35 page 2)
Maxima : on the ground — under shelter — minima —
under shelter — maxima under shelter 755 millimeters
(1.007) maximum + 5

Abbeville — Ajaccio — Algiers — Anger — Antibes —
Belfort — Besançon — Biarritz — Bordeaux — Bréhat —
Brest — Calais — Chartres — Châteauroux — Cherbourg
— Dijon — Le Havre — Le Puy — Lyon — Marseille —
Montélimar — Nancy — Orléans — Perpignan — Salon
d'Automne, Grand Palais — French Association for the
Defense of Animals — Pasteur's precursors — martyrized
or kidnapped children ... and the Christmas message —
A.C. of 35 and 285 R.A.L. artistic matinée at 2 p.m. — after
the call of the war dead and the minute of silence — it is
often indispensable to insure their health and sometimes
their life the delicate features, the seductive force and the
sex-appeal of the charming little household — the flame of
remembrance — migratory birds piping and hopping about
before taking off, the left, leaving behind them figures yet
again ravaged, hearts suddenly closed up again, an ennui
kin to pain

What S.V.P. is went about it like a child. She is found expir-
ing the head the chest caught under an armoire a pater
familias shoots at the door nearly wounding the boss the
mysterious death of a nurse and that's not all! He wanted to
drink they didn't let him in he had drunk too much and
couldn't pay a pater familias wanted to play at KIDNAP
PERS it's the newspaper talking and answering for he alone
destroys without pain ooh Fernand — ooh my colleague
a woman I reclothed sap liqueur à la fine champagne
Demars St-Amand (Cher)
"Le Journal" 8.12.35 page 3

(page 2)
milk givers the opening session of the conference on intern-
ship chatter society pages a world premiere fish journeys for
the little Italians' Christmas tree the jubilee of the French
squadron weather-report what an annoyance! the lovers
from below will leave us! engagement marriage necrology
marvellous and muscadine what-a-shame!...

[II]   on the back of the huge slice
       of ardent melon
       tree a piece of river
       laughing table
       under the threat of the wing which
       tightens for the pleasure of seeing
       expire between its teeth
       distracted from its ennui
       a blade of grass
       the two little prunus buttons
       fallen so low
       embrace for the last two or three days

irritated by the cries
of the little girl

[PJ]

15 December XXXV

the knife's blade burns the wound that this knitting afternoon's
sigh gashes with its drops — the smell of the mouse caught in
the trap — the clock's molten butter — that the sea — plumb-
line attached to the sun — hanging from the day's neck — the
earth — wakes up love-dove colored temptation and tears the
fan's end into a thousand bits — S.O.S. of the shadow placed in
the middle of the table by the poor little palm tree — offered as
a gift at Easter by the friendly florist — but if the smallest
silence each day torn a little more grabs on to the veil the hour
drags along — sew these lips with a blond hair attached to the
needle of her eye

[PJ]

16 December XXXV [I] [II]

[I]   nothing but the color
       the bee champs at the bit
       just the odor
       the bird milks its sickle
       just to see them twist on the pillow
       love melts the metal of the swift's rail
       just a hair

[II] if suddenly the regiment of claws of the girl of the fat
       drum-major burns in the cup the splinters of the butterfly's
       flower of the mirrors the naked bee and decorated only

with its festive rump gnaws the chicken bone of Sunday
stew blanched in the light of the pigeon wing's passage
yelling on the roofs and the mirabelle pies her pain and
then shuts up when the deafening smell with the scottish
colors of the bird tasting of honey milks the milk at the
sickle's teats

but if over water the reflection sings "tender night" "blond
hair" just to see the image of her arm twist on the pillow
and laugh

love melts the metal of the swift's rail waiting to appease
her thirst to see floating in the river's water that the laugh-
ter of a mouth shows these lips

repudiated?
that she stinks!

[PJ]

17 DECEMBER XXXV

the ball of bulls weeps in the ivory cradle — telling disreputable
stories easy to tell in leisure clubs — and glistening shoe polish
in the wine square before the mother-of-pearl portrait of the
torero oil lamp and moon eye — scattered bunch of carnations
cutting out the brandy potato — with its boar-bristle brush —
thirsty like an eye forgotten atop the tower at noontime — for a
water-crazy summer night — carries the ashen virtue of the
arena tied up with a half-league of chorizo — Valentian
firecracker quail son of a whore old skillet and northern belly
button — underpants biweekly of songs — with all due respect
my best regards most affectionate and refined — when the must
boils and the blackbird is already warming up its lifestyle — and

not making soup with Estremadura ham but with four cloves —
shoots his arrow over the roof and receives the applause of the
palm leaves — which laugh at the joke and wind up non-stop
even at noon the blue phonograph — while drips upon the table
— the word which slowly corrodes the tablecloth — happy to be
lying all day long with nothing to do — calls out the numbers
issuing from the Madrid lottery drum and cuts off the eaves to
the tile roof in La Mancha — for otherwise despite the spites
and not having at hand the wheat which poisons the cloak —
embroidered with so much gold on almond-green silk with its
purple top — rubs the nose of the hobby-horse — and all he
does is fling himself from his whole past through the window in
the mirror — and even so and with all that since his graceful
body has left the rope — which the pea flower wraps around
itself — just in the yearning and in the bad music egged on by
the frying pan — the face provoked by the lamb's rage has
stopped frightening — the commercial firm clears up the smoke
and wrings its billion hatreds — while the cuckoo sings and the
kite doesn't let the key go through its Malaga eye — to the top of
the horn top — on which is balanced the sun where anchovies
fry

[RN]

19 December XXXV [i] [ii]

[i]   now the kitchen is all the time bawling and screaming not
letting the garlic soup settle in peace nor the music of splin-
ters in blue stitched with white threads and mended with
red and the earth friendly bond of two coifed caballeros
exudes from the other baked batch with his memories
drawn out in cords rightly nailed heart of malaga raisins
and olive oil sugar cubes banderole down on its knees on the

fire so simple it is to say mass and to scare him to death with
the tip of the candle wick nearly snuffed out full of black
and blue children kicked out of the noisiest dances the bob-
bin of silk a greek amphora placed where nothing ought to
be placed with no bread and no water for the glint of an eye
that begs handouts for playing the fool and the death so
bullfighterish should he be lacking the grace to dress up
like a bull his bullfighter's suit of lights luminous smash-
ing pikes down against pile-ups of sand made with ragouts
of so many massed banderillas protuberant dribbling out
from the body's harmonium sketched on the run and left
stretched at knife's midpoint above the blood stain on the
altar cloth going off burning the wreath the flames make
for him flames that their love held as prisoners dead drunk
now kept up all night by the snorts out of sight in back of
the bull pen nor does he have faith nor the will nor the
shadow that whips him nor art nor the will to be saying his
name nor reading it writ on the walls

and if his face on the small tambourine no longer casts a
shadow for the feather in flight to retrieve and the light
from the bulb to distort — nor does his nose stick out from
in back of the color he lacks and will not reach his hand out
— except to scare off the sound that the little goat makes
when it jumps on his neck and stretching its legs out it rocks
him — and now being heaped up in back of the broomstick
whatever he failed to say stings him — if the mortar doesn't
smell of adobo the ringdove whose ear the zambomba has
scratched cannot sleep from such sorrows — yet what
should we do if today is a day of mourning the bell elbow
deep in the sand — with the afternoon dragging its guts
with a smell as of noises and copper it leaves on his tongue

[II] lover man's ashes
     forever erect
     spreading roots out sustaining
     the cypress

                                                              [JR]

21 DECEMBER XXXV

I mean a dish a cup a nest a knife a tree a frying pan a nasty spill
while strolling on the sharp edge of a cornice breaking up into a
thousand pieces screaming like a madwoman and lying down to
sleep stark naked legs spread wide over the odor from a knife
that just beheaded the wine froth and nothing bleeds from it
except for lips like butterflies and asks you for no handouts for a
visit to the bulls with a cicada like a feather in the wind

a thing behind another thing with raffle numbers dropping
from a drum so sprightly so unlikely with its smiles and scowls it
terrifies the muses huddled underneath the eaves along the tile
roof of the house across the way who then get happy looking at
their faces in the whorehouse mirrors hobbling off to gather
flowers with no fear of shooting stars $-1-2-27-32-31-40$
-23

like a battalion (1) in transit (2) in lock step (3) like turkeys (4)
and in addition (5) with onions and carnations (6) and at the
same time the potatoes boiled with nothing more thrown in
except some thin applause and escargots and chitlins that the
babe's screams in her crib stir up and (7) fury jammed in all the
corners of still quickened quicklime mending her cat costume
(8) with shouting matches clean and mean and scratches that
the horseflies pay him back with every day the keening of the

clock the beds half made and unmade sheets entangled scorched
with fire with their silver color and the rose buds where the
bugle has passed wind already rubbing it around the frying pan
the bullet of the ballroom sweet red pepper of her love (9)
smashed to pieces by the scepter (10) of Sorrow of her solitude
by sad songs sailing off like papers thrown into the air descend-
ing from this afternoon's dream of this month December when
the dog howls and the blind piano hides so not to spread its cape
out in the face of all the fury in the full-length portrait of the
bull the etching of its years atop the sea propped on a chair that
sticks a pair of mid-sized banderillas in there where they stick
without the leaves (11) of the bell tree that would hurt him (12)
nor for their eyes to cheer the jest by which the glass door jostles
him nor does the smell (13) of tar of urine of the unpaid bills
(14) that dangle from a nail that screws into the soft dough of
his heart the cow's hoof and the owl's talon (15) that neither joy
nor song on boatride drenches the senility that bears the year-old
wheat wrapped in a grape leaf nor the jabbing of his pilgrim
name against his forehead these can make the straw that's hang-
ing from the roof over the passageway (16) destroy the shadow
playing the dead woman and she gathers up the pleat as maybe
life would and the shoeless foot that runs her through would be
imprinted (17) without a thought of being vanquished and
would hone in on the ash that covers the left portion of the sub-
ject of the painting (18) never bothering to place there in the
sunlit window the announcement of the revolution floating up
above the pennons on the tile roofs of his native town (19) with-
out the crash of hammer lusting after sickle that explodes and
blocks the cante hondo and the plainchant in the kiss gone head
to head against her mouth two balls of fire

(1) made of melon slices and decked out in colors of a small town bull ring 7 by the clock the month september at the bullfights on a weekday afternoon

(2) cautious and accredited with snot that soils the gilding on the dress for dingdong holidays put out to sop up moisture overnight out on the rearview balcony that fronts the garden

(3) the smell of scabies beaded through the eyes and spouting sighs from his guitar like parchment and alfalfa

(4) royaloyals lugging chains to all appearances of weird realities, glowing white hot redder than his cheeks

(5) aflame with icy fires of his sword

(6) they simmer down and hide from shame provoked by stripping naked there before the placard half torn from the wall circling the bull ring

(7) like the seesaw that the sun shakes in the blood erupting from the horse's breast death flinging the door open with her horns

(8) a convent of drunk nuns flaunting their garters

(9) castle of cards of a summer dumped in hot water as hard as a stone and dumped in again at a clam's pace extracts two bits from his change purse and buys himself a clutch of illusions

(10) who's conducting the concert

(11) clandestine

(12) the molars of judgment

(13) scorching

(14) now already when the cruddy things are sprouting flowers and the worms have left already from their rich old lady's face and turned already into little doves and when the dirty rags

(15) inside the picture frame that's gilded by the shafts of celery
     that wait in silence in the orchard
(16) tight as a strand of wire
(17) of the desires that he carries on his shoulders ground down
     by a load of flour and will plod on chockablock past every
     little hole left in the ground to lay his egg
(18) done on the run and quicker than a babe's game
(19) which is the same as everybody's

[JR]

24 DECEMBER XXXV

never have you seen a tongue more vicious than the loving
friend's who licks the little bitch with woolies twisted on the
palette of the painter ashen faced and dressed in colors of a hard
boiled egg and fortified with gunk that makes a thousand mon-
key shines down on his bed when the tomato warms him up
no longer and no longer worth a damn now that the dew that
doesn't know the winning number in the raffle pins a posy on
the mare while cooking his arroz con pollo in the frying pan so it
can tell the truth to him and extricate him from a jam while the
zambomba sings to him and gets him ready for a night of carnal
love with giggly gloves yet if around the half-done painting
of the shameless line a hooker's daughter ravenous and never
gorged with licking and with eating dead men's balls the
firecracker banderilla put to death by lightning more offensive
than it seems and such a pallid worm inside the nankeen cheese
without a shave and haircut more than seven months now makes
it to the summit of the prickly pear still smiling more than ever
having seen the christmas night bird like a ham that doesn't
smell and cheese that's all aquiver and is coveting the bird that
sings and wrings the curtain and by now he doesn't put a jacket

on or play the pianola crouched beneath the piss pot of the
roustabouts and dead but standing up he neither cries out for the
goring by the bull that afternoon nor does he trumpet the big
winner when the mortar tired out lies down to sleep and dreams
and fans his one and only face and rakes it in the snow so that
the swallows tired out from reading grow so nervous when they
hear the casserole made of aluminum and baking its goat melon
ribbons of all rainbow colors in the flute the cup and sings to
him a death song followed by another death song just as if the
skull could sing in horror of the ham that jerks and throbs out on
the griddle cognizant of bird smells in the wine it pulls his leg
and bites his hand and if the weather doesn't clear up soon it just
stays cold and there's no wit nor grit if he should carry her away
suspended in between the saw's teeth by the ring that Neptune's
cousin gave him wrapped up in the sound of fly wings full of
caramels they make at midnight when they kill the cock so that
the note that holds the roof in equilibrium and that the violin
does not allow to breathe while showing him the knife thrust
squeezing on his throat with windy doughnut paper kited hands
with claws in canvas shoes at three pesetas 75 centimos each it
gnaws the knife wound as it takes the train the first to leave his
chest each morning more and more in love and that swells up
the cables lost to sight and the balloon strung up with wieners
from estremadura urgent logic of the sky so blue so graceful
spitting at the crabs the island's mouths the nuns who melt
inside the ship's sails the defendant seated on his curule chair
who lets off farts each one a winning number in the raffle tuck-
ing up his skirts at every juncture with his forks of antique silver
without teeth with wrinkled skin disgusting baldness when the
arrow whizzes by so fast the bishop soils himself and sprinkles
him with salt and pepper jumps the line and reads the future in
the bull's eye snails a broken pot-au-feu made out of boxwood

and a wrist watch laurel and oregano a silver basin

[JR]

28 DECEMBER XXXV

astride this afternoon that's running out trailing its guts and liver on the forget-me-not lake open at random supporting in my arms these two broken wings along the tambourine of screams I take a walk when suddenly the cigarette wraps like a madwoman around my finger and bites me till she draws blood

[PJ]

30 DECEMBER XXXV

night
in the fountain

the dream twists the beak
of the blow struck
against the air

torn
from the guts
of the color

hidden
in the guitar

its joy
intoxicated
by the song
of pain

pulling
the threads
that support
the stage
of the scene

pours
the water
from the chandelier
down the staircase

which
the black hand
umbrellas

in the blue ear
resonates
the soap bubble
that escapes

kidnapping
early dawn

[PJ]

[1ST – 3RD JANUARY XXXVI]

1ST JANUARY XXXVI

peregrine beauty to which the pilgrim pays homage with his rat-
tle wizard draws sparks from the roast chicken with his watchful
mice by his side ripping the wrapping of the unknown object
making a fiery circle with knives and jackknives bringing out to

the window of the repulsive rag the bull's muzzle good night
and good bye it's getting late

3 JANUARY XXXVI

but if the vine leaf the feast the poppy the shoes and the black-
bird dawn's lips the weight of the hand the string holding the
mask on the roof and the eye burning deep inside the steel roots
of the sword if night lets its head fall at last upon its breast at
one o'clock tonight each raindrop bores little by little its hole
into the bronze plaque and inscribes boredom since it's too late
for the night to yield the wheat eaten up by the light and the
beads which went to bed hours ago dream of crime the arti-
chokes stuffed more with sparklers than with the boiled must's
fighting sighs first of all the light from the bulb has neither the
patience the lion has to spare nor even more so can the clock lis-
ten to the list of so much categorical balanced twaddle riding on
top of the smart one's nose the one who swallows the spring and
leaves it standing before the pregnant truth even though so
many lickings that the bunches of flowers tied with fishbones
picked up in the garbage heaps sing to him carried in between
the teeth of the tamed alligator and they neither soothe with
their perfume nor stink

[RN]

3 JANUARY XXXVI [I] [II]

[I]   III   the violets hummed drop after drop
      II   the rain's lips
      III   the caterpillar's passage over the hand
      I   the pin the hare its fear of blood which makes the fox
          thirsty

III   of the branch that hits to the grandeur of the projected
      shadow attracted by the wind's teeth
II   the nails
III   hid the view
I   steal the flower
III   and in the organ fry up the dead leaves
II   that draw blood
III   that the lake's light astonishes
I   and makes sing
III   and if a noise shows its eye
II   deep in the woods
III   and throttles silence
I   the pink of its pinprick
III   corosive *y* acid
II   the smell of earth
III   stomping its smell with hammer blows
I   black head
III   the deer
II   mad with love
III   falls down wounded

[II]   Silence dead drunk with so much laughter below the shoul-
       der concave mirror and piggybank by the wind's hairs if the
       dresser hides only the sun while martyrising it and presses
       between those teeth only the support bait of these two eyes
       at the edge of the keyhole the caravan is on its way in boats
       and illusion carries on its back only the hope to break those
       chains and plant its flag on the mountain top but if the
       table extends itself all the way through the room's door and
       if the door hides behind the hand's shadow one more time

the song of the smell of her dress will never again be able to laugh up its sleeve while standing upright head bowed low to the chest and slightly toward the left the tree what do those worries do planted like a crown around his forehead mathematics don't show the race the fox describes around the electric light bulb while madman and madwoman sitting facing each other with their laughter cutting out the leaves of the notebook great fun the cast shadow of the right hand points the beak and marks the degrees of so paternal a breastfeeding simultaneously goat and leaf from the bouquet sent as a present to the lady and memory of feathers with fingers wet from the foam of radio waves while the onion fries in the pan and the lemon's color grills in the bowl

[PJ]

4 JANUARY XXXVI

the paintings are madwomen
struck to the heart
radiant bubbles
by the eyes taken by the throat
of the cannoning whip lash
beating its wings
around the square of his desire

[PJ]

SUNDAY 5 JANUARY XXXVI

more than of honey the aftertaste if her gaze shoots the perfume of her caress and rides and sings her excursion of delights

nothing else recalls the color fanning her temple when the
flower presses its lips against the edge of the glass

[JW]

6 JANUARY XXXVI 3 A.M.

she and I
from our heart
the finesse of its hearing is such
that <u>at the eye</u> which opens his <u>wings</u>
    fearful
the pigeon in the cage
fans the feather horse stretched out on its hazel-tree
rummages among the vermin
the ends of threads

[PJ]

[6 JANUARY – 2 FEBRUARY XXXVI]

6 JANUARY XXXVI

around the well in the plaza the pins of the cries are sticking the
butterflies of the mouths upon the Magi's cake and the arm of
the heat gathers in its fist twenty sacks worth from the mountain
of wheat and spreads it out and paints on each grain a face
which in front the garden of thoughts repeats in its mirrors and
the corroded clock melts drunkenly from its fire and spills the
pleasure that drenches the afternoon on its lips the sand that
rises the dry mouth showing the tongue where the eyes come to
fill their pitchers and the solitary orange climbs up along the
invisible spiderweb and remains suspended in the air until the
plate comes out that gathers it from behind the roof on the left

and catches fire in the tinder of the trumpet which clawing the
naked breast of the sky makes it pour into the arena's throat the
milk which thirsty on its knees the body thrown back head
touching feet demands and which desire writhing in the clarion
like a fool who with his notes makes the rocket of his love rise up
as high as the skirt of the balcony between the legs of his loge
wrapped in the freshness of silk of the rose dressed with the
weight of gold the hand of the white wing of a dove takes off
from the arm and flies to his brow and wipes his sweat with his
fingertips and makes it jump sardine in the skillet at the touch of
the feather that passes the arrow of his smile outlined in the
aroma of the carnation by his nose at the bullpen that begins to
unwind the ball of silence from his rags of fear and anguish
model hearing a child cry in her cradle in the desperate after-
noon mother-of-pearl and conch shell while the wheat makes its
bread in the painter's palette who prepares his bath and per-
fumes it with the smell of the shower of his well-flexed rainbow
and launches and smears on his arrow the spree of color measur-
ing each step that leads to the breaking or binding line leaving
not a single loose end chastising the light that bares itself makes
a date and flees running at the slightest movement that the wind
picking up its skirts among the rows carries off and tosses the
worms from the cheese into the lower tiers and accelerates the
hour's movement in the village clock which explodes in the red
flags it prefers while the crystal piece of music shrieks shattering
its front in a thousand bits from the blow dealt against the sky
that burns the afternoon sizzling in the oven stuffed with horses
dressed in sadness in purple and silver stripes and in apple green
and jet black which swallowing saliva bites the cheek of the sun
till blood gushes forth which keeps in its cocoon the diamond
bull made of all the love of the loves of the blood flag shaken by

the olés from the bunch of hearts flapping their wings at the
snout showing its beauty through the blind spot of its prison

7 JANUARY XXXVI
where thousands of lightning rods end at the well that is the bull
where acrobats climb a thousand loves that are going to receive
the clouds from hands that would like to caress it touch its hair
and kiss it on the brow

9 JANUARY XXXVI
to make it virgin since it's under the glass where bees go around
making the hive of their piccolos waiting for the pigeon to see
that the coming hour is about to explode and the buzz of the
opening bread shouts its applause even more in love faints and
goes to pieces in the arms of the afternoon the kiss that pricks
the chain in the thick of the neck and makes it dance until its
colors bleed and the ribbons of the fingers end up white on the
hand that hangs and starts rubbing over the hair the dancing
and sticky game of life that kicks up a racket and cuts it when
the moment falls biting the bells shaken by the stab that the
swift delivers into thin air

10 JANUARY XXXVI
and in the tiers of wheat I'll break the silence on the embers of
the trumpets since today I'm going to write you a corrida you'll
lick your fingers if you care to listen to me until the end when
the lone ant in the middle of the arena sees the night penetrate
and stretch out its hand and run its palm over the wounds and
then apply it to the face of the ring and ascend the deck of span-
gles to the top and shake them around the plate of asbestos
turning the wheel of night at a gallop tossing its rags out the

window to see them break the line of the arrow's journey into a
thousand pieces of dream and tie the ends and weave the basket
where the bunch of games of spider threads will spring forth
that get mathematically entangled with the rope from the well
and pull the best and the worst from the ball or if not at any rate
everything we imagine to be true which is already something to
open the door of the pen and let the butterflies escape so that
they'll go tell it all furtively in the corner that hides its nose
beneath the wing abandoned on the stirrup of the gate when the
arena lifts its shadow and tears it out and fear carries it away and
passes its knife through the open neck of the lamb opening its
eye wide and leaving its gaze nailed to the point of the blade
which laughs sticking out past the eaves of the roof if the dew
drop tickles it turns over in its bed and bites its lips but for a
voice to pass its fingers through the crack in the door and the
cricket will climb on its legs uphill the abandoned piece from the
cracking of the forest and the smell of fried codfish will say its
prayer before the pepper that swells its pride in the heat of the
coals that roast it and the biting teeth clenched tight between
the two knees

11 JANUARY XXXVI

the nightfrets two twenty thirty-two six forty twenty-seven sev-
enteen eighteen forty-five and ten at two-thirty in the morning
he wakes up smells the fresh scent of watermelon on the pier
which sways gazing at the stars trembling trembling trembling
trembling trembling trembling trembling trembling trembling
trembling trembling lightens lightens lightens lighter lightens
the rose that comes out of the pale blue light blue light pale blue
blue from its darkest blue if the pale rose colors its rose with rose
that is paler still and the rose rosens with rose in the rosiest rose

yet of the rose rose rosing its rose rose rose rose in the rosiest the
rose that catches fire in the thirst for drinking in the gold that
sprinkles its enflamed rose in the fire of the gold that burns its
cheeks blazing from its incandescent rose which the gold melted
in the white red burns if the plate grows swells increases and
climbs the eye of the partridge of the lark of the quail of the
blackbird of the goldfinch of the sparrow hawk of the ringdove
and other spangles catching fire in the throat of its cries marzi-
pan of nougat of rooster and roast leg of lamb color of dry straw
thyme between the teeth of the square root of such an amusing
aubade stretching its arms passing its fingers among the trees
pissing the streams of flowers and shaking its sheets warm still
in the smell from the window her attractive body entangled in
the clear perfume of the silk of the morning that's washed in
the gaze lost in the distance of the rosy pompon cloud hiding its
light behind the bed of the cloud nine times minus four repeat-
ed in the bell of the hour's flight that opens its lips jumps on a
horse with its wings and climbs like a rocket above its song to
make holes in the tip of the blue of the ball of the poor washer-
woman of the drawing spread out to dry on the copper plate of
the etching of roses and jasmine today anniversary of this love
that is my life now that it's four little minutes past six on the
eleventh of January in the year XXXVI I write and smell the
flowers that are in front of me to the right but seated in front of
the table in such a way that the line going from the left angle
where my elbow rests cuts the waste basket in two and what do I
care about the bull and its fight at this hour now that the piano is
eating slowly swallowing serpents and toads and skinning frogs
with the sound of its silly mouse music but the perfumed fan of
its memory which will carry me away on its leaf rowing seaward

12 JANUARY XXXVI

along the filthy spoon of this Sunday here in Paris raining with its hands the song of cotton of its pearl but what can you do that's how it is and you have to let each one drag the old rag we inherit a little higher so worn out from so much rubbing along the clouds cleaning greasy casseroles pierced and gnawed by the broken bones of the rabbit made into easter and customhouse of the rubber that not even its rage chews anymore in the hatred mill affectionately licks the crystal of the wound to see the mute dance at the back of the room and the silence blowing in the trumpet and suffocating the musician with its deleterious per-fume and dressing him with visiting cards and placing him on top of the discobolus and laughing at him undo his seams and then carrying him off to roast in the pan where the monkey's ears are frying which is depicted in the horn of the phonograph if the gray sweeps the shirt from the port in the wheel of the disc of castanets the stridence of its pair of banderillas touches him in the pocket where he keeps his summer in Barcelona the beautiful and the list where I left so many things hanging on the altar of joy that I mix now with a bit of the color of the neck of the pigeon of melancholy

14 JANUARY XXXVI

1 2 3 4 5 6 7 8 9 10 11 12 13 14 15 16 17 18 19 20 21 22 23 24 25 26 27 28 29 30 31 32 33 34 33 32 31 30 29 28 27 26 25 24 23 22 21 0 2 32 1 0 4 32 1 2 0 2 3 4 2 0 2 1 do re mi fa sol la ti do do ti la sol fa mi re do sings Spanish fly its hard-boiled egg color of sermon of Lent trained flea and grudging whip of the transparent alabaster of the wings that the breadroll clutched to the little bitch that's no longer a bitch or anything that licks the ream of eyes nailed to the mirror of the suit of lights of Bengal shakes in

the morning when the serpent wets its lit candle in the gaze of
the horse that waits to be able to open its belly to the light black
sauce chest casket and writing desk hiding the fright and rancor
in the cigarette smoke breast of laurel leaves and crown inserted
into the embroidery of the drawing of the cape of soot adorned
with onions peppers and tomatoes the eggplant and garlic paint-
ed lifelike with their smell and their sayings and manner of
dress which in the wish to imitate the narcissus flower will burn
their wings in the flame which the tip of the horn of their key
will snatch the bolt from the curtains that cover the touch of
silence of entrails that swell and overflow from the bed of the
trunk that broke its straps exploding the sound of reveille of
death with its gala outfit head crowned with keyrings full of
complicated little keys of the drawing of its twisted snail curiosi-
ties of biscuit and Malagan *churro* and its necklaces of bunches
of anchovies and over its net tunic made from the guts of squint-
ing cats wears tied around its waist the rope from the well that
threads sixteen sea bream heads through the eyes and each end
retains with a knot the dried skin of an angler holding between
its teeth on the tongue sticking out a Sevillian nickel one and the
other a cigarette butt as for its feet it wears galoshes and above
each one tied with some green ribbons a handkerchief with the
Spanish colors painted on its four edges and in each corner the
portrait of a bullfighter Costillares Pedro Romero Conejito and
el Chico del Pandero who are singing and playing guitar doing
somersaults juggling the pears of the elm tree when the ma-
chine starts to move and the steam hides it behind the shadow
carried on their shoulders by the matador's entire team who are
coming out of the boardinghouse now carrying in their throat
the weight of unseeing eyes and the metal taste of the cry of the
ball of cotton that scratches their ear with worry the slap of

street breath collecting garbage in the gold and indigo silk plate
the plum red and the black compressed in green by the silver
embroidery that celebrates it and by the ivory white

16 JANUARY XXXVI

writes on the jawbone of the balcony with the smell of fried
eggs and potatoes the landlady's paper which in French in the
text tells the true story of the strange event that took place sud-
denly in the Jewish quarter in Avignon and says *la fille du
marchand entortillée au doigt de la pâle chimère secoue son
édredon taillé dans du cristal de roche* with the sneaky sneak of
the street informers the flood of pennants and the panting of
the color of the flags with the sole intention of harvesting organ
pipes that play such a bullfighting march with its music of eyes
in measure and time to the hour that digs its spurs if the rooster
dressed in its tomato and pepper has left in the skirmish besides
many illusions its bones which the cigar lit in the pealing of the
clocktower bell that forces its way amid the cymbals and bass
drum erases the shadow which the fall of the clapper caused in
the brow of the silence and the car flies more than it runs and
grows intoxicated with its heat with its smell with its gestures
with its desire the faun the colt and mounts it and its thighs
squeeze it tight burning its skin the wave that the sea carries off
and draws at the bottom a heart with two open wings and two
bull's horns and between the teeth of the mouth an arrow and if
the ace of diamonds doesn't come out first when he tosses the
cards from the deck through the clouds he takes the bow and
arrows and starts piercing all the cards one by one until they fall
dead upon the roof

17 JANUARY XXXVI

which if the mother-of-pearl why go looking so far at the bottom
of the mine what the stream still sings in the hand of the flower
face to face the breeze blows shaking its fringes tells me the
truth straight out covers its nose and hides between the folds of
the reflection that the passing of its hand through the sun's ray
that blows out the crack on the inner left side of the refuge and
decomposes its bounds that the clockmaker with the first lash he
delivers will cause to leap wings together beneath the wheels
that weave light on the grain of sand that the slipper carries off
embedded in the left edge the arena opens its belly wide and sees
in the horn the key that splits it and sets it dry raisin on the
cane that goes fishing for the needlepoint that the color wipes
the plate clean of the potato omelette heart grasshopper heart
laughs open-mouthed heart is content crust of bread sprinkled
with olive oil rubbed in the flying gurnard's eye Pandora's box
tambourine accompanying the chimes of the feet hanging in the
tree made by the pieces torn from the afternoon that rubs its
nose in the arm that a lily's sigh reclining at the edge of the
creaking and the flavor that in the bull's eye the cinnamon lifts
onto the tip of the blue nailing it with bayonets hammering on
the nape of the neck the stool where seated he is writing his vile
garrote story of the bull explodes at four in the afternoon the
fiesta

18 JANUARY XXXVI

and the song of songs appears inside the crystal clear cup of the
bullfighters who are full of thousands of rainbow castanets of
guitars of silk of hearts bells of fires of Bengal and of rockets of
butterflies of lips flowers that dancing singing clapping and
exploding and flying go in against the crystal to break the

breakwater of olés that applaud their forms upon the sail that swells pregnant in the twisted panting that receives from the thousands and thousands of concentric circles made all around by the thousands and thousands of mouths that start nailing above their bodies the sound that awakens against the crystal the kiss of the design that embroiders the gold or silver that will dress the capes boleros and bags that coat bullfighters and tore-adors cooked in the heat of the threads of the coffin of the clever worm dyed as the stellar specter that the colored wings that hold up in the air like the mules that the tickles that the bells season mince with their vinegar throw a net over the body stretched out in the sun and haul the seine of the miraculous fish that shows amid its mesh the monkey's leaps and mischief and the matador's team appears in the world dragging behind them the centaurs centurions

19 JANUARY XXXVI

and from the table of flames from the bonfire of music the cloud of transparent locusts rises precious stones that fly through out of their machinegunning necessity to possess the key to the main problem central point and eye of the needle beacon rain of stars whip drill and taste of hate in the mouth bird beribboned arrow comes to peck in mid-flight from the burning rose of death that the purple and almond green gauze of the light of its wax in the plate gathers the venom that the swan scorpion will sing now so twisted at the fluttering of the silk against the face of the air that laughs at the saying he drops his head rolling to the bitter shore of the aloe of the color given by the punch of the sun that has gone away fugitive from the night from the bed where with a bicycle in a house of ill repute in Barcelona he leaped with the lance and thrust banderillas sitting in a chair which now that the monkey the parrot the drumsticks the saw

the hammer the sickle the scarf and the thistle the trumpet the
clarion the jetstone the cry the light and the curl the feather and
the smell under his arm cook together in the cauldron the light
the feather the cheese the rice the breadcrusts and the ice the
chirping of the swifts at the bottom of the blue soup tureen and
the tra la la la la they shoot the necessary shots and the omis-
sions that drown in the ink and the blind man sees his image
portrayed in the foam of the few pieces of silence that fly strung
along on the threads of the air and entangle the pale skein that
stops and waits and halts its silence and stops for a moment the
clock that turns such a pale yellow faints and bleeds its hours
from the unhealthy sorrow learned by every school and wakes up
egg sun brighter than the sun made into a man bull host sur-
rounded by twenty-six white eagle wings wrapped in iris circles
that keep growing larger as others appear and grow infinitely
and since infinitely others and others that appear grow larger
as well over the India ink of the infinite which comical as it
may be the accuracy of what was said it shows its bit of irony
and smiles at the written page because the truth is laughter
which in a pure guffaw quarrels with such a funny chimera and
water under the bridge since it's time to come out now for the
first tough surly black bull wild-haired muddy dapple-gray
cowardly and outlined clockmaker and bearded affection blood-
drenched carnation pipes of Pan and slice with its sardine in
marinade on top and northern arch passing its finger along the
edge of the scythe shuts the bolt and turning it twice like a goat
chaste satyr unaware of love even by sight sun within his sun
and I laugh knowing what he is climbing the mountains uphill
setting himself like a flag on the highest peak shaking it drunk
with joy choking in its folds the birds that later at night belly up
dead will keep counting their pesetas and playing to see which
will toss them the furthest from the vertigo that makes it fling

from the crate the dark ball of the bullpen that gives off the
smell of love cuckoo bird which by the handful cherubs and
chubby angels with no backsides accompany and fan with their
wings the jingle and perfume they offer to the indigo blue of the
clarion with their farts which in the water of the fountain that
fills the crystal glass already described ascend in a balloon the
basket filled with the bunch of the most insipid jokes and flatter-
ies so high that the baba made with eau-de-vie flour anisette
sugar and olive oil kneaded a long time the dough cut into
square pieces and folded twice fried in hot boiling oil and when
you see they're a nice golden brown you take them out and let
them cool and melt some honey and while it's hot roll them in it
draining them well and then when they're almost cold pour
rainbow sprinkles over them in front of the mirror of family
memories that for me have this flavor and that my mother some-
times sent me knowing how much I liked these things when I
was still a boy so long ago and that now at one-o-eight in the
morning on the twentieth of January in the year XXXVI lying
in bed in my room that looks out on the garden in the Rue La
Boétie number 23 in Paris I don't know why I remember all this
that has nothing to do with what I'm writing or maybe it's only
the apparent embroidery of the threads running wild with hap-
piness from floating freely without being tamed by the pattern
tickled out of it by the bullring attendant

20 JANUARY XXXVI

and at the first shove the bull gives to the horse the curtain rises
and all the boats full of footlights go on with fireworks from the
sheaves of rockets that reap lights spread-eagle between the
sheets of the colors that make its bed and of the bunches of
flowers of the cup of glass banderillero who nails his fan who
gets tangled up in the open skein of the pattern of his dance and

the bull with its key seeks the eagle eye of the tambourine that
rings from the blow given by the horn in the spree of its
abdomen like the deliberate chiming of the binge fine and deli-
cate banquet of death and opens the door of the deck of the
belly wide to the mare lifts the curtains and discovers the feast
and arranges the table and chairs and collects the forgotten rags
and with its snout cleans the tablecloths stained with the collect-
ed blood spurts into the cups along the paths and lanes of the
guts braiding them so carefully and arranging them and tying
them to the ribs hanging Chinese lanterns and flags on them its
eye gleaning the inside details discovers the back of the cave in
the deepest inner depth stuck to the twisted roof of the dry tree
and sponge drowning in blood the hard-boiled egg of the little
white and blue horse wrapped in the sugar and honey of the
purple anemone and the poppy full stop and briny bellflower
and saltpeter caught by the teeth in the whitewash of the wall
that stays up by a miracle in the jostling dealt by the panting
that swells the blackberry basket and the white become rose of
the little horse jumps its blue that pecks the lilac color from the
light that bites it on the neck and in its chest the fanfare of the
bass drum and the cymbal the trombone bursts out hands tied by
the ropes that pull the net of thorns and of eyes that pull
through their veins the broken boat shaking its legs and undoing
the mess of the bloody intestine beauties that get tangled up
each time more in the labyrinth of the mainmast of the captive
pain of the game of chess that swims champion among the
waves of olés and the cries that tear ostrich from the open book
frightened in the sun that opens its mouth and looks at its throat
its tongue speaking truly now tossing out plans perspectives and
drawing lines of flight its head turns around and says look at me
now that you're looking at me look at me since you're already
looking at me look at me since me already you're looking at now

look at me since you're looking at me if already me now look
since already you're looking since if you're looking at me and if
la look now la look ti now look la ti la la ti mi ti la mi ti ti mi ti la
ti ti boat lying on the beach cut out by the scissors of the mirror
of the silk of the cape and flower stinking from the twisted fart
bells hanging from the neck of the slap in the curtains of the tail
cake of pierced bone in the part of the tiers that are to the right
of the left hand of the ashtray that's already playing with flames
in the highly prohibited game 32 33 24 0 2 21 golden in the festi-
val of the tender dove the niche laughs at the rope la ti la sol re
breaks the dispatch and the clam lights the chain of the clock la
ti la fa mi re ti la shuts in the touch of silence beneath the needle
that wets its finger in the drop of water from the spigot 2 and 2
are six and three reales more and 2 are 10 and six 498678 and in
addition the washerwoman's accounts with her wheat and her
wheaty asparagus and her packets of pure sentiments and braid-
ed ornaments and the complications borne on the shoulder and
the throw-me and leave-it and don't say there's a reason to sit
down and not do anything more ever that we'll have to see
what's good and bad and the bad flavor left to fear by burdens
and bugs that's good the clock is fed up with giving so many
alms to the hours that don't even listen to its drowsy ringing of
the bell when it hasn't slept in a century and a thousand others
that her hand covers the mouth of the drain that gushes from
the belly of the one I was telling you the tale about and that
each little curl on the nape of the neck taking the shape of a let-
ter combined in a certain way here is the hard part would form
the complete page of the truth of the story passed through the
sieve of the mathematics of the exact poetry of its eye

22 JANUARY XXXVI

stone bronze steel blood fire black soot punch hammer cable iron
chain dog wolf fried squid black record of cante hondo rust the
bell's barking lip eye whistle arrow shout if the silence fades
away it's all ready say a hundred times a and then b and then a b
a a and then a b a b and then and then a b c d leap of the toad
that falls drowns and passes the feather duster tired at this hour
and doesn't let the bunch of grapes bullfight its wine today since
it's already one twenty in the morning on the 23rd of January in
the year 1936

26 JANUARY XXXVI

without order or measure without taste without smell the eye
will close its wings and sing the prayer for the dead hand placed
on guard of laughter dies if the awning scrapes in the light of
his neck the displeasure of the color that punishes it bites over a
slow flame the finger that twists the shadow that the fan makes
of it but let the air come to awaken the glass that ignites it and
then the crackling that would be the joy that cheers it on and
reddens the rag scratching the box would skip with the meta-
morphosis of the blood and the thrown dice which if the sword
leaps hitting right in the middle of the host and falls apart in the
middle of the rose the pair of banderillas that dance saffron flint
the blue disc caught in the mesh of the rain of hands and gath-
ered in flight by the sharp beak of the somersault of the captive
steel in the cage the boat leaves its bed and goes out through the
world trailing its cape and if the grief and regrets and the blow
they strike at the mirror can nail their keys in a crown upon its
brow the halo of kisses burns in its bonfire the distant sound car-
ried in the beak by the reflection of the stone in the ring sniffing
its armpit

27 JANUARY XXXVI

it's raining along the thread that bathes the destiny of the fold of
the leaf that flies when it crosses the piece of linen the perfume
that intoxicates with its cries the eye placed on the anvil and
with each blow that transforms the color of the colors the blood
of the flame burns inside the crystal of the goblet

the handful of kings and queens from the playing cards that he
tosses against the passing cloud the joy that roasts its chestnuts
weighs its old rags on the scales and puts the bread darned with
red thread and nailed with thorns in the oven hangs it from the
mainmast of the brigantine that goes out wings extended from
the earthenware bowl from the gazpacho from the corrida and
hides its hour in the flyer stuck to its prison wall cuts it and
crumbles and puts it on guard atop the horn that crowns with
abysses the stroll by the seashore in the afternoon around six in
the silk of its pearly arm shell from Compostela beside the 3
flowers that vomit the green tongue from their mouths heads
tousled from the reddish tulip and from the two other yellow
tulips singing around the silver and gold of the suits the hard-
boiled egg and the anchovies the onion and the oil and the
elegance and the confections the grace and the poise and the joke
and the salt that they offer to the blockhead who stretching out
his hand asks them for a little alms sitting alone on the ground
in the middle of the plaza who swallowing saliva rises to heaven
among the clouds of bullfighting music hauling the rope from
the well and the bucket full of the sun's laughter that spills and
drenches the piece of the plaza on the left from the blow of its
lance while the stroke of the bell and the blackbird at the stroke
of silence wakes up and sticks out its nose behind the veil the
light keeps quiet and an instant puts its hands in front of the

noise and throws the cotton above the frying pan and combs the hair of the silence with the feather that the lilac color has stained and rubs the glass with its breath and erases the plaza with its hand and rocks its sleep by the eye of the pearl in the tie-pin and sings into the mouth of the goblet the secret that takes its siesta spread out at the bottom which if the white dissolves in such a pale blue it sighs in the rose and in ecstasy the yellow faints floats its image in the zephyr and the cambric and a scent of violets sways along when the clock moves its spider legs to catch the fly

28 JANUARY XXXVI

225.818 zero three twenty-one thirty-three plus the zeros and all the rest that's added and does the account that complicates each time more the mess of messes of this life which neither one nor the other nor the one beyond nor the most distant memory that hammers around the cage and makes the goldfinch tell its troubles typewritten so wet and drenched on the moss of the piece of the old cobalt blue rag spoils the tale and drinks a shot of light to everyone's health and if it's not the eagle the doorman who receives him on the doorstep of his house and collects his hat and cape when he arrives and the lion who licks his hand at the festoon his caresses make shaking the flag of salutations that the sparrow hawk flies the cape flutters about from the swarm of bees haloing the bull's head and carries it away enamored of the washed-out blue in his eyes behind him like a lamb adorned with rosettes and colored bows

1ST FEBRUARY XXXVI

love is a nettle we have to mow down each instant if we want to have a snooze stretched out in its shadow

2 FEBRUARY XXXVI

once again the beak of the bull opens the skin of aged wine in
the horse's belly and the cellar lit by the blood's oil explodes the
bass drum of the fanfare of pain cooked with the finest needle
from the fringes of its eye in the flag that the terror has nailed
inside and that the fear shakes desperately trampling on the cur-
tains of its entrails tangling in the threads of the curtain of its
theater the illusion of the drama that stakes its life on the last
card and builds its house of cards on the razor's edge of the
sound of the swan song of the clarion that dies of sorrow swim-
ming blind diver through the green guts of the lake where
Ophelia goes searching at the bottom for a piece of paper and a
pencil to start gradually doing her overdue accounts of the list of
the stockings of the shirts and pants and the handkerchiefs
soaked in the sound of the flower torn from the flute of the
inner blue that covers the window gripping the bars a bouquet of
hands bites it and twists it when he offers his cape to fill the
horn that the bull presents to him and wrapped in the incense of
his cape the panting of the silence enters which the cotton sinks
in its wound with the sound of cymbals death which opens the
faucet where the little white mouse flees which robs it of the
grain of rice where its pure horse history is written while the
cape sprinkles its purple and coats the tip with the caramel the
finishing touch of the diversionary maneuver on the trivet the
cauldron begins to make its soup and sing very funny and cheer-
ful tales to pass the time and distract the respectable public
disgusting and rotten caught in the prongs of the fork that
scrapes the bottom of the paella if the gold rains its saltshaker
and stamps in the puddle where the harp floats its tongue rub-
bing the mud the cup spits the reflection and doesn't sing
through the veil the prayer for the dead which time nails to the

poster that peels from the wall the infernal machine of the
fluttering where the butterfly laughs

[JW]

3 FEBRUARY XXXVI

if the flower inscribes its design in the color huddling in its cot-
ton-wool nest and suddenly wakes her up with a blow of the
whip to the cheek the scream vaporizing the song of the baby
bird eats the seeds of the little bit of sun sprinkling the o so
gauche corner of the tablecloth and lays a hand on the back of
the chair that closes its eyes and falls asleep after lunch letting
the shadow's blade cut in half only the regrets which without
saying a word the distant sea's breath by pulling out the four
pins keep them nailed to the wall will let them fly away like a
petrified musical tune rises and lifts hooked to the zephyr hold-
ing on its balanced tray the irritating caress of the wound's
perfume whose lips harvest a certain uneasiness scallop stitched
on the hem that the raindrops stew in the pot-au-feu of the gaze
into the mirror with the angry beast's hair bristling hiding the
rising flood of the desire to piss openly on the passably incor-
rect lesson indulgence wearing the clogs of its old savoir vivre
transfers the reason not to mock the enchanted flute of the
calambredaine's hand-kissing

[PJ]

6 FEBRUARY XXXVI

the toothache of grimacing color and these o so mathematically
convoluted homages so adroitly planted along the lines of chance
meetings in the shadow of the attitude taken by the drawing

caught in passing by the light that under its thick thumb crushes the line put to sleep by the reflection of the vase with a shove of the shoulder pushes back and sacks the desired order and spits all scorn overboard to the coquille Saint-Jacques well displayed on the slender gas-burner

[PJ]

[10 – 12 February XXXVI]

10 february xxxvi

I

at such an hour spread out on the color spread that bleeds this silence on the light's sound perforating it if the scream in the night of her hair doesn't roll through the air the wave bathing her nor can calm down pierced by the small heap that gives the necklace of smiles deposited in the wound's nest by the tempest which with its wing prolongs her caressing martyrdom aurora borealis evening-dress of electric wires and throws her in my glass to plunge in full swing sounding her heart to pick the branch of coral fastened to the mirror that holds its breath

12 february xxxvi

II

crystal slice of the moving reflection well spread over the authoritarian temptation of space loosely colored by the light perforating it the black tempest clutches it in its claws so caressingly rocks and licks it behind the ear through the disk's tulle

III

around the disk shining from its crystal temptation assassinated by the prickling of the light the burst caressing with its claws

slides the shining blade of its desire to the bottom of the glass
and bites the grain of the musical tune ready to germinate

IV

if around the circles that color assassinates the swarm of bees of
the disk's tune punctures with its stings the bloated balloon of
the budding lightning storm floats in the spread out and tattered
light the bewildered perfume of its image

[PJ]

February 29 XXXVI

the raft of the medusa unties itself from the sea to take the wash
of the bird's pocket mirror in its arms

if the raft of the medusa finally unties its chains flies through
the dark its forehead hooks into the pocket mirror's wash

if the raft of the medusa divests its body of its chains and lets
the rags of waves float hanging on by the fingertips its forehead
grinds its caress on the stone of the wash cut by the detached
wing of pocket mirror

if my raft of the medusa divests its body of its chains and only
lets the rags of waves float hanging on by the fingertips its fore-
head grinds its caress on the stone of the wash cut by the
detached wing of the tender wounded bird singing sitting on the
tip of the great amorous buffalo's horn

[PJ]

3 March XXXVI

string the thread through the needle with your bamboo sword
and prick it from the right side through the fat nape of a glance
concealed behind a glass of limpid water stopper that sets free its
fingernails from face and aggravates the wound made by its
laughter claw devouring the paper that ignites and bursts and
twists a beak at bottom of the ivory lake if the venetian blind on
sentry duty dissipates its sadness that the sugarcoated color of
this afternoon wipes with its finger at each note coming from
the hungup piano dangling like a rag the very hour that the
clock sets back

[JR]

8 March XXXVI

with peels of bells cover the boredom her stew of devouring eels
and rub her pepper on fringe of tears at the telescope of the
rocket suddenly stopped in its run opening wide its ears to the
mice of the flag flying drums beating the drinking glass full of
clear water to the rim of the nearly absolutely necessary need to
illuminate its spring night with pin heads drop her hand and
distractedly caress the sharp edge on her forehead of the blade of
the knife planted on its two legs in the middle of the desert this
dawn of day eight of the month of march breathes in the shut-
ters the tune of the song of the feather-duster discovering the
face of the secret rolled into a stinking ball thrown into the dark-
est recess of forgetting flower fife smelling of the final period

[PJ]

9 MARCH XXXVI

Sabartés you who count the hours off one at a time tell them at
half past 8 to jump into my bed until I wake from sleep
(now that it's just turned two a.m. the 9th of march the year
MCMXXXVI)

[JR]

17 MARCH XXXVI (IN THE CAFÉ DE LA RÉGENCE)

the rasp the tongs the fist that drives in the knife the mouth of
chains that burns the finger of her hand pressed against her
temple the cold that tears the lightning bolt into shreds and the
smell of creosote the violin-bow of the hour bloated with thorns
caressing the piece of cloth swaddling her prostrate body the
swing suspended from the gallows of the sound hooked to the
perfume striking the hundred beats announcing the raising of
the curtain of fire in the pocket mirror if the splinter glitter
howls its distress and rolls its drawing into a ball and nails it to
silence

[PJ]

22 MARCH XXXVI

breadcrumb so gently deposited by her fingers on the rim of the
sky as blue suitor as the chained shellfish playing the flute beat-
ing its wings at each drop flowers in spring at the rent in her
dress made by the window inflating and filling the room and
carrying her away her long hair on the wind

[PJ]

24 March XXXVI

<pre>
pot
      saw
my   lady
      gay
laugh   sand
</pre>

[PJ]

25 March XXXVI (on the train to antibes)

think evening <u>angelus</u> to see you <u>broken</u> in the mirror exploding
from clog kick blow-pipe <u>to see you nailed</u> on the pond shivering
detaching and rolling itself into a pill unhooks the hanged body
of the naked loved one from the festoon of mouths untie your
hand your hands

[PJ]

Juan-les-Pins 26 March XXXVI

the slender sojourn of the secret price of pain simmers on the
low fire of memory where the onion plays the star if the hand
detaches itself from its lines having read and reread the past but
at the crack of the riding-whip caught straight in the eyes

[PJ]

Juan-les-Pins 29 March XXXVI

salaried characters of the drama that plays this comedy for itself
topsy-turvy they tumble over each other infesting the stage with
their rejoinders imposed by a stinking slave logic in decomposi-
tion chained and dank turning language into goo whenever a

true scream gets it to flower and when one unties the pathways
that gnaw the wings of her hands the words not immediately
spoken petrify on the branch of liquid coral and dry up the milk
in the dugs of the aurora borealis hatching small rainbows in
their nests imposes the list of actors on the ladder braided with
the skein of her black hair love the begging reasons the hand
brandishing a river held by the middle and burning at each end
— the sheaf of vegetables broken by fatigue for having chased
two hares at once on the lake clattering in the wind attached to
the roots — the king — the queen — the jacks — the losing
numbers of all national lotteries — the tight men and the loose
girls — huge crawfish hanging out in the worst places Ophelia
laughing like a madwoman — six pairs of point-lace curtains
sown onto the marble of the dissection table of the flight of the
first swallow seen this spring and the tears of a little shellfish
girl — the shutters one closes in the face of evening come to eat
soup — boredom boredom boredom terrible boredom and the
bouquet of flowers hanging from the bow of the pigeon's neck
falling from the ceiling dead center on the roulette wheel — all
of it ground, crushed, powdered dust in the o so tired green
hanging from the point of the knife of the palm pinched by
rosy-golden cloud finger-spread on the blue eye orphan bell of
hours holding out her hand at the mercy of capricious alms

[PJ]

JUAN-LES-PINS 3 APRIL XXXVI [I] [II] [III]

[I] go ahead and let the blackbird sing into the soup absorbent
     cotton fleas are thrashing and with tears that sear its pearly
     nest its iron belly buttons and its lettuces its stairways of
     white marble sugared innards made of gold and flowers
     jacket gazing in the distance gazes lost amidst the brazen

wish to bring forth breakwaters and wheat from crash of
tambourine against the shard of memory tied to the wire
floating swallow-like through veins and ringing out the
hour making casseroles of bread crumbs a la andaluza dish-
ing out the bread and lard soaked in café con leche to the
medlars spinning in and spinning out his bedroom at each
cry and from behind his back disposing of the remnants of
the feast he grabs the globe and splits it into sixes throws it
in the mailbox that goes crazy little sand grain whirling on
the point of nail that bears the full weight of all life and of
the tales recounting its great deeds

[II] *the evening star* <u>*sophistiphies*</u> *the blue red spiral of the
crystal marble in the answer brought in on the morning tray
beside the tree branch flowering and visible outside the win-
dow doubling up with so much laughter and breaks up the
scent of recollection on the choppimg block of the lethargic
centipede*

[III] gold of water tap and hip * sugar and mustard * spider's
thread and wheat inside his gaze * death leap of prickly
pear * wheel of fortune linnet and umbilicus in flight * silk
shirt and rice with chicken * pierced palm with rose's song
and wheat asparagus of his true love * owl's aroma and
mint's essence * garlic * lettuces and goat cheese * a paint-
ing set up on the shore of the mediterranean color of
turtledove * water drop * feather bed jangling of keys * the
clock on fire

[JR]

italicized section translated from French

JUAN-LES-PINS 4 APRIL XXXVI [I] [II]

[I]   * portrait of a young girl * on an old tin can flattened by a
truck * attach a piece of broken glass and paint on the
profile of a woman's face * hang a pair of small doll's gloves
at the bottom * plant some feathers on top * pin the whole
to a bitter orange * make a hole in the box's lid *

[II]   lilac colored sapajou extremely ceremonious faced with the
circumstances — kneeling on chickpeas milks the moon's
lying teat a reflection of the tower on his hand — listens to
the smell of each blow the wrapper beats out on the box
which of course the name of the gendarme suggests to him
and laughs wrapped in exotic shawls at the marble that
derides the grimaces the schoolchildren's screams make —
rolls up the flap of the wave and sits down on the sound of
the bell that swims on the clouds' wrinkled sheet and glues
its eye on the almond green envelope of the flowering tree
if the bars' gray melts its tenderness at the geranium's
urgent call — but if the rose stripped of its linens washes
and delouses itself the ragman's trumpet strangles the
flute's melody stewing on the kitchen fire and speaks its
mind to the poster inured to the play of all the truths
learned and forgotten according to the chance of encounters
— miracle of quicklime and quicksilver* hand deprived of
its lines eyes made by riding whip blows solitary sail on the
high sea detached from its boat the jugged rabbit chases its
fate among the thyme of the music pinned to the organ of
the fountain of youth's smells

[PJ]

---

*According to John Richardson, quicklime and quicksilver refer to Yvonne Zervos and
Paul Eluard.

8 APRIL XXXVI

I

eyeglasses nailed by the arrows of love in its individual dance
cell — fried the corsage of red mullets eggs and tomatoes in her
hair the breasts shaft of her flag in oil its thyme smell trans-
pierces me — fixes the hour and defeated in the skein of the
raven's wing long rain drops — and with his fingernail pricks
the infernal machine sewn with the flowers from the basket to
the hem of her dress's desperate scream

II

each garlic clove nailed by the arrows of love a halo around the
bonfire of the fried red mullet with eggs and tomatoes dance
thyme flag fleeing the skein of long raindrops in the raven's
wing transpierced by the smell of the hour fixed by the scream
of his fingernail pricked the flower basket by the machine's
infernal hem

III

nail garlic love arrow of thyme skein flag long rain drops dance
in its individual cell the halo of the red mullets raven fixes the
hour and pricks at the center his fingernails

IV

skein of the red mullets of thyme dance the halo of the ravens
long rain drops and prick in the center these fingernails the hour

V

the hour dances in halo — the skein of the ravens in the center
of the long raindrops these fingernails

long hours skein of long rain drops pricks horse in the center the
fingernail's halo

[PJ]

9 APRIL XXXVI

I

it's the almond green tone the sea to quaff laughter gillyflower
seashell bean window pane negro silence slate corollary medlar
buffoon

II

it's to sea laughter seashell to quaff gillyflower your almond
negro bean window pane silence slate the green buffoon corol-
lary

III

window pane negro silence sea slate green bean to laughter it's
the gillyflower seashell buffoon your corollary

IV

negro bean silence green seashell slate your almond sea gilly-
flower the window pane corollary it's to laughter

V

corollary it's your laughter seashell sea gillyflower slate the
green negro silence window pane almond

[PJ]

10 APRIL XXXVI

alone sun toothache doubles the ante and paints sea-bream on
the feather of the gaze fixes the drop point and dilutes its finger-
nails by dancing

[PJ]

11 APRIL XXXVI

git along and may her little brother kill her if he wants to muck
his hands with all that honey and that treacle and the french
toast looks so happy on its plate and waiting for the moths to sop
it up and for its crud to smell like flowers and for hunger to turn
escargots into miura bulls to get a writeoff and to shoot out
sparks and practice death defying somersaults atop the clouds so
furious that with so many torch songs the guitar would crack in
two and leave its lightning flashes in arrears with dirty hands
stuck to the silken curtains in an air that breezes by at dawn
above the long knife blue line cut of time while passing pissing
on his hands the portion of our daily bread and that of every-
body every day and tapping with his heels the jabjab of his spurs
around the aureola of his hands and throwing wheat to the
ceramic pigeons frozen in the form prescribed by life insurance
given to the poet by the light descried in irises in depths of the
lagoon and now let's dance because it's time for madcap capers to
peal out olé olé olé and full of grace

[JR]

12 APRIL XXXVI

dining only-on-shit room the sideboard turned eagle opens
its wings and breaks them against the soft-boiled blue of the

wisterias' sweetest memories and dragged by the feet all along the moldings of the chairs rolled up into balls and sleeping one eye open on the alert for the almond green's jump the sleight of hand the swallow the conflagration shook up by his anger with the slender paws of the gazelle soberly writing his thoughts on the plate ball pumped up with oxygen a famous farter pythoness pinned to the curtain by the truck that wounds her and bleeds her on the dish of lentils tank with wheels of women's teats running in circles around the edge of the tablecloth spread for lunch on the table balanced on the skinny point of the sharp angle of the scent so much the tragic actor it pours with open throat its menstruation into the cup where the champagne foams and pulls the chestnuts out of the fire the sad-sack color that the bronze rubber erases at the four corners of the table of the set piece of the sagacious shadow collector of cries and folded orgies submissive to the play of light and the whims of drawing that the blinded groping sun complicates with its seeds the previsions of the fruit-dish filled with caresses and offends the savoir-vivre of white lounging legs spread wide on the middle of the secret cipher mouse hole ultraviolet ray of the what-will-they-say prism

[PJ]

13 April XXXVI

miniscule boat made from cloves sprinkled with pastel roses and greens fixes shines and glitters aromatizes and colors enchants and pours winged flag into her cup her scarf the small leaf of the cherry tree's flower fallen to the ground under the tree all her under linens tucked up bottom spanked by raindrop mice

[PJ]

19 APRIL XXXVI IN JUAN-LES-PINS

a midsummer night's dream stung by the diamond point of the
glazier's scream on the bull's neck wrapped in paper from public
conveniences turns the beam of his spotlight on the fishhook's
edge scratching the wound outlined by the flies circling the
bouquet of the bugle band and roasted over a live fire the little
hope of bringing the boat back to the harbor flanks chock-full
with the language of the miraculous fishy draught of ther-
mometers swarming in the net shaking off a rain of stars sifted
through the rainbow biting the lips of the good weather dawns
represented as leaving the cabaret's arms drunk and pale a sheet
nailed to the four corners by wind roses burning at the end of
the arums with their Scottish designs and colors filled with the
sweet peas germinated in the softness of her corsage and bloom-
ing in the perfumed nest of the halos the flute's song drowns its
sadness in the curtains' reeds and teardrop after teardrop follows
each drop detaching itself from the telegraph wire on the night's
drum covered with the veil of the first rendezvous of wings
arriving as loose parts to the boomerang flights in blue black
conflagration of space

[PJ]

20 APRIL XXXVI

to the summer saults carping and monkeying around the cata-
pult tied to the hair vanishing at top speed through the drain of
the bubble of hope's sigh thrown to the wind by the window's
shoulder heave breastfeeding her little ones the letter detaches
itself smoothes its feathers and locks on to the ultraviolet cocoon
of the electric chair's down

[PJ]

21 APRIL XXXVI

powder of paradychlorobenzine plumb-line of the dance tune
from the bridge its moorings loosened camellia in the ropes
entwined carries away in its hands the mutilated head of the
marble statue stretched out on the sand near the edge of the
water advancing its fingers pulling them back into its sleeves
nails bitten by the inhuman form of the imperative body fixed
in stone by the capricious desire of the dream a flute player
marked with a red hot iron by the siren gnaws at him and drags
him fishing sail at the tip of the arrow that follows the heads-
or-tails of its flight circling the sound of the water drop falling
on her chest and breaking its forehead against the echoes of
that rotten silence's stink smelling of marshmallow benumbed
by the stabbing perfume of grilled sardines caramel color of
shadow through the Venetian blind shut tight target practice of
inquisitive starlight listening in on the feast of torn off flags
umbilical cord of the impassionate source of the drawings of
small bells spiraling around the sunbeam planted right in the
middle of the feast spread-eagled in naked foam arm tying gaze
in blind flight mouth open caries sand swallower of the period
hitting the forehead of the untamable beast's monster dressed in
sunday best clogs in swallow horn legs covered in sugar-cane
stockings under small pantaloons of spider lace taken from the
flies' throats shirt made from strips of cheese held together by
electric cables locked in crystal balls inscribed in the circuit of
the veins of the Lorraine ham resting on the shelf holding up
the brassiere garden bench painted green where the wet nurse
and the soldier are sitting playing hopscotch hide and seek in
the circuit imposed on the nooks by the she-monkey dressed
as a canteen-attendant — oak robe made from great planks
nailed with carpenter's nails and held up by welded wrought

iron wedges — hat made from granite rock attempting to hold up and balance the bloody neck feathers of a chicken run over by a car full of oranges turned over on the road — a necklace of onions and breath savers and Pan flutes — a cigarette case excavated from a doughnut fastened to the dress by hooks hanging from small radio apparatuses good weather for the cherries locked into their pits and beautiful among the beautiful floats proud beauty standing up on the clouds' mother of pearl ladders that laughingly tour the domain of the seedy cottage of the infinite her loved body

[PJ]

23 April XXXVI

I

bugle-call of the harp stuck in the mud in the middle of the road no exit octopus fastened to the core of the warm ball source of the river of feathers earth welded head lowered

II

dissolved in the flakes heart shoved in no exit to the octopus fastened to the road in the river of feathers boils in the source the earth's lowered head

III

* to the helmet taken to heart * octopus shoved into the harp * the road * warm ball of the river of feathers * fasten earth is lowered head *

[PJ]

24 APRIL XXXVI

legs in the air the rainbow in the middle of the starry night
wringing its linens cradle with astonished eyes pure goldfinch
from the blinking hammock of the games round of nails ham-
mered into the fire at the prism's throat rope held by the ends at
the burns of the mud-stuck wheel in the pond biting with rage
the eye of the expiring bull

[PJ]

28 APRIL XXXVI

Venus having left her flat to buy sardines in oil from the grocery
suffers sunstroke becomes a shell

sheet of mauve silk paper a kind of Venus leaving her flat by
chance in the morning in her little everyday dress feet naked in
her slippers unkempt grease stains on the sleeves buys sardines
in oil from the grocers a flute song on the electric chair forgotten
in the Venetian blinds shaking her body to the sound of these
swear words becomes seen under the magnifying glass a kind of
shell if the tone the sea lends the scream glazier carries off with
its tongue the bitterness of the artichoke leaf and with the foot
kicks the ear of the marsh-mallow curtain that glues its mouth
to the pane the oil drop broke and through its wing sees the
dream of its geometric wound for and against sharp angle of the
crystal locked into the mathematically illusory perfume stolen
from the blind sunbeam holding out its hands to catch the smok-
ing platter of potatoes on the table on horseback on the blue
thread flying among the garden flowers this afternoon april 28
of this year XXXVI where a great hedgehoggy happiness serves
as ball to bat around and to repaint the rainbow locked into the

water glass at the stroke of hope given to the avalanche of eyes racing at top speed along the lacy edge of the salt mountain established at the bottom of the cloud of the orange tree flowers arriving at the pace of rain biting the lips of the masked ball fixed to the granite wall by the rose's thorns wax figures their faces covered with gobs of spit

[PJ]

29 APRIL XXXVI

all lines removed from the painting that represents the image of a young girl's head appears floating around white aroma of blows hitting the sky's shoulder pride white cheese poppies white wine fried at the pigeon shoot of the white fife-player yellow yell of whips reflected by the flight of a swallow over the eye of mauve milk nettle winged horse at the end of the yellow foam at the white corsage of the mauve pike pencil streak with goat's leaps white star mauve yellow spread at the edge of the moon mauve dish of flageolets arc bent at iris yellow cobalt blue indigo blue in the mauve nets from slate yellow to feather white blue put rope to neck mauve yellow dove at worst decapitated blue bites mauve hand yellow lake at white lip blue detachable collar rat devouring the mauve ear of corn yellow blue mauve yellow blue blue blue blue line wrapping its spiral the bridge stretches arriving first and breathless at the target's center

[PJ]

3 MAY XXXVI

do 3 re 1 mi 0 fa 2 sol 8 la 3 si 7 do 3
do 22 si 9 la 12 sol 5 fa 30 mi 6 re 11 ½ do 1

do 333 si 150 la ¼ sol 17 fa 303 re 1 mi 106 si 33.333.333
mi 10 si 44 la 9 sol 22 fa 43 mi 0 − 95
the hand makes the cast shadow that the light let him make and
stuffs the sum of the numbers 3 − 5 − 10 − 15 − 21 − 2 − 75 − full
of silence and the floating scarf carried off by the claws of the
hair its spread wings spinning drunk with freedom in the blue of
the corsage's stripes under infinity's open skies

[PJ]

4 MAY XXXVI

all the shredded shadows peel off the bodies with the haste of
the start of a journey and faithful to their appointment with
light they spread out in the smoky thickness of the crystal spi-
raling downward to the bottom of the ocean of their kingdom
here's her story I was born to a white father and a small glass of
Andalusian eau-de-vie I was born to an unmarried mother a girl
of fifteen born in Malaga in the Percheles* the beautiful toro
who engendered me the forehead crowned with jasmines with
his teeth had torn from his hands the lines of the cage that
imprisoned the people birds of prey with beak and claw tearing
the naked shoulder of the lemon tree's flower girl dead from
fright broken wings blue heart striped with red in spirals with
eyes of a night moth wrapped in the apple-green silk paper of
her dress and shoed with pointy owl ears leaps from one wave to
the other and bounces on the foam the marble head of the enor-
mous mutilated statue planted in the sand at the water's edge

[PJ]

---

*Percheles: name of a district in Malaga that once had a bad reputation.

5 MAY XXXVI

tightened around the bottle's neck of the chair's lake made from
the sounds of the hours the clocks of the arm chair which
blooms in spring this morning at 10:30 leaning against the
fireplace on the heart swallow perched on the telegraph wire
rose from the final bouquet body hanging by the tongue from
the discrete fire of the rain of sun seeds from the artificial ardor
of the palette thrown over the windmills into the nettles unrolls
the roll of the rainbow's threads and cuts out the drawing of the
profile of the head on the stone of the arums and rubs his gaze
with garlic and onion and unties the ribbons of his hands in the
heat of the lump made from the molten mirror that encloses the
immaculate image of the toro's jump over the barrier and all
that to say that it be well understood never again to believe nei-
ther in numbers nor feasts nor in the gilded flights of pain going
to make its honey in the sewers on scraps of lime winged with
the smell of the slab of meat hooked to the grill over the fire at
lunch hour hotel rat coming in through the window of the room
a set piece set up piecemeal on the stage of the bronze paper
cradling its ennui and the hearing bowl of the sail of the flower-
adorned palm of the liquid dove but let us wipe the bottom of
the dirty pots clean of the languorous eyes of the partridges and
the calf's nostrils let's do the torture room of sweet harmonies
colored by the set-square's compass from the corner of the
frame's cornice by the lack of affection of the torn rag maw gap-
ing at blows to the kidneys by the whip of the flags stretched
along the window and of the silence nailed to the four corners of
the ripped off door teeth shattering and covered with fleas aping
the robe and the veil covered with shit of the oh so ceremonious
young-girl-to-be-wed costume cut into salami slices served up
venison-like plus the registration fees and the charges of the

boleros of the gypsy gitanes and matches bit by bit and the ter-
ror of the flame caught in the hair by the teeth of the shadow of
the horse belly slit open behind the shutters in the tepid heat of
a little sun bestrews on a flute tune of the corner of the mirror
sitting under the olive tree of the white curtain on the evening
of this day Tuesday the 5th of the month of may of this year at 5
minutes to 7

[PJ]

8 MAY XXXVI

rolled up body of the bronze dress with pearls of laughter from
the fire bubble appears in the middle of the square the pink dirt-
ied with sperm and crowned with flowers of a young girl with a
toro's head clad in a white feather dress standing on her boat
made of marble slabs drifting in the liquid air of the eye of the
egg at the sail of her veil of buttered noodles of the bleeding
mirror that her hands daily push deeper into shit and in the
nests of seahorses harvests the ribbons of impossible colors sunk
straight like swords in her hearts with rope ladders and landings
crawling with bird flocks of musical notes that melt along can-
dles dragged and with ropes around the throat tied to horses
covered with banderoles on the thick layer of red daubed around
the circles of the wheels of the overturned car emptying itself in
agony of the fireworks bouquet of the ripe and the unripe splat-
tering the sand at the blows of the hours' foreheads exploding on
impact hitting the ground the poppies detach themselves and
form the bouquet that fills the crystal vase on the world propped
up by the sheaves of rocket clusters filling the sail of the boat
hanging from the neck of the clouds swimming above the waves
that try to fasten their lips to the keel and chase it under the
stretched rope of its course a fan open to desires and passions

black quicklime from the deep grottos where flutter the linked
butterflies of hands loved in the absolute black of the sun cov-
ered with snow the angle of morning hides under the pillow

[PJ]

10 MAY XXXVI

where gooseberry clusters flood the walls of words with the acid
savor of the light hitting naked buttocks the periwinkle-blue
body of remembrance hanging from the nail planted plumb in
the middle of the pink toad's leap across the silver plaque grilled
alive on the harp's strings torero wetting the edge of his cape in
the hollow of the hand detached from the arm of the begging
mummy at the closed door of hope a farandole snows on the
open fan slicing the orange at the lunulae the tambourine's
mourning caught between the teeth of the horse on fire egg
dancing on the water spout noise in the garden ball rebounding
in the game of the mauve young girl dissolved in the azure of
the so tender green of her dimmed white dress wrapped in the
slate leaf goes ferreting out the evening along the rimes of the
sonnet of the palm tree a kind of beach with fine sand of death
heads filling the boat stranded and bitten in the belly by the
tamer torn from the claws of hours attached in clusters to the
main mast by the pan-pipe's sound laundry hung out forgotten
by night on the ropes chariot of joy made of clear water with
wheels of perfumes pulled by gazes filled with the savor of the
colors of the rainbow of songs and laughter

[PJ]

11 MAY XXXVI

but if the dress loosened at the shoulders falls like a stone to the
bottom of the pool and shatters the drawing's pane the watch's
spring catches her eye and blinds her and abandons her in the
hands of the hangman dead leaf lighten up the advance of the
medusa's skull between the pages of the book male-voice bil-
berry choir acrobat petrified skeleton of the fog rising from
the meadow black marble column liquid overflowing from the
bowl of rice à la valencienne from the corner of the cornice at
the sound of dead drunk numbers falling drop by drop on the
flagstones of the fire sponges it's laughable especially because
one has to sing all one's life the ba be bi bo bu of the bu bo bi be
ba of the philosophical soup gone cold on the corner of the side-
board where the sun eats it with a fork

[PJ]

13 MAY XXXVI

the blue feather of the liquid smiling with acrobatic light mem-
ory of winged hand wiping forehead so sweet to the gaze and
caresses of the perfume of her movements evaporate his open
palette of a coat flowery in the spring of the star of knives
formed by these colors and awaits the song of her dance on the
carpet of the girl's naked body dissolving the mauve reflection
in the lack of attention of the blue enveloping her and pissing
the stain of her rose on the fading blue in the hollow of the
almond green surrounded by the crown of orange blossom
leaves to the regret of the raised saddle-stitch of her dress sitting
next to the poet writing at his table on which rests the old shoe
brought back by his muse's grief together with the six francs he
is owed in relation to the price deduction on the order of two

pairs of sandals prepaid that very afternoon before mailing his
sister one of the already made pairs as a present

[PJ]

Paris 16 May XXXVI

no longer hits the aroma of the savor of yellow on the sound of
green charm sighing at the touch of pink at pearls of laughter
the gaze of the faded perfume of the blue of emptiness models
the liquid dove of the faded chant of light blinded by the scream
of the heat gazing at her body in the fresh air tolls the sweet bell
of the absence of hours torn from silence

[PJ]

18 May XXXVI

the aroma of the flowers of the branch torn from the lemon tree
petrifies its shape in the hollow of the hand resting on the tem-
ple at the heat of mauve hidden in the cheek and points its barb
at the left nostril of the young girl far away in her dream

[PJ]

20 May XXXVI

ah if the bird made of garlands woven from the hours asleep in
the bronze spider's belly could make its star fritters up in the air
of the sea of numbers at the angry blows of the billy-goats
dressed in feathers and sing on the rose telegraph wire of the eye
of the egg's blue of the scarf hanging from the fiery nail planted
exactly in the middle of the forehead between the horns of the
toro's head what silence

[PJ]

23 May XXXVI [i] [ii]

[i]   faun that pulls the chariot of oblivion its garland threaded
      on the toro's head

[ii] pink disk of the perfume of geometric forms void mathe-
      matical object of the abandoned tight rope of flute tunes
      dead birds falling into the lake detached from their wings
      that remain stuck to the clouds' temples the sole the rooster
      the flint the lemon and the almond the ivy the sparrow-
      hawk the chair the naked body of love spread over red-hot
      coals and singing *Ma Paloma* the letters m.t.* floating at the
      mercy of the waves and the bird's cage opening like flower
      fix mirror caressing blue of evaporated corsage her cheek
      on the mirror shaped over this afternoon breaks into several
      pieces the magic wand of silence hidden beneath the pillow
      and nails it to the breathless wheel turning at top speed
      flames the bouquet resting on the edge of the window
      detached from the house lost on the last card in the game of
      who loses wins at the sound of laughter made by the falling
      scaffolding of the tower dead drunk with boredom if the
      boat that's waiting for day on its misery doesn't immediate-
      ly punish its sail with the harp of assassinated weeping
      picked in the fields laid out to dry in the sun of the music
      held tightly in its claws by the eagle drowned in the liquid
      dove

                                                              [PJ]

---

* m.t. = Marie-Thérèse Walter.

6 June XXXVI

in a goblet   sleeves of a harlequin costume
knotted around its stem   the toro's head expires embroiled
in the scent of verbena and candles stand on a drum
balanced   by a prism's   deceptive stammer

[AH]

7 June XXXVI

on the curtain   received from flying hands   by the open sea's
        hair
a verbena leaf perfume ladder   attached by swallow chirps
to geometric flight patterns of desire
the galloping prism's beef stew   flower weapon   thrust into
        heart
breathes out its indifference   its garment powders the goblet
shaped like an eagle's head
snows music harlequin arrows   false harvester of stars
arms in embroidered blouse sleeves   undo the nest of vipers
in the tree of dormant candles
cutting the scent of silence   on the gentle lights
hung from shutter slats
drum summons to love's mathematical apex
wings spread wide   in the toro's astonished eye
skinnydipping   in the scent of blue
wrapped round the neck of the sun as dust
hiding   under the jangling bed
enveloped in whiplash shadow   mumbled by anemic green
curled up   in a ball of memories   tossed into the ashes
at the very moment when the wheel
balances chance

15 June XXXVI

garlic laughs at its color of star dead leaf

laughs mocking at the rose the dagger that thrusts its color
    into the garlic of star dead leaf

laughs maliciously at the dagger of roses the smell of a falling
    star dead leaf

garlic on the wing

[AH]

13 August 36

nothing else now but for the aloe the gall and the thistle the
lime the nettle and the mallow on top of the quince that smells
like a burnt wooden shoe   and the amorous song of the raven
frightened by its shadow shattered into a thousand pieces   the
drunken bell that falls into the well   the hand that tiptoes dry-
eyed to the fair   the horse the broken wings and the big open
stomach   showing the ballroom of its entrails   full of lights
and flowers   spiced with the music pinned to the star's center
the star of prismatic feudal castle lights   in the colors of his
palette   drenched in the dew of the songs of the gori gori gori
in the machine gun's kisses   and the weight on the back of two
hundred pounds of feathers   dropped by a silence that rises
from the white paper   reddening every word that spurts   onto
his bare back   with his suit of worms and his tie-pin laughter
today 13 august of the year 1936 this afternoon that untangles
the web of the pattern   dances the tarantela for him shows him
the muzzle   seen through the bull's eye   and sparkles at the

bottom of the cup   hides behind curtains of silk and honey
the bullet that speeds through the hour   suspended from a rope
attached to the balcony   pitiful now

[AH]

translated from Spanish

[SEPTEMBER] 1936

so moving   the memory of the broken glass in his eye   does not
strike the hour on the bell   that scents the blue   so tired of
loving the sighing garment that covers him   the sun that may
from one moment to the next explode in his hand   reenter his
claws   and fall asleep in the shade that outlines   the praying
mantis nibbling on a communion wafer   but if the curve   that
animates the song   attached to the end of the hook   coils up
and bites the heart of the knife that charms and colors it   and
the bouquet of starfish cries out in distress in the cup   the flick
of the tongue of his gaze   wakes up the tragic ratatouille   of
the flies' ballet in the curtain of flames   that reaches the
windowsill

[AH]

3 OCTOBER XXXVI

miserable shagreen enclosing the body   torn by love that bleeds
so cramped in the crown of his nest of thorns   miserable memo-
ry of jasmine scent   pinned to the bottom of his eye   sounding
the alarm on all his bells   biting the neck of the rainbow
storm caught in a trap   comb mirror letter of comic alphabet
drink from a wineskin   hand distance color deleted   from the
rolls of the living   when life boils   in the great village hall

smelling of cabbage   its stew of hopes   and under the table
smiles at the lie   all the chairs sitting around it rise   and glue
themselves to the walls of the director's office   waiting for the
dogfish to finish licking up the hours   that gum up the sails of
his nice umbrella   and to hear the crack   when in my chest it
breaks   the stick of the sense of alarm in his gaze   with the
electric aroma of stars   you crush under your heel

[AH]

6 October XXXVI

in the painting of 30 april canvas # 15 F. woman seeing herself
in a mirror puts down a comb with some hairs in its teeth and
some lice in her hair as well some lice and if possible some crabs
in her pubic hair

(charming idea to add to the package)

[AH]

10 October XXXVI

[1]   flesh decomposing in its miserable shagreen accordion
squeezing the love-torn body   rapidly spinning the wool
bleeding so in the despairing place   in the crown of thorns
nest of twigs   at the sound of the tambourine awakened by
the miserable memory   left by the vomit that smells of jas-
mine glued to the back of the eye wearing cafe tables as
sashes wrapped round her neck   sounding the alarm
reproducing her image in all the mirrors with all the blows
struck on the cheeks of her bells   the tralalala of the
tralalalettes   biting the rainbow's neck   the bra of the

tempest caught in a snare now whistles between the comb's teeth and twists in her hands the mirror asleep on her breast   abandoned to its fate

[II] comical alphabet letter stitched on hot coal   drunk from wineskin   hand distance color   deleted from the list of mortals   sinks claws in the saving copper of forehead against stone   if life cooks great banquet hall feasts of cabbage smell on its knees in a corner his stew of hopes sing Carmen sing and you Cleopatra and mice on the big fishermen's bodies lined up on the bank of the canal under the table open to the lie   the chairs around it rise and attach themselves to the walls of the director's office of the young villa Marie-Rose waiting for the frog to lick clean the hours that make the fabric of her pretty umbrella sticky   and if the weather is clear listen to the crack when in my chest breaks the perfume of the stick the arrow painted on the fan tossed on the bed   the luminous alarmed panther sheen of her regard   with an electric aroma a most disagreeable noise   spreading a dreadful odor of stars crushed underfoot

[AH]

11 OCTOBER XXXVI

[I] ∗ wearing tied around her neck like a scarf a bathtub filled with boiling water ∗ wearing tied around her neck like a scarf a mirror wardrobe full of dirty laundry

∗ wearing tied around her neck like a scarf the dining room table set for lunch the tablecloth in flames

[II] bedside lady dove filled with clear water with liquid
plumage lit up by an image burning the oil of beehives

[AH]

[11 – 17 October XXXVI]

11 OCTOBER XXXVI

flails crazy   her bedsheets in flames   hips flapping wings
bedside lady dove filled with clear water with liquid plumage lit
by a lamp burning beehive oil   wearing tied around her neck
like a scarf a bathtub filled with boiling water   in it swim tan-
gled eels   her body wrapped in the folds of a young mirror
wardrobe full of dirty laundry   her waist held by the dining
room table set for lunch twisted around the small of her back
shaken by the sun's scissors striking right into the middle of the
bouquet of dried flowers hung from the middle of the ceiling
in the cuttlefish bone of the light through the window   sing
caressing the soft hair of jasmines   musical notes attached to
curtains hung green and mauve against red brick   submerged
in the ash that coats the rest of the scene   eyes biting with all
the teeth in their jaw   the lump of coal in the toothless mouth
vomits her hair into the jar full of milk set down on the bed
whence the head thrusts up open-mouthed leaving a trace of
light   clad in her pillar of salt robe   in the depths of the
wardrobe mirror   creased by her caresses   a party wall between
the pile or face of reasons scratching her crabs   or a feast half
fig half raisin   summer eternalizes her tendernesses on the
astonished eye placed on the hand pierced by the quills of green
dragons   launched by flaps of the tongue   tedium tickles its
ribs

13 OCTOBER XXXVI

losing at every turn of fortune a piece of the Chinese robe hung
on piercing cries   fine-tooth comb full of lice and a few hairs
but here an exact copy of the text "6 october XXXVI — in the
painting of 30 april canvas # 15 F 'Woman seeing herself in a
mirror' puts down a comb with some hairs and some lice in its
teeth — some lice in her hair as well and if possible some crabs
in her pubic hair" and in parentheses "charming idea to add to
the package"   but what silence is louder than death says the
cunt to the cunt while scratching the front of his anus in an ele-
gant manner   I don't give a shit I don't give a shit says the
beauty   orders from above   gilded I do a balancing act on the
edge   shit does not smell like roses it may already be time to go
to the table eat soup of curtains well-cooked   then thrown into
urine stored in the cellar for six months   and steeped in it twen-
ty-six dozen rosaries of mother-of-pearl coral ivory   and of olive
pits and six hundred little rumps   well-washed in salted holy
water   each one placed on a Brussels sprout and into a bag of
bitter orange skin   perfumed by a nun's big fart   plus one
thousand snail-forks tied together and heated to the point of
melting   plus some old missals a hotel ballroom curtain   cur-
tain rings set aside in a pale pink satin purse   plus cut into small
cubes   the friendly hands that salute the procession

17 OCTOBER XXXVI

passing inside the bar of soap farted out by the big dead crab on
the deserted beach

[AH]

26 October XXXVI

painting a quarter azure that lights up sufficiently the lamp of
corrosive sublimate that extinguishes Spring with its hands
[and] burns with [...]*

[AH]

4 November XXXVI

mathematically pure illusory image of the terrifying throb of
the piece of lace detached from sight of the vaginal burp fart-
ing at top speed the drawing reborn in the folds of the powder
compact hidden under a layer of the gateau of lies glued to a
tear-skittle reason that burns in the middle of the foot of the
nose of the painting   immersed in the silver soup plate
presents its back to the desperate blows of love removing its
blindfold 3 4 5 10 29 0 10 224 3 3 0 10 11 23 32 34 35 38 22 tell
me colors proofs presented against

[AH]

11 November XXXVI

spleen of a quarter of Brie in its sleeping-car

[PJ]

12 November XXXVI [I] [II]

[I]   one anonymous to the other the party in full swing on the
seafood plate

---

*The last word is unreadable.

[II] sucking thoughts of forms within sucking forms of
thoughts strength without muscles

mouth full of blood of forms sucked from thoughts

[AH]

[25 JANUARY – 25 FEBRUARY 1937]

25 JANUARY XXXVII

noise of footsteps illuminated flowers samples of gazes sapajous
through the closed venetian shutters of hands laid in the shad-
ow of her cheeks so colored by force by music thinned in the
luminous fountain suspended between heaven and earth on the
balcony hooked to clouds of dust reflected to the four corners of
the map foundering with all hands under the petals of a carna-
tion meat-grinder-stitched all that to say good night before
going to bed to her blue corsage bought for 35 francs in the flea
market always thinking of her tonight exactly at 8 minutes past
1 in the a.m. on 25 of january of this year 37

26.1.37

orange blossom jasmine cabinet perfumed with pine scent little
sugar cube stuck sentry-like on point of bayonet drawn from his
gaze and bleeding honey from his fingers on the dove's wings
burning at lake bottom in the skillet of his eyes shows up exactly
at the happy hour with its flower needle pin prick poised to
touch the sea's snout blue bull wingèd incandescent spread out at
the ocean's rim

1ST FEBRUARY XXXVII

escarole if the forgetting and the thousand reflections of silence
hidden in the shadow of its claws and the pimping song melted

into its leaves break the monotony of its color smear and borrows
from disquiet spread out to dry on the barbed wires forgotten
by the enemy of his happiness all along the clacking of the sun
drawing its bow over the venetian blinds the cries of his drawing
startled awake are moved to tears by rubbing the eyes with
onions getting on their high horse next to the frying pan

2.2.37

when the light arrives counting its steps so tired and charged
by so many wrinkles to introduce its nose into the lock of the
large chest full of petticoat accessories to the great interior dance
of the household objects wrapped in the hot and cold bandages
in his looks but the whip lashes given to his shoulders in the
reflection of the lentil dish besides the shadow of the potatoes
doesn't take a grain of love from the solicitude of desire
stretched out in the folds of the dish-cloth

4.2.37

for as far as the sound of the hour hooks the wings of forgotten
colors to its beak among the disorder the fluted bread stretches
out its hand and with its irregularity wounds the perfume that
floats under the turnips pissing their rage through the sun's dia-
mond put on the burner on the blackest corner of the sugar no
longer so so white if clear

5.2.37

without forgetting the pink flag waves with pleasure in the blue
sheet of the fire and lights the almond green dragging its tat-
tered rags on the nails leaving shreds of its dress on the spikes of
each slap of the rod on the water that boils redoubles its desire
singing on the wing to hide its true image behind the bronze veil
shaking her hair disheveled by the hands of a blue so tender

dying at the bottom of the milk bowl leaning on the triangle
that cuts the scene in half and a full-mouthed call to arms at
angles scalloping the enchanted circles dragging their misery to
the door of each object the rain beats the panes tames the wild
beasts sauce pans plates water jug forks and spoons for home-
made soup of rock crystal smelling of violets mince-meat of
colored aromas at knife's point passed drop by drop through the
large jar's filter full of suns cuts the throat of the dish-rag's
white which holds out a hand to the armful of black thrown
through the open corridor door with so much love so much
heartbreak soft caramel crucified plumb line and celeriac scrap
of newspaper and bone of dog dead of rabies names of rats of
mongooses of wolf of carp of house warmings pyrotechnics fes-
toon of la si do la re mi doubly grateful doubly enchanted doubly
sad and so tired the little color the lilac adds caresses the fore-
head and smoothes the hair of the little light that yawns rising
from the cup's handle smashed by the bludgeon stroke of the
shadow cast by the passage of a hand but without thyme or rea-
son light insinuates itself in the room and nests in the beams
without a cry of anguish and dies and rots in the drawings of the
mirror without recognizing them anymore famous feast choking
fête of imprisoned objects and illiterate vegetables bullets that
strike them in the heart crack up laughing as they hit the mark
what a shame what a shame a thousand times a shame the
threatening portrait of the drama plays between the lines if the
head when it falls from six miles around the reasons for being
watch from the ceiling and built a complete system of defense
whim of a king of a pope and of a pig a thousand little candles
and a thousand torches and this morning's light skirt pulling
its net from the sea so hellish a drink from so many heart-
breaks washed in all the waters of hazard and chance numbered
alphabetically twisted ground hacked pressed reduced to dust

infallibly disappeared effaced from the face of the world of
appearances enveloped in the black cotton wool nothing but the
smell and not one gesture harder than stone the blue immobi-
lizes its clarion at the edge of the simulated abyss if loose rock by
the weeping dish-rag crying all the tears of its eyes in the mad
gaiety of its dances and *salto mortales* clear sweep pale posted
at the battlements gracious smile immobile swept up asleep
in his arms easily recognizable by the wings of the peeled pota-
toes arriving in the nick of time in the middle of the discussions
and heated disputes freshness of the raindrops on the forehead
mountain air

6.2.37

vipers' nest brassiere poppy pity camouflage corsage trash gilded
tomato sting center of circumference bitter savor matters not if
the day necessarily knows how to find its favorite place under the
pillow and how to relieve itself in scent of mathematics rose
irresistibly aggressive mean and blacker than the orange the
rumpled music of mustard smell in her eyes the last word of the
song quickens the section of the wall to the right of the window
of little pride fixed with two nails at the spot where the sun
strikes with might and main on the curtain's rising by the wind
hanging from the window what clarity what happiness lift the
skirt and show the belly of light melted butter of the bells at ten
o'clock dipping the pen into the inkwell the shadow of the leaf
moving across the blue of the paper imagined by the heap of
ashes

10.2.37

fine salt spirits famous cresol drugs of kaleidoscope yelling
aggressive napkin surface petticoat negro lint cotton nose
chamomile armchair sparrow-hawk fin ship's hold twisted

thread whittling sand fly arrow whistle next model cucumber
urine hat rock must one say it hides gorilla shear mirror earth if
the light if the night if the blue swept over his face if ennui
shivering at the door if all the gold and the silver if all the rest
and all and all and all my dear caress and spit and smoke and
grate and ooze and stink and illuminates and reeks and in its box
crawl the festoons of the soup and smash and crumble and snore
copra tol-de-rol of the fol-de-rol-de-ridos the plate crushed by its
weight by the knots its fingers knocking at the door licks the
hive that comes undone in its mouth stings jumping with both
feet over the cord of the molten lead tied up by this winter
afternoon and gets written confirmation when the silk hammer
rings on his cheek the retreat of the jack painted on the edge
of the knife's edge of a furtiva lacrima after all and with that
thank you Madam I'm delighted and so proud and so polite and
so tender and so dressed to the nines and painted spic and span
gamboling to the right pythoness undone at the bottom of the
cup well endowed in chain mail of her corset of peanuts redo-
lent with verbena and musk and dry straw without a criticism
without a learned breath without a mid-lent sigh and so straight
in the middle of the plate of the spit gobs of the sincerest
homages offered with so much distinction and eagerness just out
of the oven piping hot how to say and explain well to you in two
words with the fingertips the end end of the lights sealed over
the leg sans order or reason really indifferent to the interested
visits of the color on the subject of history's bottom of the heart
which has us by the throat neither more nor less the temptation
that photographs the inside of the inkwell weighs the reasons
and jams its [olfat] between leather and flesh of the piece of
sausage cooked with cabbage with undulating ass and a thousand
daintinesses faced with the tyranny of the savor of that poppy
red color flaunted in the middle of the room good morning to

the canary you've finally arrived all covered with dust the feet so
black tell me you pig didn't you by any chance roll all naked in
the coal you make me laugh go and wash up immediately in the
sink of menstruations itineraries with the red yellow and green
fringes of the dial pulling its hours out of eider-down and hop
hop on to the white knees the desire of the hammer blow among
the steps of the sky's blue wiping its clogs on the lips of the tit-
tle-tattle and through his ignominy making bright the frank
talk of stars barely cooked filthy language ugly and knavish not
knowing how to speak a single true word and so ridiculously
dressed courtesans vile hunchbacked and one-eyed hypocritical
and inane nobodies door openers enveloped in a horrid smell full
of lice and bedbugs and so stupid

11.2.37

thirty thousand candles cabbages cauliflowers and olives black
and green ochre burnt and raw sienna vermilion and burnt
umber lemon orange noodles motor oil a few drops and stirring a
silence envelops in passing in the present moment the piece
being played opposed to the obtuse angles of sad truth reduced
to dust and glued to the spider webs of gummy reason that insin-
uates itself under the armpits of the dish of shit just picked from
the tree of good and evil planted in the heart last season proud
all marble barque a thousand thunders presenting themselves
any old way and no trouble in evening negligee tonight at five
thirty exactly at the meeting of the hands over the eyes of the
wood split in four dangling from the highest branch of the cot-
ton in the ears of the badly combed ennui filthy hobgoblin
always between the legs of the chairs and the feet of the table
and how much courage does the miserable lamp need to suck the
endless dregs of the black canvas in oilcloth unnailed from its
frame enveloping the drama under its pleats

12.2.37

and what hidden strength in the water of his gestures' liquid
marble feeds the source of so much laughter freshly cut hay
perfumed breath of the large piece of wall lethally wounded
expiring its color in the pile of plates hidden in the shadow held
firmly by the waist by the shock of the bricks' red half-spread
over the table sinking like a stone in the puddle of the bit of
newspaper torn in a thousand pieces *costa rica* bonfire fixed bal-
ance at the exact point of the prism and the tone detached from
everything from the everyday dress of the characters threshing
about so clumsily in the middle of the ambushes and so many
irritations arrayed like onions above prayer mills revealed to the
day discovered naked inside out like a sock begging and proud
milquetoast shaking their sheets out the bull's-eye window of
weariness dying his beautiful death at the sound of the flageolets
the kidney beans the chick peas haricot beans and turnip cab-
bages sleepwalkers amidst the laughter and jeers of the drawing
whipping the order established fearfully by the law in equilibri-
um on the taut rope of the well attached to the sympathetic cut
of the fields stung by the beautiful language of the garbage in
its gilded frame assassinated at the wall of love stretched out
under the sink sweet marshmallow in its nest hatching its words

15.2.37

antipathetic firing range azure crab-louse and turnip-cabbage
canticle phantom of bronze riveted to the granite of the clouds
shit and shit plus shit equals all the shits multiplied by shit
mucus of glosses pestilential breath of the wind rose's anus dou-
ble cream cocoon spinning perfect love hanging from its pustules
slowly stewing on the so sweet fire of her eyes horror and despair
a piece of black pudding resting on a wad of cotton the opera-
tion having succeeded perfectly turned away from every thing's

line of sight holding the nostrils of the heap of tensions and the remains of the remains what pleasure what happiness and what a piggish trick doesn't he turn the crank creaking in the joints of the outspokenness of his belly larded with old newspapers filthy and disgusting old pillows spitting fear and stinking of snot and rotten wisdom teeth what a party what a feast in the bowels of heaven down on its knees on earth and what laughter shakes its paunch after crossing the heart the horn of plenty of the beast now at last made mute by love and frozen by happiness biting the lips of the bouquet gone mad the immense spread of the winding cloth disappearing under the snow melted from the cracked powdered ice plus four chairs a table a dresser two shelves a wall-cupboard painted white staircase to the left the whole lot one price so many francs 90 centimes plus transport and tip

18.2.37

but what horse drags its guts with so much grace sending so many kisses and smiles and so many inflaming glances and so much flatulence so odoriferous and perfumed and so many aromas at the moment of death that the edge of the rag so worried yet so wise doesn't unroll in the history that preoccupies us right now as evening comes hiding her intentions glues eye to ear of so many stifled musics under the cotton-wool of the color promenading on its arm and what a wallop doesn't it give the oily cream of the sky that spreads its blot on the everyday dress of the kitchen the match opening its beak to its heart by the roots cozy warm well washed well heeled nails pared ready for the dance disguised as public house at the big number of this day's date at the smell of rancid oil being fried in the noise of ant bites gnawing the silk paper enveloping the scene being sung on the anvil of the bouquet of roses the spitballs of the lilies and the brioches macaroons rye rolls orange marmalade as large as a thumb's nail silver and gold basket of diamonds and pearls sapphires amethysts of cabbage cauliflower and carrots melted butter and salt and the exact measure of the sleight of hand the wing beat to give the fire to light the torch of cold water sliced like salami devilishly seductive in her disguise of tears and smartly hatted by the blows of fate andouille stripper of wrongdoings and perfect knight sweating fear forgetting himself in the clouds and not old-fashioned at all in his crystal costume put out to dry under the shower of the eccentric circles of the thousand and one reasons of relaxation and all the others

20.2.37

tooth ache in the eyes of the sun pricks — pricks ache of sun teeth in the eyes — eyes of teeth pricks of the sun of ache of sun pricks eyes of teeth ache of teeth — of sun pricks of ache eyes flower passed through the clear air filter of the red iron song contained in the bottle riveted to the plaster sprinkled by the atmosphere's heaviness nailed to the large pieces of timber holding by a thread to the scottish cloth fallen who knows how into the soup of the story's interwined hair sweeping the light hiding under the drawings pretending indifference vis-a-vis proper nouns that designate the open maw of things showing themselves in full anger a paroxysm of rage and prettier than seeing a woman in a mirror putting lipstick on her lips than if the little attention of the onion cooking on the fire and the smell of the cabbage turnips carrots potatoes the table the chairs far more enterprising far more skillful concerning caresses and so reserved grabbing you by the throat in the softness of their velvety paws the colors are numbered in hierarchical order go a-dying one after the other by touching upon the reality of the objects that designate them as the companion destined to

unravel the strings of the drawing that imprisons the images of
the phantoms hardened in the fire of light with so much eager-
ness and joy and cries of pleasure and happiness not knowing
where to turn first head dizzy ass topsy-turvy and the veils on
the eyes of each one letting themselves fall from the ceiling to
the floor on the bouncy tits on the window panes breaking them
hurting and cutting themselves their blood staining the walls
the floorboards the ceiling the fire in the kitchen cutting it into
bits hacking it into tiny pieces pressing it with their weight
spreading it with their hands in disorder and just about gone
crazy and all of a sudden hiding in their shadow having become
fearful trembling and stinking of hot excrement sing Carmen in
her laughing pan sing and weep the rottenness of the chi lo sa
fandango hunts the slipper steals the magpie in its nest of thorns
and carries it away in its cage wings on the forehead old shoes on
the feet coat of moon cloth shirt of coal rose water hot peppers
artichokes strawberries hair feathers muslin noses cheese and
rope ladders words of love tears and tripe of rum beans and
incomprehensible signs of fat earth cotton chunks of stale bread
and of wind and rain plus all the overdue accounts kept up to
date on the fingertips comfy warm on the kitchen sink of his
dreams smelling of the sewer fat and shiny happy to be alive on
horseback on the four pins of his great tralala draped in the
beautiful courtly coat of his shit enveloped in odors threads of
the most infamous smells the masked ball of white threads and
farts unravels its procession and spreads out its day flees at night
from Saturday to Sunday preening himself in front of the pit
audience and bowing low to salute the entrails hang as garlands
on the nails hammered into the heart of this story with flags
torn by bullets throttled screams of the forks and spoons in the
panic flight of the concrete fact of the ruler-drawn lines and the
set-square the plumb line the compass the play of parabolas the

fun of hyperboles guaranteed pure olive oil nothing added tangerines oranges pears cerulean blue apple green carriage green light yellow drawn by lots and winning at this con game only a moment of the tunic caught in the window trapped suffers as much as the twisted arm of the blue by the pincers of the bouquet's center

25.2.37

extremely attached to the proprieties gobblito oval passed through the lake's sieve nailed to the apple green smelling so good of the wise man's hand reflected on the broken bottle neck flaming colors suspended by the feet at the bottom of the molten water fleeces by its screams ripped from the beast's hair the farandole of knuckle bones and stupefies them rhyming the birds' songs — so then nailed sieve smelling so good the reflection broken by the colors of the beast's screams and the water of the birds' songs sculling the flames forgotten by the hand detached from the head by the noise of the door opened suddenly to see its feathers spread to the flea tree on the wave of ribbons ruffled by the wind shaken by the wings of the water laid on the edge martyrizes the coming of the good samaritan from his good woman of Samaria and blows up the breath balloon of the cocoon emptied of the meanings of pyrograved passion founding its drawings on the twos threes and sevens inscribed on the black list watching themselves laugh under the filthy paper put there evidently voluntarily to the right of the cup half full of milk under the domination of the force contained in the shadow that coolly cuts it into slices of the arm thrust into the unnamable liquid of the table coagulated on the ground monkeying about in the rafters and how pleased I am my friend to see you how beautiful you are more beautiful than ever you smell so good but you should have said so write me you are charming I love nothing more than to hear you laugh yes yes sit down stay a moment I have so much to tell you just imagine yesterday what a plump fat sun what colors I am I remain your greatest admirer and please accept dear lady the most beautiful of spankings ever given to such a gorgeous ass and I mark on my notebook one three pound bag of potatoes so much a quarter pound butter kitchen salt cotton coffee 10 plus sheets spoons cheese darning thread 390 total 3.000.000 plus 3 plus 9 equals zero zero 10 after all's counted it's to my advantage

[PJ]

26.1.37 translated from Spanish by [JR]

THE BLACK NOTEBOOK
[6 – 19 MARCH 1937]

6.3.37

the cuttlebone bites its <u>throne</u> at the lamp that lends its ear to the sun's calls and strips off their flesh

11.3.37

velvet egg-cup burgeoning from the sea of mother-of-pearl cysts between its lips hides behind its bars desire so cramped in its prison the band striking up lit by candles

lit by candles behind bars velvet egg-cup burgeoning mother-of-pearl cysts of the sea between its lips hide the desire so cramped in its prison striking up the band

velvet egg-cup lit by candles behind bars burgeoning mother-of-pearl cysts of the sea between its lips hide the desire so cramped in its prison striking up the band candles lighting up the mother-of-pearl burgeoning the sea's cysts between its lips behind the bars of its prison so cramped desire striking up the band hides

candles lighting the cysts of the sea burgeoning the mother of pearl of its prison between its lips behind bars hides desire so cramped velvet egg-cup striking up the band

hides lighting up from the sea the mother-of-pearl of its prison so cramped desire

the sea so cramped in the mother-of-pearl of its prison under its arm hides desire

so cramped in the prison under the bars of the sea desire strikes up the band

prisoner so cramped
under the bars covering the sea
prisoner
strikes up the band of desire
strikes up the sea

desire makes the sea strike up so cramped it imprisons it and lights up the bars

the long procession of bars lights up from its prison where so cramped in the sea desire hides tolls the bell against the velvet egg-cup

17.3.37

desire so cramped in its prison explodes the eggshell of the sea
and lights up the bars that confine it tolling the bell against the
velvet egg-cup

15.3.37

the little girl watered by the folds of the woolen corsage yells
and writhes. Its paws cling to the water hanging from the ceil-
ing. The mouth caught at the faucet of the tune's flame spread
on the plate bordered with flies from the little bag of secrets rot-
ting in the shadow of his elbow leaning on the frame's perfume
square of the mirror reflecting ennui

19.3.37

test the resistance of the steel that dandles her and in passing
takes away the wind rose that grows in her window so surprised
and caught in the kissing lips' mirrors. Who with all four paws
leans on her flame with all her weight. The hand hides three
quarters of the sun and squeezes its juice on the tongue sees
coming out of the mirror a landscape without a scratch the
naked body of the blue sheet flapping its wings caught in the
leafage's netting. Calls him and stretched out at his feet caresses
him with sweetest words and licks him

[PJ]

19.3.37 [I] [II]

[I] l'hache-chat d'os 7 carpes postales porte mâle heures
    a) the cat-axe of bone 7 carps postal carries male hours
    b) the buying of this postcard brings bad luck

[II] archive of rotten farts in his heart rotten bacalao full of worms on his tongue a prisoner inside his mouth filled with hair pot grilling squid's ink

[PJ]

section [II] *translated from Spanish*

13 APRIL 37

divinely left to dry atop a dish of lentils in the eaves with prickly pears an icy tongue for company his cross athwart his back his skin the old rag of the dry moth-eaten skin and toothless madly gulping down the sword that chokes him spitting in his eye

geometric figure that's dissolved in the corrosive acid grabs it by the throat between his claws with scorn that fights the bull up close that doesn't wipe away the cloth that overturns the cry which grows inflamed in syrup bathes the flourish of the cape with tears from skin stretched out for laughs and face up to the sun

pile of breasts gone green from earfull of their cheers caught in his claws with banderillas poised there face to face in a bullfighting sun the laughter steaming up their feathers in a jug and hurtling from the eaves to make the kill

garbage truck filled up with flowers with its wheels like cups of red wine pulled by tearful horses whipped by laughter from some children sitting on the ground in middle of the street dividing up an orange

looked at through the key hole face that swirls around over the pane the colors soaked in brine inside a wine glass laughter

dipped in slime that cries a bucket full of tears left out to dry
legs open screwed into the earth

split in two aroma of the shadow that the bucket full of laughter
gives off screwed onto the rose bush showing off its tears via the
silence that devours it — the handerkerchief that covers up her
breasts is opening its window lighting up the little lamps with
slice of watermelon scorching calamares in her cazuela

[JR]

14 APRIL 37

licks the eye with a warmth that sticks it to the bottom of the
skillet as it gobbles up the ear the blue that saturates the horn
inside the mirror

in the watermelon slice they light their little lamps the claws
that slash the bottom of the mirror chanting fortunes and mis-
fortunes showing off its snout via the eye scorched in a night
shirt on the cotton of the stone that blows apart the hand that
holds it captive

sounding the festival the bottom of the wound that chants his
happiness with legs spread open screwed down by the net that
sweetens his unhappiness and licks the tolling of the bell the rim
of the cazuela where the rice is cooking

cuts cotton in a hundred strips that drinks the bell the net of
waves and of the dance that sweetens up his trauma's happiness
minutely tallies up the details on the wall an image chanting his
unhappiness

upright on its spurs the rotting codfish shuffles off the worms around its head then crowns itself and plunks its shotgun odors on the gaming table's baizy surface

[JR]

16 April 37

snails in garb of bishop peacock's nose and seated on a drum white lilies painted there a herring skeleton a purple velvet purse that holds three and a half reales a stonemason's ladder two guitar strings one silk petticoat two children scratching at each other's face one dressed in blue the other in a load of bricks the lifelines on an ocean's hand hung out to dry up on the roof ledge covered by the shadow of a bull licking a wound that's bleeding on its foreleg

[JR]

The Dream & Lie of General Franco

15 – 18 June 1937

owl fandango escabeche swords of octopus of evil omen furry dishrag scalps afoot in middle of the skillet bare balls popped into a cone of codfish sherbet fried in scabies of his oxen heart — mouth full of marmalade of bedbugs of his words — silver bells and cockle shells and guts braided in a row — a pinky in erection not a grape and not a fig — commedia del arte of bad weaving and smudged clouds — cosmetics of a garbage truck — the rape of las meninas cries and outcries — casket on shoulders crammed with sausages and mouths — rage that contorts the drawing of a shadow that lashes teeth nailed into sand the horse ripped open top to bottom in the sun which reads it for the flies

who tack a rocket of white lilies to the knots spliced in the sar-
dine heavy nets — lamp of lice where dog is and a knot of rats
and hide outs in a palace of old rags — the banners frying in the
skillet twist in black of ink sauce spilled in drops of blood that
gun him down — the street soars to the clouds its feet bound to a
sea of wax that makes its guts rot and the veil that covers it is
singing dancing mad with sorrow — a flight of fishing poles
alhigui and *alhigui* of the moving van first class interment —
broken wings spinning in the spider web of dry bread and clear
water a paella made of sugar and of velvet that paints a
whiplash on its cheeks — the light blocked out the eyes before
the mirror that make monkeyshines the chunk of nougat in the
flames that gnaws itself the lips around the wound — cries of
children cries of women cries of birds cries of flowers cries of
wood and stone cries of bricks cries of furniture of beds of chairs
of curtains of casseroles of cats and papers cries of smells that
claw themselves of smoke that gnaws the neck of cries that boil
in cauldron and the rain of birds that floods the sea that eats into
the bone and breaks the teeth biting the cotton that the sun
wipes on its plate that bourse and bank hide in the footprint left
imbedded in the rock.

[JR]

[JUNE] 1937

inside the heart they pave the streets of the village and the sand
that flows from the hour-glasses wounded on the front when
they fell out the windows serves to dry the blood that spurts
from the astonished eyes that look through the keyholes if the
air asphyxiated by the stench escaping from the nostrils of the
fatty papers trailing on the ground and the music hidden under

the vine leaves does not keep the dance of death from effacing in one fell swoop the imprint of the voices hanging by their finger-tips on the bread crusts marinating in urine

a brilliantly illuminated interior newly paved dripping with blood held up by hour-glasses filled with eyes seen through the key holes typefaces laid on a vine leaf effacing with its feathers the smell of bread crusts marinating in urine

the light paving with its blood the hour-glasses of the key hole of its eyes effaces with its feathers the smell of bread crusts marinating in urine

the mix of colors paving the eyes of the feathers torn from the bread crusts marinating in urine

[PJ]

2 JULY 1937

what a sad fate the fate of the pierced chair of the old mandrake — one-eyed — hacked to pieces — sown with obvious white thread to the wedding dress of the sword thrust given to the flame of the lamp-post of the aurora borealis spread out to dry on the faded flower of the mauve silk cloth of the lemon yel-low laughter of the tall stories and of the orangey weepings machine-stitched with night marsh-mallows

what coquettish desire to fry the heap of reverences in the angry animal's hairs listen with ear glued to thyme's aroma the whip lashings on the ankles and what a sad fate the beggar felt in the caresses that of the chair pierced with a thousand springs brings the mirror's regrets of wound to the spider web shirt of the old beggar woman inscribed on the back of free will eaten by the worms of the pin piercing the orange tree's flower pinned to the middle of the curtain covering the mandrake

[PJ]

5 JULY 37

what a darling cream puff of coquettish desire to fry the heap of reverences clinging to the angry animal's hairs listen carefully listen with ear glued to thyme's aroma the litanies of whip lashings jumping with both feet in the ankles and what a sad fate to beg felt in the caresses of the odor of garlic fried with onions and tomatoes in the eyes that of the chair pierced by the arrows of a thousand springs brings the mirror's regrets of wound to the spider web shirt of the old beggar woman inscribed on the back of free will eaten by the worms of the pin piercing the orange tree's flower pinned to the middle of the curtain covering the toothless mouth of the shit-covered flag of the chasuble smelling of monkey's rot plaited in a thousand buttons around the neck screams screams mandrake whistling hands

order was given to the soldiers on the ramparts not to darling cream puff litanies jumping with both feet from the odor of garlic with onions and tomatoes in her eyes arrows from the toothless mouth of the shit-covered flag of the chasuble smelling of monkey's rot plaited in a thousand buttons around the neck if the enemy shows his nose and if the clarion sound of the coquettish desire to fry the heap of reverences clinging to the angry animal's hairs listens to the at attention alone in its sentry-box the fire at will and the orders of the generals numbed to the bone with jam ear glued to thyme's aroma barrage fire and shells whip lashings falling on the ramparts in the nick of

time on the ankles and what a sad fate begging prisoner attached
to the execution stake at dawn felt in the caresses orange flower
pinned to the toothless mouth filled with the hairs of the shit-
covered flag bleeding all over the chasuble smelling of monkey's
rot plaited in a thousand buttons around the neck

in the middle of the night on the palm of the hand the order
was given to the soldiers standing on the ramparts not to shoot at
the eyes of the fat in the soup given over body and soul to the
pirates darling cream puff litanies jumping with both feet from
the odor of roses of garlic fried with onions and tomatoes song of
the rooster in the eye of the arrows the toothless mouth of the
flag covered in chasuble shit smelling of monkey rot plaited in a
thousand buttons tightened around the neck if the enemy shows
his nose and if the clarion sound of the coquettish desire to fry
the heap of reverences clinging to balconies of the angry ani-
mal's hairs listens to the at attention alone in its sentry-box the
fire at will and the orders of the generals numbed to the bone
with jam ear glued to thyme's aroma barrage fire and shells of
whip lashings falling on the ramparts in the nick of time in
the labyrinths of ankles and what a sad fate begging prisoner
attached to the execution stake at dawn felt in the caresses
orange flower pinned to the toothless mouth filled with the hairs
of the shit-covered flag bleeding all over the chasuble smelling
of monkey's rot plaited in a thousand buttons around the neck of
the screams of the hands that whistle in the look of the gift that
brings the mandrake

[PJ]

[5 – 24 JULY 1937]

5 JULY 1937

wing assault tank mired in the blue thrown to the gift fixed to
the mast of the sailing ship in distress flower clothed in yellow
gold fine red rain of the bonfire of the precious present carrying
in her hands in an old newspaper the excrement of the rose farce
practical joke hit by the bat plumb in the right cheek the orange
screams of the livid festoon stars on the sleeve lilacs of her cor-
sage homage of the almond green sigh of courage locked in the
cape in the ice cream cup dozes carmine facile and comfortable
desire around the light blue of the stone mouth of the white
rainbow sun drunk spread out to dry burning image mute
mauve love star created by the gunshot in the mirror pale yellow
dragging the shreds of her bitter dress in the earth color of her
pain azure whirlwind thinned in the red milk wetting her
fingers in blue velvet drop by drop water distills on the lemon
slice the cozy warm caprice of the butterfly wing tender black
heifer the pigeon breast eye of laughter you slyboots rosewood
kneeling dead of fright turning cartwheels

6 JULY 37

then the canons mounted atop organs themselves attached to
heaps of cheeses dipping fingers into the cream of concrete fact
flutes and barks piled up on colanders and they burned incense
and old rags soaked in benzine and the lieutenant said to his
men as long as the enemy doesn't show his face further ahead
the flags we have put in brine can wait for the hour of reveille
hands linked feet warm the general's wife sleeps and her daugh-
ter is doing household work outside the battlements on the wall
facing the soldiers who are bathing in the drapes of the rocks the
wait was tough and the quarts of raisins and mulberries make

wound salve the tree being full of preserved fruits and the reveille watch stopped at lunch hour the first service bell carried death roasted and stuffed to the chicken-ass-shaped mouth of the gun barrel frozen hands stuck to the stones and the nose rummaging in the dust under the furniture trembling from fear laid on the curtains a sweet smell of naked feet and armpits confounds its design in the rows of algae covering the oilcloth with its wings love pillow in the lining of the coat makes faces at the corpses the tips of the large nails of the slate softly push her song into silence brushing her teeth against the background drop of the subject of the battle suddenly woken up the soldier brides count their breasts and the infantrymen's members benumbed by case shot trash and tank trash of all trash heaped up on the beach the barrel-organ shits its colic on the wind rose of the wedding dress of the priest disguised as a girl hops the grasshopper on the drum and sinks its nails into the plumb line rooster cotton sword of savoir-vivre the announcement of the raising of the curtain melts the beams and freezes the waves the clarion calls in the sleeping bed and the partridge smashes the shot glass against the prow

12 JULY 37

standing up end to end dead from sadness the frying dough ceremoniously salutes in front of the altar of cheese lightening her corsage the commander's daughter delivers her thoughts to the buttons undoes the vipers' nest of folds soaking the soup to the nails that come undone in reverences * the wine list raises itself on tiptoes at the risk of receiving the announcement made to the militias to go get hung elsewhere and the hand caressing the back of the landscape doesn't manage to put life into the party grilling on night's teeth * a taste of lightening in the mouth and armpit perfume at the fingertips of the flag waving in the eye of

the expiring goat ✳ Turned nails the piece of silk paper repeats
its song along the edge of the grating laid flat on the ground
hands crossed behind the execution stake stuck to the guard post
✳ but the *troulaitou* and the bread flutes in the distance and the
la oh la la the mussel à la mussel of the children playing hop-
scotch and the desperate cries of the birds glued to the keyholes
what horror what distress and what a coldness in the bones and
what a disagreeable smell floods it ✳ if feeling the ice of the
knife tear his shoulder the taste of aloes whispers in his ear her
somersaults and broken doll laughter against the bamboo stems
of the cloister lilacs displayed at the barracks door great gift
great lie doesn't take part in the feast and doesn't light the wine's
bonfire in her throat open to love and to the dances on the rope
hanging from the balcony nailed to the sheets stretched out on
the waves ✳ but that the boat trembling all over from fear man-
ages to hold on to the edge of the abyss of blue stuck to the
snows covering the dress of flames and the partridge's empty
cage and the marten and the rope ladder and the fallen cigarette
ashes and the mortar filled with garlic aï oli braids will burn
united in a torch ✳ wild spree weird party that night cuts into
slices of children's swing ✳ the ennui the ennui of the festoon
and javanese cuddles will never fill up the depth of the sigh torn
in her silk stockings ✳ nor the apparent calm of the lights of the
wide leaves trembling nor the hour nor all desire nor the dregs

17 [JULY 1937]

and later the fall of the lace come unglued from the ceiling and
the oh so bland smell of the stars falling into the vase filled with
scales and the bits of smoked bacon oh so friendly and well bred
and so calm their charms died from fright in their court dress
with tar spots that hand resting on the sword's muzzle lips glued
to the blade while uttering a thousand thanks and reverences

and one thousand three hundred fifty one smiles despite the time come unstuck from the hours fixed to the clock and the ensuing weeping before love run over by the carriage wheels unable to undo the knot of glances pinned to the mirror the tree of life frowns in its shell and looks through

19 JULY 37

the slit of the wound the dance of the innocents set on the set table and doesn't steal a second from the bitter orange juice rising via the rope at the edge of the crust if the flood of shreds of percale floating on the boats anchored on the plate full of cherries and the flower hiding its shadow on the street corners from the back of the corsage at the call of hands beating against the tree trunk the whole landscape racing at full gallop among the algae of her white-hot secrets among the words of love the cries for help tear with great appetite the tripe torn from the canvas put into a coffin drying on the wharf in its frame of envies and desires browsing the herd of sheep gently spinning their wool for neither the extract of myrrh nor the black currant salve nor the grilled sardines nor birdsong nor flute nothing but the spectral odor of the stars reflecting in the mirrors doesn't permit nor allow that the order of the lines tangling up the subject of this baleful comedy would throw its own light on the bit of wall in shadow hanging by its nails at the edge of the abyss into which the sewer of life empties if by chance the rosebushes spitting into the figure of the naked body the gall of its graces envelops in its excrements the little hope attached to the top of the greasy pole

set on the set table the miss set under the table like a mouse runs the ferret and smoothes the feathers at the back of the feather duster foaming with rage at her finger and to have thousands upon thousands of miles in the legs at the millet grain sentence upon sentence at the carrousel of roads and at the fangs tangling up dancing the jumps and leaps in perfect catalepsy but pray do tell me young man did you study in depth the odor of evening farts at dusk by the sea in the woods among the clematis have you thought through and licked the digestions of your fathers and didn't you fall backwards fainting in admiration before the beauty of the colors shaken up at the depth of thoughts raising a hue and a cry inside the nuts tell me don't keep your secret it belongs to us and you owe it to us set yourself down gently thus gently leaning against the post they will shoot you and offer you a dozen macaroons very fresh don't move you are immortal he is at the end of his end and wants to tell you only the main facts and if this day's afternoon despairs and winces if the weather spoiled by the thunderstorm stinks in its bowl

20 JULY 37

and enchagrins the third of the quarter of joy and the pain and the weight of the pitch glued to the feathers of the aimed for heart

24 JULY 37

go for it guys the piglet's fat the batter of concrete facts and the daube and honey-comb tripe and chitterlings emerging from the foam of the bouquet of suns will not pay their debts to half-burned rags swimming in the pond — angles cutting the thread of the circumference at the stridency of the color of the bit of cloth floating hanging from the coral branch of the clarion's sound dying swiftly on the mourning wheat and the hundred and some thousand of thousands and hundreds pulling on the cords of the harp eaten by worms sinking like a stone to the bottom of the hair covering the clouds

algebraic operation flayed alive vociferating all its vinegar in the
pierced chair of its prayers astride the open maw rural rose lost
by the vibration of the arrow come to lodge at the center of the
hive of blue stripes of cabins offered sacrificed to the redoubled
blows of the blisters exploding between the frozen fingers of the
black pole of the closet's doors if the music received by the nos-
trils for dinner on the battle ground nothing but whiff of what it
could seem the image as shortcut for the shadow of simple truth
and the aroma of rottenness that surrounds it and veils it and
makes visible only a bit of the quarter of your of her simple
apparatus empty shell in which the butt of the joke chews the
punch line that chokes him and paints in the liveliest colors the
linen cloth that girds him to the clocks chaining him to the
arabesques attaching themselves to his footsteps a sort of sugar
cube soaking in herring brine grilled on the square of the pow-
der box

[PJ]

[JULY] 1937

the syncope stretched its long paws around the neck of the
asphodel nicely displayed in the center of the pipe smoking plat-
ter of ribs

[PJ]

MOUGINS VAST HORIZON
12 SEPTEMBER 37

at the end of the promenade jetty
behind the casino the gentleman
so correctly dressed so gently
stripped of his pants eating his

bag of fries of turds
graciously spits
the pits of
the olives into the face
of the sea
threading his
prayers on the cord
of the flag grilling
at the end of the swear word
that illuminates the scene
the music hides its
maw in the arena
and unnails
its fright
from the frame of wasps
legs spread
the fan melts
its wax on
the anchor

[PJ]

[SEPTEMBER] 1937

portrait of the marquesa of the Christian ass throwing a nickel
to the Moorish* soldiers defenders of the Virgin

[PJ]

translated from Spanish

---

*Moorish soldiers: Moroccan regiment serving in the franquist army during the
Spanish civil war (1936-1939).

[1938, NO DATE]
WRITING WITH UNKNOWN WORDS*

---

*Written on the stationery of F.I.A.R.I. (Fédération Internationale de l'Art Révolutionnaire Indépendant), with André Breton cited on its masthead as the Secrétaire Général.

10.1.38

leave to a stealthily sneakily arriving spring the job of buttering-
up the love that seeps from the eyes around the glacial cold that
pearls along the back of the sun held suspended by its four cor-
ners nailed to the great beams holding up the sky which lets its
fist fall on the casket that, grilling its light on the soft fire of the
strip of cloth dipped in the urine of the roses covering the divid-
ing wall of the perfume of their excrement, knits the bramble of
the plumb line of the stone arc ripping apart the naked corpse of
the girl stretched out to dry under the mauve sheet of her image
hanging from the banner attached at one end to the greased pole
of her bronze throat minutely sketching on the shadow of the
scent of the lice-covered tree tearing up its comic envelope of
anguished cries that cut the stiff cord of the rock crystal mask
gnawed by the stings of trucks fixing below the hive heart gorge
hill stake measure odor river spiraling around the word sleeps
the arrow of the lamp sliding over the paper crossing it joyful

[CS]

14.1.38

gangrene of the shadow of the wardrobe falling straight down
into the soup tureen holding between its clenched teeth the
throat of the white prevalent on the top chair bandage envelop-
ing with its absorbent cotton the wound open to the frame of the
wall hidden by the hand agitated by the peach color of the blue
chiffon asleep in the hollow of the quarter of brie breaking the
cut of the steel festoon melted into the design hung on the tune
of a flute drowned in the cacophony of the awl of the trip-wire
stretched out across the chandeliers of oranges and the desires
hidden in the tin box of ruled lines and the squares twisted by

fire so fast the angles hung from the handles of the milk jug
nailed to the canon aiming its rage and counting it off on the
ends of the fingers of the flying hand that drives the caravan
sort of slice of ham and fruit tart without a word of reproach
without the least wince of sloth without the least glance of hate
twisted around the tissue-paper bag filled with honey caramels
neither cross-ruled nor decorated à la more or less modern with-
out a comma and the ass more or less provoked by the itchings of
the verses neither more nor less moved than the curtain shred-
ded by the tongs that turn it over and heat it over the mad
misguided letter dipping its soup and its feet into the river twist-
ed by its hands on the bedsheet already cold and soaked with
fear before the firing squad tearing out the tongue and with its
own hands tearing up the bandages glued to the sealed lips of
the coquettish little drawing so minute painted in large horten-
sia blue on the bottom of the neck of the vase abandoned on the
sill of the open window which looks out on the garden of the
house for rent entered on page 2.389 of the register item i just
where a drop of coffee has made a brown stain that the herds of
details that came later to sit around will start to be disturbing in
their own way without ways and of their cries and capers so
innocently placed so delicately on the ground like stones on the
plate trembling and pink and healthy dressed in new linen clean
body smelling of soap and lavender regularly entered in the reg-
isters of good and bad the folds of the slacks cutting each thread
at the foot of the ant attached to his job and if the bell sounds
the dinner hour inclining very respectfully and lining up neither
sad nor gay but rather something like a colored drawing thrown
burning into a pit very ceremoniously buried in the sheet of
cardboard that shit and shit shits it

[cs]

[2 – 7 FEBRUARY 1938]

2.2.38

hanged by the neck with the coaxing
cord
silent
smelling good the vervain
the liquid arms
exploding the drops of sweat
sounding the alarm
in the streak of light
glued to the temples
the reflections of the mirror knocking on the door
hiding the scent from the rainbow's rays
to the pigeon's wings
augmenting the coal merchant's accounts
arriving just in time

2-7.2.38

hanged by the neck with the coaxing (hanged because his fingers are rays of blue yellow green mauve light)

cord (because the sinuous drawing coils up the finger and bites to the blood of its toothless gums)

silent (because the cord at the end of which she balances whips her thighs and tickles the ash of the face of the clock suspended in the flame of the candle between her toes)

smelling good the vervain (the cavalcade of plates forks spoons and dishrags piled on the fire firecrackering and bucking the traces biting the fishy hands of the jailer) the liquid arms (are the arms of the word barely out of the mouth and already drunk on a little attention enveloped in the absorbent cotton of the tune trailing under the pillow)

explosion of drops of sweat (means love grief and a little of the scent of the fan's sandalwood)

sounding the alarm (I imagine an all-season carriage pulled by painted red heifers imitating the bricks of a wall)

in the streak of light (equal to 137.840 minus the stamp affixed to the edge of her wedding dress)

glued to the temples (the lights across the shutters shot down by the baskets of mandarins placed on the dining room table already dead)

the reflections from the mirror knocking on the door (half-fig half-grape as they say)

hiding the scent from the rainbow's rays (order in the ideas smell of coal blinded by the light from the headlights of a car arriving to remove the reasons glued to the oar of the boat breaking away from the ceiling and served hot on a cloth thrown over the chair)

to the pigeons' wings (the arms of the citizens who died for nothing buried in the earth and eating the worms of corpses)

augmenting the coal merchant's accounts (to hear far off in the country the cries of three little girls attacked by vipers)

arriving just in time (reading the list of winning lottery num-
bers out loud)

[CS]

6.2.38

surrounded by the teeth of the jaw of the sun planted in its flesh
the square of the water-filled arena supported by wax candles
shivers its fur and shakes the ash fallen onto the rumpled table-
cloth already covered with stains after the lunch glued to the
ceiling of the hail of arrows of the bugle fixed to the mast of the
sword that goes right through it and bleeds it his wide open eye
pinned by double hairpins to the movement of concentric circles
fleeing the center of the cry pricking the stretched skin of the
drum veiled in black mouths full of earth the pigeons' wings'
fingernails ripping the covering of flowering rosebushes off the
lice the consent having come so late on the surface of the piece
of marble representing it standing in beach clothing the
extended arm pointing to the exit next to the men's bathroom 10
cents ladies 1.340 plus the registration fees and a lunch paid to
the mistress of the house photographed with exposed breasts
arms raised holding a vase of flowers in her hands perfectly imi-
tating the comparative study of the interior of the opened
abdomen of the injured mare fused to the interior of the ice
block and the bronzed dress thrown across the back of the chair
broken into a thousand pieces under the curtains stinking of
farts of hearts held way up at the top of the flagpole.

[CS]

8.2.38 [ɪ] [ɪɪ]

[ɪ]   to say without trouble without fear without closing your
       eyes simply algae mistress crossbeam supporting the river
       sewn to her dress precariously balanced plastered on the
       chalk painted wall lying stomach down on the bronze of the
       hair stretched out under the boat tied to the brambles
       minutely describing the details in the streak of light melt-
       ing the plump one's wax to make the peelings thrown into
       the mouth of the drawing that would like to shred the illu-
       sion of the leaping carp of love rolled up in the bobbin open
       to all the winds lilac color color of violets butter color melt-
       ed color of the door ajar color of olives starch and garlic
       color of caressing palm unguent soft sweet on the mountain
       of ear-pink cotton the chair after walking it slowly in the
       hands to move it to the left of the room and to throw the
       light of the ceiling on it to devour it and notice on the azure
       tint of the wall the imprint of the wooden shoe represent-
       ing it sitting at the table between two columns one pink one
       yellow holding up the almond green crestfallen look of the
       [   ] injured by the sun dying on the buffet and not mak-
       ing the slightest movement during [   ] of the sincere
       birthing of the ground reflected on the corner of the foot of
       the table neither uneasy nor reticent [   ] made the care-
       ful and timely arrangements more than natural but tossed
       any old way into the bottom of the drawer of the armoire
       completely at rest under the [   ] hidden in the closed fist
       tapping on the point of pride.

[ɪɪ]   pink pink of garlic pink pink
       blue pink ceruleink
       lit by the pink lampshade

watered down earlier in the stretched-out pink
of the truck stopped at
the corner of the barricaded road

of the bronzed hair laid out across the boat lying belly down
the river sewn to her dress the wounded arm of the sun
entering at top speed spots the imprint of the wooden shoe
on the table and throws the olive-colored garlic-colored
palm salve light of the ceiling softly into the hands the blue
that oozes a pink pre-dawn

neither more nor less glued to the chalk-painted wall the
bed of brambles of the bronzed hair laid out under the boat
of the sketch tearing up the river sewn to her dress neither
more nor less boat melting the wax of the bronzed hair laid
out at the feet of the table the color of lilac the leaping ear-
pink cotton carp of the chair softly moves the hand that
strangles it

to move the door-ajar-colored starch to the left of the room
and to throw the ash of ceiling light into the mouth of the
sketch that wants to shred the illusion of the wooden shad-
ow shoe holding up the crestfallen look of almond green

[CS]

10.2.38

global price given to the ragseller for a scale filled with armoires
of chairs of petticoats of Pan flutes of toes of brambles of fishing
rods and of the palms of the hand for an ocean sea of filthy old
papers tied up with stinking yellowed pink and mauve ribbons
dipping into rose water covered with black hair the sum of three

hundred and fifty and one small rye breads if the shell the
flower and the coal of the worst sheep in the air across the bars
of the chair don't ignite the flame of the flute and destroy the
colony of sighs and tears cooking in the pan of the open arms of
light crushed in the mortar festoon of the music glued to the
stone of the sink spinning its sand at the foot of the pink hill
buffet [   ] kiss planted on the mouth of the open window

[CS]

[12 – 19 FEBRUARY 1938]

12.2.38

accurate representation engraved on the grain of sand of the
raindrops' silence this afternoon of emptiness on the laundry
laid out on its feather bed of a wax figure imitating a child at the
edge of a river having fun with a *prunus* branch teasing two bee-
tles she sits on potato peels on the sink of her shadow reflecting
on the hairy back of the marble hand reproducing the image
accurately molded from the imprint of the foot of the chicken
wing singing far away in the oat field curled up on the portrait of
the cat molten into the wax of the ink dish's corner sheltered
under the left arm of the armchair blue wetting the large loaf's
crumb biting its fleas and I want tell you the boredom the joy
the songs and the laughter at the wind's colic of love climbing
up the rungs of the ladder playing at knuckle bones at trundling
hoops jumping rope playing hopscotch freeze tag playing knife
playing numbers old sun torn by scabies shivering and freezing
covered with snow hidden under the closet licking its wounds
hand held out begging for alms plus three hundred ninety three
hundred twenty seven meters of cotton cloth 387 zero 250 and
three hundred pleasantly warm dinner rolls butter carrots oil six
chairs a sideboard a kitchen table coal garbanzos bacon a drum

its sticks old newspapers brushes a meter of hail a bucket a cage
bed a gallows the executioner of wounds and sores and a clothes-
brush a dog an old woman delousing herself a tree and a huge
mirror in the middle of the kitchen reflecting a battle two horse-
men attacking each other with lances covered in sweat and blood
another one his horse wounded dead on the ground and the spec-
tators clapping on the table covered with a wax cloth the wine
spilled on it flowing over the floorboards grabbing on to the win-
dow panes tearing the nails of the light of the wolf trap of the
dress wrapping it up completely in its chains of children's
screams

19.2.38

and by a tar painted boat cut by the frame the detailed descrip-
tion of the events of the month days hours of the plus and the
minus and of the garlic sauces with marsh-mallows with pep-
pers and with caresses on the naked trunk of the morning air of
this burning day finely chopping the edges of the handkerchief
of this sky spread out to dry on clouds flowing through the slits
of closed shutters the snails of the mayonnaise of petrified light
dirtying happiness with the licks of its tongue on the furniture
stretching woken up by the bells' ears budding branches shoot-
ing out covering themselves with leaves flowers giving fruit
poisonous birds biting into silver pieces ointment covering the
wound opened by the colors of the rainbow assassinating the
milk jar hidden on the shadow of the oh so sour wind's opened
fan of the rope beating the window pane thick mattress of
buzzing bees slit open by the horn of the liquid cockcrow burn-
ing falling drop by drop from the philter of the curtains' raised
saddle-stitch on the azure triangle planted on the lemon larded
with the flames of the one thousand three hundred ninety and a
hundred colored streamers eyes fixed on the floor but don't get

up be all ears you won't leave without having a little something don't say another word and count the steps of this dance you must have fun be happy truly will you have to have your belly tickled to make you laugh if you don't like entrails you'll be served anal fish bones well peeled and washed in almond water throw in a little starch butter a pepper corn salt four dried figs a quarter of well degreased bacon shallots black pudding a cuttle-bone a bag of coal two melons and the price of a countryside rest home bring to a boil over a low fire hit it with a large hammer and piss all around it for an hour and don't give it time to sigh let it crust over and scratch the skin until it bleeds now serve half cold in dreadful weather on gloves of freezing horsehair

[PJ]

1.3.38

black sunbeam knocking at the door drawing on the proffered hand the eyelet of the herd of the folds of the shadow tensed as touches the noise of the fan hidden in the buckram of the honey pot of the powdered sugar burning on a scrap of celestial blue sweet almond milk of the pigeon flight wipes the mirror caught in the vice of the keyboard of vibrant knives stuck in the back of the sun oozing through the closed shutters cerulean filth of marine cobalt

[PJ]

9.3.38

I

wag mirror jasper crow
petticoat acanthus dilemma citadel
snout udder opossum

II

naked leg of the mirror stretched out
on the flames of the hairy back of the sun flat on
its belly on the cheek

III

painted at the edge of the abyss of the grimace of the itch
little wild flower pink and violet with black spots
in a glass at the scale of certainty of the sweetness
of caramel of the wheel's fingers

IV

covering the lemon yellow with the blood
running from the truck loaded with birds
under the blue sheet of the pile of oranges

[PJ]

19.3.38

I repeat characters 1 and 2 the 1 before the other sitting on
chairs hands on floor reflecting at times on the liquid marble of
knees put in irons by the underside of the arms in the armpit
hair of 2 the eyes of 1 and in the honey folds of the belly the
fingers of the mouths stuck to the two anterior legs of the chair
of 1 teeth covered with hair of the hollow oranges of the gums
of the sailor suit of the child kneeling on the back of the table
burning around the edge of its circle the blues of the convolvu-
lus completely surrounding the body of the 2 and I'm saying sit
down the 1 in front of the 2 on chairs hands on floor playing at
throwing the feet of the other at each other through the mirror
inclined at sixty thousand degrees for a whole winter afternoon
that seems like spring

blue square of the orange larding its wings with mauve butter holding tightly in its teeth the hot coals torn in the waves' flames at the gums of the sailor suit rolling the big heap of flames up in a ball

[PJ]

20.3.38

come down from the table it squeezed between its knees the sailor suit puts itself under it lips glue to belly and at its dugs sucks the bouquet of immortelles of the hive neither flesh nor faggot of umbrellas nothing but clean picked bones but what smell doesn't organize the music vomited from its four paws by the peck of a rose so mimi seen at the end of each branch under the flagellating laughter of the sun's kiss I only tell you that much what an orgy of lampions in the frying pan of this morning exactly the twentieth of march of this year 38 doesn't cook the silk shirt to shreds in the stroke of the pen of the flight of the eye of garlic broken hair crowned with roses and blackberries the head of the adolescent the song hidden behind the spokes of the wheel smells of mint of thyme of imprinted canvas of the hay wagon filled with bits of smoking ice covered with forget-me-not of eagles tearing flowers from the flesh of the refuse of a fox's corpse spread on the ground shadow shards of a large puddle of mauve ink drinking the mud of the cockcrow in large gulps with no leaf stirring

[PJ]

26.3.38

grocery establishment described in great detail with pen on acanthus leaf in violet ink on the fly-leaf of each leaf of the great tree of the lotus leaf for one whole spring the piece of curtain to anybody who'll listen by the genesis of the strings of the purse open to all winds unsews the hem of her dress and inscribes in the great book the great hullabaloo on the stage of the theater of the great cycle of the heap of garbage covering the dress in dung of the majestic garden-party given in honor of the great mass of slaps in the face to be given for no reason to the leaves of the branches in the garden showing their buttocks through the slates of the closed shutters at the tears in the curtains wiping the dregs of sugar of the old lamb of leg bone caught in the vice of the wallpaper covering the left shoulder of the wall to the left of the side-board when the fingers of the left hand of 2 ripping the teeth of the sailor suit tightened around the cranks traversing the neck of the mechanical horse with the regularity of the heart beats' jolts of the saw cutting the sun-drop falling on the tip of the knife sitting on the angle open to the breaking point of the great round table dissolved in the straw mat covering with its laughter and yells the ceiling hanging by its four feet from the corners of the room overflowing with mustard pots of paint reduced to pap by the wisdom of characters 1 and 2 chewing its nails behind the girders of the shadow fixed on the relief map sweet and bitter words stuck to the kites circling the lamp hanging from the threads of the line drawn on the mirror by the lightning bolt of the kingfisher on the plumb-line of the half-open door of the orchestra playing *Ma Paloma* let me repeat large square room used as dining room furnished very plainly but with a beautiful view on the entrails of the disemboweled horse rotting for centuries on the lawn to rent for the season 395 plus cleaning and inventory fees to be paid to the concierge the statues and the tulip beds remaining the possession of the inheritors for the first two weeks and suddenly standing up the 2 sings the 1 accompanies him beating his

heels on the floor he sings I'm the very detailed description of
the lack of desire to fill the hot-air balloon with sand to make a
nest for him to piss on and set fire to the lake great vessel full of
very poetical excrement of stars a croissant in a large bucket full
of old urine howls at the moon all of it said in a very sweet voice
and very respectfully bowing to the audience which sleeps stand-
ing up on the edge of the first-tier boxes a drop of blue publicly
spreads the lie bogged down in the grain of alcohol the handle of
the orangey bites the acid of the pink his fingers brush aside the
danger of the rain of birds detached from their wings and tilts
the mirror of the wardrobe to dead center let me tell you says
the 2 and please more clearly says the 1 wiping his mouth with
the back of his left hand Darius says the 2 great philosopher
from Mougins living in Alcoi on the 80th of march says the 1 of
the year 07, ninety says the 2 proofed Q by Q says the 1 that the
gods and the rivers having come out of their lairs become
incomprehensible to the sages says the 2 if the light of a lantern
says the 1 that one would put on a diet says the 2 salt and wine
says the 1 and that the heat of the sun would mildew for a thou-
sand years at the center of the oceans says the 2 would take away
the power of prediction and here's the proof says the 1 back to
back the numbers 3 and 389 crushed ground cooked and cooked
again minced and put through the mill said the 1 and the 2 at
the same time will provide the exact weight

[PJ]

30.3.38

kneeling immobile white dissolves its cream in the brain driving
at top speed surrounded by swallows painting the finger tips of
the light showing its eyes through the slats of the shutters the
handkerchief waved by the presence of an apple croaks in the

middle of the almond the high jump of the orangey so periwin-
kle blue of the nose of the mauve and stretches its arms around
the indigo the kiss of the power-hammer attached to the emer-
ald of the dish-rag confirms the sentence before the knife's
reflection

[PJ]

31.3.38

sugar of the halting breath of the shutters jumping with a single
leap in the naked expiring body of the sheet of paper the laugh-
ter of the bouquet bleeding all over its song the tone and
cadence the nest of anemones in the heat of the brush of pastels
thrown grappling into the tussle of lines tied to the luminous
poisons sowing their wild oats among the thistles comb out their
hair

[PJ]

2.4.38

right now the blister opening a door to the room in the sky
bursts and spills over walls and ceiling his military musical juice
on the two window shades the glass chains attached to white
karma covering his tears' flower shroud the hour has come late
lunch is served roasted new suit's blue collar surrounded by steel
vegetables cooked in their own sauce the curious weeping willow
raw parts aloe muscles hands clasped wisely on the lookout
determining limits of the closed field reabsorbs what's left and
sucks the drawing sweeping the play of light whisking the colors
hiding under the strangest aspects in jokes about the end end of
history the door is open to everyone laughter coming in forma-
tion gripped to take a place alongside two miserable characters

hanging from their shadows' gallows chairs leaping at the closet throat disguised as Ophelia linens rolled up losing many pieces of lace vigorously sounding the alarm to the hens smoldering inside ice tearing her fingernails on oil images trickling the objects looking for their eyelids folded over stars' stomachs encased in a big piece of bread wrinkled in the pool of sunlight sustaining the wet building cotton in the mouth of the square lilacs the unexpected hour scribbles in the folded flag hanging by an end to the key fresh butter sardines radishes anchovies purple cotton sheet blue azure of the orange kisses crushed by the heel a vase bursts with joy in the hands of green almond rays and pale rose of the wallpaper that holds it pricked by thousands and thousands of apple blossoms it faints it dies and sings and while coiling up around the beams coming from the window across to the table and falls dead on the parquet floor the machine turns around the subject pushes it forward by its cries excites it invents it with the slightest look left stuck to each object and sorts it folds and attaches each color dragging in the air gives it a name a number and a definite place lights up the corners of the furniture with small flames and edges the angles of the buffet with forget-me-nots and throws out several buckets of blue ink haphazardly from top to bottom on the ground in a corner which awakens with a start jumps in front and hits the clouds dragging in the deserted streets the rest of the room set-ting fire to the furniture crying mid flames covered with Spring dew tearing the woods dressing them in branches and flowers leaving them naked bald cropped neither more nor less torn apart with relish by cigarette ashes rising from the bottom of the written page

[AW, LW]

translated with Katie Ahearn

28.4.38

right now the First inflating his head vomits the phrase written
on the slate of her apparent tongue you'd have to think about
lunch my friend it's getting late and we should clamor about the
arrangement of these plates drawing nudes from pot of beans to
get near megaphones and break away from its stenches the good
samaritan's ears hidden under the buffet counting his fleas what
shall we do a soup of nails a slice of beams a nest of dust or
rather an old ragout of spiders scorpions polliwogs and some
debris heaps of stars and milky ways I know you prefer the gen-
tleness of aloe to the strong pressure of the rose-bush's hands
beneath your palace vault but if you wish there could be a good
roast of victims not said the Second lets go out to the restaurant
the little one should wait for us the thawing of his gnawed gums
set in his scrawny teeth and let's carry the cats we'll find at last a
gracious means to incorporate them with jazz tunes come I'll
quickly tear away the huge nails the sun stuck in your coat to fas-
ten it to your body and you can change clothes and put on your
beautiful Cheshire cheese outfit but the First rolling about the
table legs seated on the puddle of fire falling drop by drop holds
up peonies

[AW, LW]

[28 APRIL — 1ST MAY 1938]

28-29.4.38

open door half-open closed closed again half-open closed half-
open closed open onto the hydrangea patch aping the anguished
cry the cock drawn with the tip of the hour drawn from the shaft

of white chained to the stairs sticky with spit going up the
jar's contour cast in blood that burns at each tread of the mob
flax seed stuck to the skeleton's keel the vulture wrapped in
prism streamers twisted in spirals by icy pungent sand soup
under its wing foot crushing in the egg polygon of laughter
flogged against the center's edges mongoose dilemma goldsmith
baby's bottle colocynth crab-louse halberd piton brackish dyke
celestial azure blue and step by step tread of First and Second
going down the stairs and then the street

1ST MAY 38

who evaporates on his linens and soils them let's go a bit faster
says Second let's put our legs between our teeth and set them on
edge we must hurry if we want to arrive in time for the evening
soups and bite with the servant's lovely curly hair with mince-
meat heart story of our loves decomposed by acid singing hands
stretched out behind their heads at the bottom of the barge
shooting to the edge of the path eyes caught on the sky spitting
in their mouths word by word each word and my friend do you
want say again Second after having spent several eternities with-
out saying a thing do you want me to play you a military march
to keep you warm and fresh like the statue of sperm you see here
in the middle of the square I begin a long sigh from it distant
reflection that living jeers cuts the long sausage moon that
pounds the wall that approaches the restaurant with wolf's steps

[AW, LW]

9.6.38

the rose sings at the top of her lungs over toasted bits of bread
spread over butter erasing extended blue spread legs cast a shad-
ow cutting in two the eroding song end of poppy finger caught

on the beam and loosened knot flowing squeezing the throat of
the letter received in earnest

[AW, LW]

22.6.38

on four corners of the room nailed to light's mouths to yelps'
awning washing the bricks with sun with sweat pale dawn dead
from sleep sheep's head expiring beneath the bloody shower
from the bugler posted under the wheels of the flag of the
disheveled bed meat scraps of rose bouquet at the finger-nail tip
imitating the laughter and cries of the jasmine scent enveloping
the blue hydrangea streaks and green almond upright chair
boiling on the shared cock-a-doodle-doo look scrap of coffee-
soaked fabric the rainbow's axe the square of the song's holey
outfit what do you want my love my mistress my life to fool
boredom and burn the veil torn while nails rusted in the
tree's trunk melting butter to the sound of military music
which passes through the sewer if hand and foot and mouth and
eyes and cotton that floats inside the closed crystal fist and heat
arriving completely frozen with fear and the fire currants drag-
ging thread full of anchovies and guitar melodies in the gust of
grains of rice snowing on her cheek

[AW, LW]

25.6.38

string of moons fan of oil of swallows fastening her sandal in
the imperceptible watermelon smell the *aqua viva* of her min-
gled hair lights up dregs of breath of hand that shakes up the
flute's wings

[AW, LW]

2 JULY 38

drop by
drop
hardy
pale blue
dies
between
the claws of
green almond
on the rose
trellis

[AW, LW]

28 NOVEMBER 38

gouging her teeth into the wound desire's architecture spreads
her wings love's livid banner that sits in the darkest corner of the
sink's drainage pipe halo of rainbow fireworks of her gaze the
sun lamp hidden in the ice block which draws its shape onto the
fingers that stroke her bronzed hair kept chained in the drawing
that fastens it to flesh that spills out over her body and pulverizes
it nailed to her eyes if spring cutting her silhouette out from the
sulphur curtain that ruffles the blind in the window crushed
against the sky by sad checkered blue cries the stone makes cir-
cles beating its drum organdy sails wrapping it in laughter the
steel corner of the scattered buffet on the sopping duster its
nest of vipers in the soup rises to the mathematical square the
appearance of not touching there the choker of excrement
jumping tiptoe on the bouncing sphere in the pit of the void and
neither tears nor heavy sighs nor sobs nor [   ] flags flapped at
the ends of pikes nor gallops of horses on fire through gasoline

puddles nor liquid of bugles flowing from their pulp risky eyes
riveted to eagles' hands unfastened flowers colors strewn over
fabric hiding most of the room serving as common hall in lieu of
rendez-vous and reunion of geometric shapes arriving drunk
pale and disheveled on time

[AW, LW]

9 DECEMBER 38 [I] [II]

[I]   torch chair left lying in december sun one evening in the
month of azure laughter coquette villa for sale all conven-
iences blind drunk to frighten [   ] 10 bonfire posted on
the ochre prison wall of azure blue sleeping in the hollow
of her gaze flea carnival flames inside the castle palms of
the skip of the opaline wheel galloping ropes hung round
the neck of the sword clash orange desire body to body of
[   ] entangling its neon shafts a.b.c. 3.4 radio 1 x 3 at the
thrust on this day distant whistle fingers of the day that
falls asleep rope cut loose falling to the bottom of crimson
pits cage full of water boiling in the window hung from the
blinds moon scent of shadow stung by swarms thousands of
hostage wasps flower of coffee beans spilled out on the floor
on the mauve scarf caught on pikes desire a thousand fleas
devouring the bridge's skeleton suspended over two rivers
of the night triangular field covered with dew with train
whistles siren lips game for thirst so that I kindly give you
between a hundred thousand to drink

[II]   sky sky sky sky sky sky sky sky sky violet violet sky sky sky
violet violet violet sky sky sky violet violet violet sky sky sky
sky violet violet violet violet sky sky sky sky violet violet
violet violet sky sky sky sky violet violet violet sky sky sky

violet green sky sky sky sky green green sky sky sky sky
black green green sky maroon sky sky sky black black black
black black white white black green maroon sky sky

hands hidden in her pockets the night sky aloe flower cobalt
sky of rope bedside book sky heart violet fan evening sky
dress violet bouquet violet violet sky moon rock sky black
green sky maroon wheel of fireworks pearl black yellow
green sky black lemon tree scissors yellow shadow snow
green snow maroon cream filled with brandy canary flight
blue green black wolf sky sky sky yellow linen embroidered
green night sky sulphur white silver plate ploughed earth
sky sky white sky sky sky white sky sky sky sky white white
sky blue blue blue blue

[AW, LW]

14.2.39

noble streetwalker wild arab joy all crystal the Louis XV of its
smoke shakes the flight of pigeons quilting her naked body
which bleeds on the blue tambourine filled with sand shed by
her tears on her mane blazing at the tip of the black flag's staff
caulking the chinks of the rainbow spread out to dry on the win-
dow shutters of the bow of her eyes' noise knocking on the door

[PJ]

29.4.39

the chair at each word his memory chews in its brambles sharp-
ens the knife of her tears in her hair's perfumed linens nailed to
the liquid of her dress if the 1 parades rubs the garlic with his
eye scratches the urine of the bouquet of lilacs and wraps the

coat with arrows of the vest's blue square spitting out the shad-
ow of the open window and if the balled up noise oozing from
the bare wall cleansed by the sun's licking doesn't imply in the
eyes of the wicker cage the presence among the ruins of blood
stains tolling the bell deep down in the hole made in the curtain
by its feathers the wound which the 2 snatches out of thin air
and instantly soaks in a brine of pants' creases aped by the draw-
ing of the flames' frame imitating the rainbow on the plaque
corroded by the acid the 1 tears up around the great heap of tan-
gled fingernails shivering and stinking with fear the image cut
out by the lash of the whip of the sirens' songs melts its wax on
the bronzed lemon of her lips the 2 then infinitesimally more
polite wiser and more wedded to convention than the barks
howls croaking and farting of the set-up of the stage mixing
with the juice the stews and the sauces standing up on the
table shoving his fingers down his throat and vomiting his
thoughts toads and snakes speaks these words the feast tell to the
flutes those organizers and patronesses to organize tonight under
the high patronage of vanquished armies and the rousing and
patriotic organizations of plain speaking and of the lumpy gold-
bearing fat slobs the associations of young and old assholes the
crippled and the healthy the tiny ones the tall ones the 3-cents-
a-pound ones the girls in attendant parts with no weight
detectable by scales the crabs and lice the fleas and sow bugs
the cockroaches lambs pigs and billy goats the white worms the
flies mosquitoes butterflies flowers the sighs and tears the white
bread the military marches and tchin tchin tralala going twice
with velvet gloves to square dance to lozenge dance the old dance
of the great frustalala around the long metal wire of the great
greasy pole of the very noble and saintly Javanese squeeze all
wings spread and catching his breath he says a few seconds after
the belly of the horse so mechanical as to be freed of all rental

and other charges cleaned from top to bottom repainted white-
hot nourished at the dugs of the concierge of building number
six or seven on the rue des Grands Augustins in Paris near the
Seine will be decorated illuminated covered with flags sprinkled
with lies and made up brand new well roasted stuffed with
white truffles completely covered with praises drawn in China
ink stuffed with stars crosses onions and some small souvenir
menus dragged in by blood-drained feet all the lamp-posts lit-up
filled with the strong smell of French fries the floor wet from
the water that washed the dishes and the dirty linen washed and
stuffed with old toothbrushes and coming from the water a
thousand lit candles the cracklings of wedding rings the voices
of bugles smothered in sardine cans and the songs and noises of
the cord breakers creaking on pulleys and all the accounts to be
painted at day at night deep in the forest with vinegar and mus-
tard on slices of smoked ham at sundown by a seaside of a
morning wrapped in limbos of linens what a menu what a mess
what a feast a fiesta sun unhinged from jaw from too much
laughter but the 1 timidly dissolved in the downpour of violet
ink rising from the floor and passing under the table from one
side to the other going back up to the ceiling save from ship-
wreck only the left hand and the thigh hooked to the edge of the
back of the chair his nose stuck to a shard of the frame in flames
his right eye piercing the cheese tablecloth that shakes the wind
in the room the other held tight in his fist by the involuntary
homicide of the blue which sticks its dart into the center of the
arena which runs its fingers slowly over the back of the furni-
ture and enervates the olive-green tone stuck on the corpse of
pink spread-eagled belly down between the two flaps of sky this
afternoon the twenty-ninth of the month of april of the year
nineteen hundred thirty nine and automatically vaporizes onto
the blotting paper the lively drop-by-drop the pale blue dies

between the claws of the almond green at the scale of pink plus
this and that and that and this the drool of snails illuminates the
long ladder from bottom to top

[PJ]

30.4.39

all four coins in the air gold's corpse flaps its carcass and farts
whole-heartedly on the toothless mouth of the serious fat slob
imitating faultlessly the grotesque parade of the odiferous masks
carried in both arms by the algae of the dishcloths hung on the
black flames taking flight in the folds of rock crushing the sail-
boat double-locked by the screams piercing to the hilt the chest
of the kitchen window's curtains which says good-bye to the
hands detached from the arms of the 2 and the 1 who fly away
instantly to return nails full of blood to the flies' nest to bite the
throat of the saliva hanging from the threads of the web the spi-
der crushes on its palms then the curses and insults of the 1 and
the 2 and the veiled drums immobile and stupid the cards
thrown up to the ceiling and the smells from the house's
kitchens when noon dribbles down the staircase and dirties the
wedding dress thrown over the banister and pisses purity into
the sewers celebrating the national holiday glorifying the shit
and the turds and the law and the rest cynocephalus enchanted
by the visit that takes the cake which in the middle of the table
reflects on its fate the spitting portrait to say only stupidities of
the reflection of the lemon lying at the edge of the table and
which in the blink of an eye wipes out the tremor of the check-
ered in the horn of chocolate spilled on the mauve of the naked
arm of the pile of plates suspended between the table and the
side-board half-way between the consequences of the blue flour
of the horizon kneeling on the telegraph wire that slices through

the sickle blow with which the sun at that moment strikes the
table and the floor but a little bit of silence rides rough-shod over
the side-board and onto the chair's shins and the light that con-
trols the room explodes and wounds the milk jar that puts order
into the laughter and nips in the bud the red spread by the pink
of the carton if the large letters of the title and the black and
white of the envelope doesn't weep and sigh but still and always
the scale and the weights of the palette that bedaubs the face of
the room pull the strings of this afternoon's curtain and wrap up
the flayed sheep's head of this gray light mincing the embalmed
cotton that winds its wrappings around the furniture and the
two characters of course of course said the 1 of course of course
said the 2 we know we know said the 1 and the 2 of course of
course said the 2 then the 1 certainly assuredly said the 2 and
let's not go any further said the 1 I'd rather not speak said the 2
I agree with you said the 1 this evening has spoiled my evening
let's go for a walk said the 2 and putting on his armor and wrap-
ping himself in the marshmallow of the wolf's leap of light
baying at the window leave me two hundred days of the ninety
centimes to piss for six months through the cross-hairs of a day
the boredom of the long feast of this tarte à la crème this long
saint savarin this marmalade this compote go fetch my walking
stick my gloves my hat and all the buttons of my suit and don't
forget the sealing wax and he starts to sing give me love the
freshness of the fire of love give me fire that lights the freshness
of love give me light that lights up the freshness of the fire of
love give me the love of the freshness of fire then gazing at his
naked body in a pocket mirror finds it suitably complete and
smells the mirror the full portrait coming out of its box and
bowing very respectfully before all the kitchen utensils in disar-
ray very ceremoniously taking from his pockets the sweetest and
most caressing words he counted them carefully kissed them one

by one wrapped them in a piece of old newspaper and threw them out the window but the 1 impatient stomping his feet on the figure of the flag of the stale bread conspicuously displayed nailed to the wall hidden by the shadow of the door and lifting his fly all the way to his neck wrapping himself in its folds like a cape he disappeared behind the vegetable basket in the scent of salads onions potatoes leaks garlic and knives and one heard already far away down the staircase his voice yell won't you come won't you come soup's ready soup's ready come on come on hurry up it's late and already black and blue and red and the quails are tired from applauding at the edge of the ramp and his voice went down went out into the abyss singing two and two is four four and two is six six and two is eight and eight sixteen and eight twenty four and eight thirty two a large net full of anchovies received the broken body of the 2 and carried it along the quay all the way to the boat made of lace and large paving stones wheels slipping on the hinges of the velvet coat of the soup mouse gray soup mauve and silver the pasta letters writing his sentence by the choice that the flight of swallows composes the hand props up the gaze fixing the center point and the laurel crown at the end of the river made to stand up by surprise and immediately surrounded by ivy sits up and begs

[PJ]

TODAY 9TH JUNE OF THE YEAR 1939

>   dollop of syrup
>   frizzing her hair
>   like feathers
>   in the middle of the fried egg
>   smelling of her song
>   of lilies

[MW]

Paris 13th June of the Year 1939
For Manolo Angeles Ortiz from his friend Picasso

The branches that the oysters weave into the song of the knife
are not the wavelength of the cry of the bit of crystal of their
smell

[MW]

24.12.39

I

the garbage can disgorges itself in the so pure azure of the loaf
of excrement set on the night sky and one by one lights the
lanterns set on the nose of branches by the mousehole of the
angles decorating the façade of the cock who sings in his eye if
the slate that peels off its wedding dress doesn't scribble with
its fingernail the ointment that coiffes her with its laughs and
with its lips caresses the border of the coat of lentils that
envelops him and the ice of his goatee

II

night disgorges itself in the azure of the loaf of excrement of
the sky lit by the lanterns set on the nose of mice of the angles
decorating the song of the cock of the slate that peels off his
wedding dress and scribbles with its laughs the ointment that
caresses it with its fingernail and licks it with its goatee if from
the border of the coat the plate of lentils that envelops him
doesn't freeze his gaze

III

night disgorges its whole body loaf of excrement the sky lit by
the angles of the cries of the cock sketched on the slate by the

fingernail of the ointment decorating the façade of its laughs of
its caresses peeling the goatee of the wedding dress thrusting its
nails on lips of the border of the coat of lentils of the eagles the
gaze takes in the mirrors

IV

the ointment decorates the emptiness of the sky with its angles
lit by the fingernail thrusting its lips in the loaf of the cries of
the cock devouring its laughs its caresses sketching the slate the
façade remaining standing by a miracle peeling its beard at the
border of the lace veil of the gaze's sail caught in the ice mirror
of the eagles detached from the lake that clacks at the window

V

lanterns lit in the emptiness of the sky thrusting its fingernails
at the laughs of the caresses sketching the slate of the skin of
the house remaining standing by a miracle the lace of the saliva
of eagles inscribed into file 39 carries the comment eagle sau-
sage in capital letters

VI

sky of laughs inscribed into file 39 the skin of the house cover-
ing the night of its saliva the eagles butchers covered by coal
dust carrying the shutter that clacks in the wind

VII

ball of wax to the touch of the emptiness of the night of the sky
empty of caresses and of laughs the ripped skin of the house
purrs its stink in a corner the coal dust folds its sheets the shutter
detached from the window mimics the eagle exactly

VIII

tangle of bees of the emptiness of the night of the sky empty of
caresses and of laughs * the ripped skin of the house purrs its
stink in a corner * the coal dust folds its sheets * the shutter
detached from the window mimics the eagle exactly

IX

tousled tangle of bees of wax of the icy flame of life of the sky
empty of caresses and of laughs the ripped skin of the house
purrs in a corner its stink the coal dust folds its sheets the shutter
detached from the window mimics the eagle exactly

[DR]

25.12.39 [I] [II]

[I]

the coal folds the sheets embroidered with the wax of eagles
falling in a shower of laughs the icy tangle of
the flames from the empty sky on the ripped skin of the house
in a corner at the bottom of the drawer of the wardrobe vomits
        its wings

clacking at the window forgotten on the emptiness
the ripped black sheet of icy honey
of the flames of the sky
on the torn skin at the house
in a corner at the bottom of the drawer
the eagle vomits its wings

on the torn skin of the house
clacking at the window forgotten at the center of infinite
        emptiness

the black honey of the ripped sheet by the icy flames
of the sky the eagle vomits its wings

at the infinite center of the emptiness on the ripped skin of the
        house
clacking at the window the naked arms of the honey of the
black sheet ripped by the ice of flames of the
stinking sky by the eagle vomiting its wings

the window forgotten at the center of the night shakes
the black sheet devoured by the ice of the flames
the eagle vomits its wings on the honey of the sky

immobile in the center of space
the ripped skin of the house
shakes the black sheet of its window
the eagle caught in the ice
vomits its wings in the sky

the black sheet of the window clacks on the cheek of the sky
carried away by the eagle vomiting its wings

torn from the teeth of the wall of the house the window shakes
        its
sheet in the coal of the blue grilled by the lamps
the fingernails of the shutters
give up the fight its wings to chance

[II]

good evening monsieur good evening madame and good evening
children big and small damasked and striped in sugar and in
marshmallow clothed in blue in black and in lilac mechanically

malodorous and cold pug nosed one-eyed irascible and filthy on horseback on crutches potbellied and bald made of sententiousness sliced very fine by the machine to make terrified rainbows just good to be thrown in the frying pan tell me my dears my loves my little piggies have you ever counted by holding your nose until 0 and if not repeat with me the list of losing of all the lotteries

[DR]

28.12.39

drop by drop the tambourine sweats the honey of the burning cheek of the house that clacks on the black sheet that displays the eagle vomiting its wings the wall advances very quickly to receive the alms of the cast shadow playing the comedy of being of the window the shutters shake with expansive gestures like madwomen the wall rushes at the call and clings to the willing shadow that lets its wings float the two shutters that support the eagle's body release their prey and abandon it to its fate the house empties its guts on the sky

[DR]

31.12.39

the lightning falls asleep lazily under the great bells ringing ringing with all their might

[DR]

1 JANUARY 1940

on the open sea of the linen curtain that sounds the hours stuck on the bottle nailed down with wasted breath the flame

underneath the copper of lemon lights the rosary of rice that
knits the little red and black box of liquorice Florent the initial
letters show their teeth to the watercolors of the windows the
light of the fly that drowns its litter of little cats in an appalling
smell of violets

[DR]

4.1.40

the bitter liquid that the king distills that powders the edge that
packs down the milk that milks the green of the shutter of the
lilacs thrown on the wall circling the house warming itself in
the sun on the stones blocks its account and fixes in some agreed
fine words shelled and dressed anew the flow and the style of fit-
ting in of the faithful resemblance that the coverlet and sheep's
wool engorged to the bristling wings by the flows of the whip of
the sprinkled color by the perfume of the roses sleeping in a row

with all the speed of its fingers the cotton of the armor's steel
studded on the mauve supporting all the responsibility of the
marked blow and all the consequences that at the fire of the
doors and windows and at the water which the light still guards
on his shoulders the trace of the obvious bite

[DR]

5.1.40

a pretty figure even that of the beloved woman is only a game of
solitaire the symptom of the foreshadowing of the heap of
entangled threads of a system to be set up no matter what on the
far fetched plans of the so delicious perfume be it of the heap of
shit that the colors of the floodlight let blossom in a retort at the

temperature of the pink that has to be drawn with the frozen
ashes of the angles and of the arches before chance doesn't
materialize to make hay cut close and bringing fruit to ripeness
in season that if at his window it doesn't strike a mortal blow in
the melee scarcely recognizable behind the salmon curtain of
ibis claw reason crazy and naked cloudy from the so delicious
scent he knows in the cup of shit that the colors of the projectors
were blooming in a retort at the temperature of the pink that he
had to draw with the frozen ashes of his angles and arches before
chance doesn't come to make hay cut close by the sun and bring-
ing fruit to ripeness in season that if at his window it doesn't
strike a mortal blow in the melee scarcely recognizable behind
the salmon curtain of ibis claw reason crazy and naked

[DR]

6.1.40

a symptom that denies the diversity of trajectories of blows so
tangled in networks of colored threads of a frequency more or
less accelerated by the metronome of + or − terrific heat going
from well being to pain made the forms of floating crystals take
in at a glance overall of the picture the required direction of the
dial established initially on the principal ropes that make the
taut veils play the angle and arch needed for the game already
won on the picture predicted by all the oracles already marked
by red fire at the desired point of the map

[DR]

7.1.40

the photographic plate turning on an axis at a faster pace
than the images tossing around it and finds already wilted the

bouquet of surprises not yet gathered but leaving hooked at each
reincarnation the larva witness that in spite of the inconstancy
of its rays of light hitting it right at the blood over the whole
naked body driving at the gallop of the memories already listed
and allowing no doubt of their identity hurried on all sides in
fire of joy the game of balancing the light the brilliance sustain-
ing all the weight of the scaffolding of the sphere of colors
coarsely ground on the transparent curtain of unperceived sensa-
tions at the beginning

[DR]

14.1.40

the long thread of silence slides the point of its knife between
the pleats of the sky painted in faux wood that oozes from the
lips of the window sucking a caramel

[DR]

20.1.40

slide along the knife's length from the point up to the hilt the
caramel of the open window's lips on the pleats of the sky paint-
ed up in faux wood the long thread of silence

[DR]

Paris 25 February 1940

The night so brutally snatched from the evaporating sky torn up
by so many pins the whiteness of its linens found itself bleeding
drop by drop bathed its shell in the echo of the stone thrown in
the well

[DR]

1.3.40

THE MEAL

The sheet gets up from the bed and immediately its wheels roaring with laughter begin tearing into shreds the skin of the bouquet planted up to the hilt on the song dragging its old shoes under the feet of the table attached to the crystal of the vase by chains and the voice rehearses the mirror stripped by the care of the tender blue to make him push the howls on the broken teeth of the window that gives him a greeting very pompous and peculiar 1st course carries tears in a heap of sand and is made to crack between the teeth by men and women chosen as among the most beautiful

END

[DR]

4.3.40

mouth bordered with mantrap hooks $\left\{ \begin{array}{l} \text{mauve} \\ \text{pink} \\ \text{mauve} \end{array} \right.$

tendered hand of a field of oats pinning the border of the mildewed sheet to the howls of expiring exsanguinated sirens the horn of abundance the nails tearing the skin of the clouds polishing the furniture under the plow of the slice of buttered bread shivering the blotch of pillows seems to shine suddenly on the angles and arches choosing to sound the alarm at the hurdy-gurdy of folds and wrinkles of the color plastered on the ground on the linoleum the pile of plates napkins of cries and tears makes of the soup and the beef drawn of its entrails the clothes and the finery of the pure air bath rising by the luminous rope of the sky painted liberally brushed and the hem of the robe

trailing on the keyboard plays furiously the song for the piano of
boats coming in at evening scaly arms in the pail of water full of
almond milk drawn from the mare its wings broken at the bars
of the cage that represents pure and simple the hydrangea veil
sequined with little silver stars serving to hide behind its thou-
sand grimaces the true drama impossible to fully display on the
void that hangs on a nail

[DR]

20.5.40

song of cocks midday or disorganized bustle of the petrified
sky changing itself under spread out arms of the nest of vipers
curtains draw the gallows of bouquets sulfur lemon wings of
flowers of irises and of poppies with orange smell of armpits
extols its hair

[DR]

7.6.40

the beauty that evaporates from its hands sets down its dewiness
in the sewer system of climbing flowers elbowing under the
green rug of the linden — the acrid emanations of the lilac cloth
that burnt at the window biting at the shoulder of evening that
thrashes about between the barbed wire — of the lemon hat the
flames race after the braid that consumes itself in a spiral

[DR]

THE CORRIDA

3.7.40

funereal hangings besilvered their hammer blows atop the box seats the bonfire burns and each beat of the tomtom that wipes out the outburst the clarion bugles lay bare shows its snout by the wound that laughs at the wings of the sky with blood puddings jolting the fleas on the face of the watermelon that melts it and singes the leg hairs and sketching the curve that is fanning the shots that are banging the door with their knuckles with thousands of fried eggs that rain down the shoulders sweet peppers and lacy tomatoes laid in twixt its breasts the candles and tapers that light up the doors and the windows and gather from garden and orchard the stickpins and studs of the flowers aiming their shots twixt the creases and doing and undoing tables and fables and weaving the metallic spider web on roof tiles and twixt fingers with the odors of french fries and garlics with so much hot love that the drops of blood trickling from its necklace of jasmines can cauterize ulcers that sing on the pallid flag *bloodless the hair tangled jammed in the wheels in the reeds expunged by the waters a gong someone bangs by the noise of the stars squashed flat by the wheels of great clouds whipped by storms the thunderstruck eyes of the bull* who bathes twixt two waters *who stares at himself in his mirror*

4.7.40

honeycomb of scrumptious honey of its flies decked out like owls very flustery and very cassoulets of calamares en su tinta and so much in rut and seasoned in the styles of day and night so fresh and with their faces masked so ugly and with such a smell of fart so chubby and made into escabeche and so shiny with their mourners' veils so cheerful and so tearful filling up a bowl

of broth and other eggy soups like castanets but lugging on their
shoulders lines and reels with rainbow colors wrapped up in a
shroud of shriveled chestnuts with the sound of keening with
their artistry the bull ring's uncorked head that bathes in midst
of the voracious cries of the embroidered hedgehog roundabout
the torte and corn tortilla boiling at the back of the blue mantel
cut to bits and pieces by the parched lips of the wine glass that
swells up and bursts a kiss upon the mouth of the bullfighting
horn blood and a heart of rice of juicy drooling afternoon with
big bear hugs teeth sunk into the neck pink colored spattered
twixt the legs that odor that comes into play that risks its own
life on a game of black jack poker hearts a spurt of blood that
gushes from the middle of the sun's chest gaping open in the
face the fear of flights of partridges across a field of crickets'
cuticles of all the prickly pears and pear trees combed and
crimped cut clean a face that's powdered up and perfumed with
its sesame of scabs and ringworms with its smells its sausage
angels with their asses soaking in gazpacho with a key that burns
his hand that opens up its wings and snares the fish hook

5.7.40

la description of the costume follows parlay and plucks out a
number from the bucket very green and oily at the pundits'
party that the casserole filled up with chitlins hauls back of the
pile of sardines and the stairway with its worms and dishes and
the string of eyes escaping from between the planks that nail it
to the sand to battle there like cocks threading the needle that
the little butterflies who swim in the crude oil will go and stick
atop the silk with all the bitterness of that illusion carried on
one's shoulders like a house that's fit to burst with memories and
skipping on a jump rope made of great white lilies air the spider
and the moth the fish and cat and rabbit and a small bouquet of

bedbugs and of bruises with the hours and the dead days petti-
coats left on the window sill to dry the air in conflict shaking
haunches in the lower depths of bedroom of the moon glass mir-
ror and of more moons still that wax amidst the waves inside its
cape its howlings at the death that spurts out from the moun-
tains of its folds nailed to the fat neck of the light that melts
down from the hole inside the well as it arises

6.7.40

half asleep and soaked down to the bone so casual and cool like
any cucumber and not a plugged dime in between the short
hairs and with balls like bags filled up with gold and whoop-
sadaisy the flea-bitten minutes fawn all over with a taste of
cockles sketching in the length of her whole body with the
twists and turns of drawings that have decked her out with aloe
and will go on freezing every flower in every which bouquet will
eat it raw they will and mash it with their thumps and bumps of
a young billy goat and carry it away by auto rolling like a silver
dollar from Sevilla to the billboards for the grill the whippets
hide behind tucked under armpits and will make a long pass
with his cape a lemon in that shade of yellow so it rolls the
whole length of that nest of woodcocks breaking thigh bones
into little lumps of sugar crowsfeet fans embroidery of trumpets
that will knock the socks off of the cypress going by on horse-
back over the cream custard multicolored magic lantern as it
licks the angularly cranked circumference while walking arm in
arm and harking with a twinkle to the chanson of the long
parabola that undermines the festival of wheat there on the altar
cloth the sepulchre the joyjoy portrait pissing the whole globe
away with smells of fat cigars or playing ball beneath black cur-
tains dribbling out its clear white egg wax daubing the glass
windows of the wondrous reliquary's chest of drawers the lacy

porker liquefied between the almond sheets a carousel with oh so
many hugs and kisses curtains for the mouse hole music tack the
strings of onions on the purple while its spoon retrieves the
clump of hair the sickle paints the green bled empty a new blue
that flees the orange red that pricks it and with shaking legs the
amaranth pulls off its socks its claws evaporated in the fish tank

7.7.40

legs of the wicker chairs there in the dining room there in the
mouse's nest in the ploughshare that's pulling a water wheel
ears of a feather mop shears that splice percale from sherbets
and take it out walking on partridge-eyed clouds in a firmament
made out of glances that writhes round the drunken boat's
masthead and turned upside down on a staircase of silver
propped up like a monkey who gives himself airs so serious and
earnest so wrapped in his odors sketched in with inja ink with
vermicelli shawl with clam shells taking his most urgent needs
out on the slip of sky that scrapes the spine twixt the shackles
of clouds of the green apple color tinting its chemise with all
the mess and complication of a juggling match the little ball of
threads entangled with the black bread harshness of the air-
borne architectures standing tall and very stiff by order and
command of the authorities perspectives showing up on time
and from the color of the colors oily tender rolls filled up with
hair and ribbon paste and with quince jellies Carmen and
toréador prends garde with a friture of bull's balls propped up on
his shoulder like a parrot the walls that dangle from the after-
noon that come loose from their cheeks in tatters sing a silent
song their patches jamming up with cotton and their windows
and their shutters the parade of mouths that with their tongues
are knocking at the door and with a ball of light spin out each
grain of rice their beaded necklaces on every train that comes

forth from the curtains full of wasps the silence nailed onto the
cloth frame of the drum bursts like a sunrise on the garment
with its paws its sparrows' nest its water flowing down the ladder
on the rocket

8.7.40

so that they lift him sprawled out on the oil cloth of the gurney
of the stinking cheese the loving curtsies and the knee jabs of
the pile-up of black ewes of all the faded blues drab colored now
that penetrates the nostrils of the pleats of the chemise shaped
like a cross the massive head of hair of thighs of spurts of feath-
ers of a net of fish scales of a handful of high hurdles of the
perfume wing that they are dragging through those dreams the
flight of oranges fans pissing wholly open glow worms licking
lips set into place around the eye exactly at the hour of the cis-
tern pulling at the blackberry mantilla at the pail that's full of
summer nights and purple silks and from the color of its skin a
crust of bread that somebody coughs up and bit by bit into the
next world it blows off in spirals on the ceiling of the room the
pleats of light of the venetian blind its wheel half drawn and
straight down to the bottom of the ocean of the bed worn out
between the beach rocks of the sheets that look out from behind
the sunlight bars caught in its claws the total clarity up to the
edge of the penumbra decked out for a masquerade a major holi-
day the perfumed faces of a pair of mirrors staring at each other

10.7.40

stone unto stone the water skeletons are swimming choruses of
grapes in clusters haunches shimmying their fricassees beneath
the anchor of the bread crumbs from a typewriter that's giving
birth to cats and mice inside a cage of flies of comings and of
goings of the rooms to rent an earthworm's burrow of a dish of
salmagundi of the flush and gush of clouds that spews the putrid

leavings of a hunk of sun dead and forgotten in a corner stinking
rag of daylight flinging from its tongue a pot of basil and verbe-
na for saint johns day with the velvet of its jewels the applauses
of its tears to light the light bulbs that will fire up the cooking
pot of banderillas with their essences of spikenard

11.7.40

black soap of the cuts of ham of sulfur with its wet compresses
covering the lake of flour galloping its thousand metal feet
inside the bowl of fruit the tree branch with its wheel's teeth it
grinds down the sun's bones shiny clean details the suit down to
the finest detail like the double ox tongues that are calf and clap-
per of the bell of menstrual purple dribbling down between her
legs a cape in rapid motion separated from the cotton dressing
that the claws tear from the redness gushing top to bottom as it
covers up the knife blow ending with his body in the midst of
the machine gun fire that weaves its clouds onto the whiteness of
the cup of milk that's drawn in cobalt blue positioned on the
margin of a hammer blow the blueness of the sky down on his
knees and begging for a handout at the entrance to the canopy
atop the roof in flames concealed beneath the drawings that are
burning him that take him prisoner behind the splotches of the
moorish blackberries bespattering himself a finger in the saffron
almond sauce and bathing on the shore the three long lances the
black mantle and the lady's hood with soot cascading from the
green sash binding up a bundle in the bull ring

12.7.40

skin torn alive from the sun's face spitting out his guts onto the
veils of the blood wedding that arises from the lopped off neck
the harvests the fireworks display the scales filled with flowers
with breasts frozen with horse sherbets and with naked wings

spread open on the eagle suits the wheels the smells of helio-
trope of melted silk of music hanging from the windows that
have cleared the decks the reckonings are now complete

13.7.40

the thousands and thousands of leagues and more leagues and
the millions and millions of millions of leagues at so much the
yard of blue indigo lace and the reckonings made come to such
and much more plus the outlay for stamps and for taxes for capi-
tal gains and for paying your way from this world to the next of
the do-re-mi-fa-sol of the hour glass of the turkey breast of the
poppy field of the prison bars of the granite globe jampacked
with worms the stairways of oil of their hands and are singing
encircling the commas and dots that are shaking the shafts that
are stringing the nips that they slap on his nape the colors that
sweat the scrapes they inflame on the fat back of pork and the
streamers with luffas that mop up the floor tiles the sky of the
giant latrine all its draperies hung from their balconies filled up
with flickering candles the lackluster sound of a rattle an oom-
pah band strolling around with its handkerchiefs over the bones
of the pile-up of thank you's its blind woman's face that is tick-
ling the chicken soup air thick as jet that's already corroding its
shoeless wings goats skipping over those oceans the angel hairs
weaving the mother of pearl of the clarion call in this after-
noon's velvet detaching itself bit by bit from the stone and brick
crust from the transparent veil that is steering its patches of
light as best as it can

14.7.40

aquiline nose a biscuit and a marzipan of sickly hue that the rip-
ples of a conflagration whistle up that consumes itself beneath
a canopy in green in ruddy flush of watermelon slices of a roof

of a salt flower of dry rawhide of a diamond of the gooey clouds above the outcries and olés are powdering themselves with pollen that rains down in buckets smell of linseed oil and of raw fish meat of a strip of cloth newly unfurled the light of street lamps broken into bits and jumbled up in corners lights like mice escaping from between the digits of the balconies an ant that's running down an arm of wheat the length of that tall chimney that has wound itself around the silk sash almond tree in blossom and is turning round in circles and in still more circles

15.7.40

death chants and chants from Sevilla syrup of tincture of laudanum mouth hanging open with painter's brush sowing its anise seeds colors strewn over the meadow rattles and tambourines clank on an anvil a call of alarum geraniums licking the legs of white marble that climbs up the stairway of light of the shadow the eye in erection of games of a prism that enters it yellow is barely perceived on the blue of their blue eyes in passing it blushes and hides in the back of the crook of the elbow the sleeve striped with shadows and coming unstitched from its tiles bit by bit roots puffed up by the apple green color have dug in at the edge of the foam that the lime paints in lilac as it holds in its arms its tendermost languors

16.7.40

liquid that strums on the bull's colored ribbon knots rattling the fistful of eels on the tracks the keyboard of bull's hoofs the firebrands buzzing of knobs of the beehive its luminous bells set down on the poundage of billing and cooing of turtledove color that drops down inside and alongside a pathway of green scarce a ghost of the green of the clothing stretched out on the ivory

flat roof the kisses and sucks of the perfumed mother of pearl
the horse color that fades from the wall in the alleyway over the
stirrup of skin from the rampart that masks it and half cracks its
head and still alive buries it somewhere in back of the banners
that smother its flames

17.7.40

ox carts crammed full from the graveyard with its curtains box
seats draped for mourning lashed with silver and with soot black
cloth

scrambled eggs with coal sacks rolling down the bleachers in
procession barrow loads of old flames lugged on shoulders tooth-
less with a plate of mussels set upon a lime stove hands the wax
of lips of lemon dresses of grimaces of the yellow rose that driv-
els ink upon the coat of ashes of the cold frost of the pyre rising
on tip toe between the fire's paws at dawn machinery so compli-
cated and so dangerous a rind of ripe manchego of the flowery
mill the cutlass the rope ladder opening its leaves to catch the
dew left by caresses nipping at it fleas with fragrances of rosaries
that cantillate in sunlit air this afternoon the small bells open up
their wings with olés crystal irises a hidden aura waits in
ambush lightning's arrow zips past lifting up her skirts her foot
can barely touch the water puddle the vermilion spreading like a
soup behind the spikes the grillwork in the sunlight combs the
cooties from her hair with dove white hands the sponges preg-
nant with the light and flying off the idiots with eyeglasses
beneath the bed of night burnt paper swinging on a seesaw that
dries up the blotter where the river branching thrusts a head
into the window with a painted face and a bouquet of flowers

18.7.40

fingers byways baskets of chick peas and hazel nuts crackers and taffies lupine seeds fresh water someone who drinks it and music with dishes of anchovies sardines in bunches and clam chowder low as a turkey's fart sets the wheel jetting off over the fire and hammers his sugar knives onto the water jug skin of a mountain goat gaping down from the flayed clouds that bleed forth a vomit of stars paper flowers long candles sky rockets freakish and geekish and scarecrows near sulfur in color one sniffs out by ear in the egg yolks one scratches what itches the saltpeter there on the wall in a corner that pulls back abruptly and lands in the shelter from blasts that the purple mattress inflicts and that sketches the swipe of the scythe striking home that one paints on the linen cloth canvas horse trappings festooned with small colored lamps with feathers the cock fight tears loose in a chorus of hand fans

19.7.40

itching powder on the skin of clear blue yonder of cream custards of the steering wheels of petticoats of stones that blow upon their piñon nut cones sulfur colored bedbugs' bugles burning through the paleness of the rosy fingered glow the crease along the sleeve beneath the arm their snails which blushes burns the wall of straw that filters out the water with its silky laces and is hammering its tacks into the arm and face that sprinkle the may garden bull ring and the guts that slither past tied to the wheels of belly or of curtain or of hunk of sky that slip loose from the nail that wears a hole in them with its outpourings necklace of small beads of outcries by the fistful thrusting out their fingernails between the cracks the flutes and penny whistles smells of burnt hoofs of the flag that's torn to shreds the linden trees in blossom of its clothing cooings from

beneath the lakeside canopy its reed ropes knotted to the planks
of wood red ochre cough that shakes the cage of blackbirds of
the life spurt that astonishes itself in midst of open flower eye
and noses the dead man the funereal cigar box bloody strips of
cloth and smell of kishkes torn out by the sun's horns branding
in black marks the veils and draperies to do their business there
midway along and show their backsides shit and piss and don't
stop letting off a thousand and a million farts that then give
birth illuminated unto hundreds and more hundreds of small
oil lamps ballrooms banquet halls deluxe and deeply grieving
of the velvet belly garnet of chorizos from estremadura of the
red sea fluttering against the marzipan glass windows oozing
from this afternoon and daubed with tar along the length of
wooden mast besmeared with honey sprinkled on the sack of
greasy poles the gold of molten watches lightly falling rain its
butterflies the odor of hot bread emerging naked from the oven
sun's face sticking fingers up his nose hands globs of mercury
and searching blindly deep inside the molten gold that pulls the
curtain down will-of-the-wisps on sword's edge for the love of
god oh love a little charity

20.7.40

the line ascending from the earth with sea smell on his shoul-
ders up night's ladder till the flower goes by banging with his
head against the steps the moistened sheets mouth open wide
worn out evaporated from the light coagulated in a salt-like
silence plays at jumping rope hands full of visions clump of sand
sends forth a death rattle his teeth clenched tight against the
dust of his reflection crawling wounded pushing from one box
seat into the other box seat one into the other hand his claws in
glory of festivities in jet a dance of wingd blood sausages grand-
daddy pianos with their cordless keys a shawl of crows spread

over the mowed field the black drape with large tears of sperm
of wax of swarms of blowflies humming on a drum skin made
of ice that lemon green so tight the tambourine reverberates its
metal disks like car wheels on a hearse stirs up the gypsy dancers
in a cricket serenade the ears of owls on a dead end country lane
a nape of kinky hair that slams the door of sunlight on the big
bass drum the cymbals in a rain of feathers of all sorts of colors
singing with loud screeches with sun's cow bell galloping a
squirrel in his cage who makes the wheels go round

21.7.40

crystal goblet crocked on star juice stars that scratch their crab
lice in the fragile moonlight sweeping up the lime a sigh a
naked body newborn sheep cheese wrapped in milky paper
grape seeds at their feet that squeeze the rags of molten steel
that wipe away the bloody smoke that plays games on the copper
breath its hair a golden chain that raises up the drawbridge with
a howl and rubs its scabs against the phosphorescence of the
water's tresses that a ray of sunlight kindles that it rises like a
madman jumping in the all together through a window in the
room above the belly of the ceiling tickling him until he's laugh-
ing gulping bunches of mint candies all atremble in a pool of
flour held up by the ship's masts as it crumbles bit by bit to
smithereens veins entangled in the wires of the wireless electric
telegraph the itch that smarts the melon slice of paper lantern
all dressed up in sunday suit a mix of leather and of flesh reseda
colored satin squatting set in place as an example to the other
straggling colors that are crawling up the pathways of the
lovesick rose the dissipated purple of the banderilla halves
ablaze and punitory of the massive skewers of sardines up front
and burning in the blackness of the sand in candles and the bed-
bugs and the lice in cots of cardboard horses covered with the

drag of clammy heel tappings of flies whose lips are grinding down the edges of the wound

22.7.40

thorns of the oil bath of the frog song varnishing with coral the wild crush of wires of a perfume gnawing at the cord tied to the ring of milk that milks off the humungus wall it hangs a shadow from that does the sha-wa-shimmy on the railing with its chasubles of feather dusters of the incense feet in shackles of the horses those whose horseshoes trample on the altar eyesore plastered on the burning candle up in flames a hand raised to salute the flowered brigantine moored in the middle of the harbor in an agony its hoofs nailed on the spume of venom hidden in between its pages

26.7.40

I

~~tongue of the metal quaking and enveloping with linens wounded head of the bouquet of flowers plucking in the crystal of the fan the bloody seaweed trickling down~~

II

~~ox tongue of the metal quaking in the lemon tambourine gigantic square with something tender love meticulous enveloping with snow with flames the wounded head of the bouquet of flowers~~

III

~~ox tongue of the metal quaking in the crystal cup the tambourine's wild flights enveloping with so much tender love meticulous the wounded head of the bouquet of flowers of the flames the fan~~

IV

ox tongue of the metal quaking in the crystal cup enveloping the wounded head of the bouquet of flowers with so much tender love

V

oxen plowing up the metal of the flames the crystal field the wounded head of the bouquet of flowers

VI

fan open to all winds to squalls of feathers of the rainbow of the oxen plowing up the metal of the flames the crystal field the wounded head of the bouquet of flowers

VII

rainbow of the oxen plowing up the metal of the flames the squall of feathers of the wounded crystal the bouquet of flowers of the cries of bells of shattered perfumes

VIII

rainbow of the feathers of the oxen plowing up the crystal of the flames

IX

feathers of the rainbow of the oxen plowing up the crystal of the perfumes of the cries of bells the flames

X

bell cries of the crystal of the perfumes plowed up by the squall of rainbow feathers in the flames

XI

squall of feathers of the cries of crystal of the rainbow of the
oxen plowing up the flames of the bouquet

XII

squall of feathers of the loud cries of the crystal of the rainbow
of the oxen plowing up the perfume of the flames of the bou-
quet

XIII

squall of feathers of the loud cries of the rainbow plowing up
the crystal of the flames of the bouquet

XIV

loud cries of the rainbow of the feathers plowing up the crystal
of the squall of flames

29.7.40

entangled in the rainbow of their feathers oxen plowing up the
flames of crystal of the howling that perfumes the angles and
the curves snared by the web of nails and begging help they
melt the pewter of the stopper in the redhot resin of the finger
boards the tinsels and the patty pies a chunk of rubber sweeping
clean the image tacked up on the glass the mirror a craw full of
ice of handkerchiefs mouths open to the smoke of arrows stick-
ing to the pellets on the wall of mercury that roll their ringlets
there above the tower of their cheeks the bread and cheese with
grapes and honey and with kisses and a belly crammed with
lunch for the siesta and for more siestas stretched astride the
great pole with the shakes and quakes of disrespect and shame-
lessness of waves that make you puke of black rags shaking from
their assholes silver purgatives fat tears the teeth inside a wolf's

jaws cloth aflutter from the windows every street out in the open
flesh stuck to their bones disheveled drag their feet along a vul-
ture at a spinning wheel who spins the skeins of wool pulled
from a flock of ears of corn of fields of wheat a curtain striped in
grey and blue and green breast pressed against a paper ducky
showing from the tiptoe of its tongue the limbs and laces of the
marches and the pasodobles night's aroma spikenard sucking at
its source the sea that sweats a highway

30.7.40

ragged and dribbling in her milk bath turkey soup with pump-
kin seeds its worms embroidered on a frame of pins a lacework
of small bells a rabbit's ears opened like wings on scraps of paper
flying in the vortex in the waters in a gust of flames an upsy-
daisy on the seesaw bugle and the banderillas sow their rice
fields in the pool of blood its feathers fondling the silk of worms
who spin their ways of life their manners and their wagerings
their alleys thick with blotting paper at the edge of shadows cut
down by the eagles' beaks the crimson paws the rosy creases
perched atop its tapers dribbling down and dribbling down its
snot flies nibbling at the open book the toasted bread crumb of
the skull sprouting its spikes unquiet agitations of the grasses of
the sky stopped on the hour garbage truck filled up with little
love dolls stinking dead entangled with the wings of brooder
hens of wool a chunk of sea cast up atop the courtyard wall and
grasping at the slash of scythe that slices through the butter of
the tiles in petticoats festoons and there it glues atop its plasters
noodles of the sun tied to the buoy dancing its illuminations up
above the boat's hull moored out in the spangles picking at their
lice atop the finch's cage that sings in tiny snatches salt and pep-
per frying pan of stars that runneth over toasting up their
eyeglasses with hammer blows that bash the cardboard of the

belly of the door the bang bang of a knocker and a sense of hor-
ror in the rats' nest of the guts ripped out and drowning in the
darkness of the shattered light stuffed in the mourner's envelope
the lamp switched off by inkstained hands that licks its wounds
a flight of partridges over the clumps of thyme of veils black
robes for rituals a turbulence of air the wings of bats are fanning
in fart castle muddy waters wetted by the ribs tongues trembling
from the cold and scratching their designs onto the blackboard
raining down their quicklime on the mountain pasted on the
ruined houses of the flesh torn into shreds the rags of skin
detaching from the shipwrecked ark in middle of the bull ring
hawk eye aureole of flags unhitched from masts fly free over
these countries night penned up inside the sun fiesta footlights
skeletons of chairs disposed around the dead man yawning
laughter tube of blood that drops down in the middle of unrav-
eled hanks of whoopdeedoos eyes glued upon the thrusts the
horn delivers to the big bass drum of skin of belly of the horse
and overspread with sheets of spit of lights of wax of shit that
vomits forth the marble of its columns garlands of the tremors
of its skin and juggling acts of lights in hot pursuit teeth
rammed into the boards of the arena artichoke a hole in life that
sinks into the soup of an indifferent earth the windows open lit
by thousands of small lamps its limbs all on the outside with
incomprehensible hand signals throwing kisses at him bruised
by stones hooves soldered to the sheets of copper struck by cym-
bals from between their manes combs shaking out the centipede
their hands dipped in the dust the algae smack atop the horse's
stirrup and the air that with its cape is brushing the arroyo
where a shadow lizard's playing with the light and swallows it
all up the final reckoning

music in passage through the sieve of cemetery screen still silent
seated on plush chair of deep green velvet of the horns of sun-
rise with green still exuding from its jasmine hair atop the spiral
staircase of the chord that sounds the call to arms at bottom of
the hot pot of the sun there dunking buttered toast into the
milky coffee of the bamboo flute the cloak with yellow and blue
squares the forest with its kerchiefs powdering the stable shad-
ows' open scissors scooting behind curtains a jack rabbit hanging
from his arm a hand upon the velvet of its lips the shaky naked
banister jabbed in the guts in middle of the beach yanked from
the bundle of wet rags of well placed stab wounds of the solar
belches when he eats and drinks his fill a finger slipped between
two buttons on his fly and scraping flesh against the floor where
his own hairs dwell perfect moment of vulgarity that knows no
limits everybody in accord and in stupidity of all-out battles
of the skyscrapers with perfect knockouts dentifrices water-
proof silk stockings for the coughing hundred hundredweights
of writings teeth venereal diseases syphilis the little sisters of
the poor bounce apples off the phony sky of globules passing
through the pinhole of the padlock on the lime dark black room
and the furnace filled with water and with aguardiente quince
paste with the color that the mouth sans teeth barfs up the heat
at melting point and stretches out his legs atop the cushions and
the skirts the poison pill love potion mouth that's open to the
thirst of saber that entwines it

2.8.40

lily that climbs the staircase on all fours to the woodshed that
wallows around mid the honey fronds bursts when the globe
falls down flat on the boiling hot oil in the skillet egg fried with
a fan and a watch chain years snagged on the keel of the long

mountain range with its wolves come unstuck in his hands pale
mirrored wardrobe propped up on the wallpaper holding it tight
in his arms all the while it expires a hangman with head lopped
off hidden behind the huge shadow torn up from the house
mantle fleeing on horseback quick gallop away from the sun
screeching over its folds swiss chard fields of the ocean split into
two equal parts by waves with odors of eggplant of silk colors
sleeping under the grapevine diverting the light with its stories
so will not escape by a leap on the spiral in midst of a puddle of
flour green lemon branches of dusters bedangled with ribbons
convulsive a game of smudges and drips of the varnished hair
tousled and floating on well burnished metal of taste turning
bitter unleashing its light on his forehead the curtain drops
down and snuffs out the street lamps

3.8.40

of toes of their eyes sinking fangs in a spoonful of starlit aïoli
mashed unto death in a mortar a chorus intoned by hushed voic-
es so slow and so careful removing their clothes and unsticking
its colors each flareup of flame with saliva with fingernails
offers him prayers for the dead quicklime painted with thrusts of
a broom its bells sounding by ear with twenty some quintals of
yellow so that they wake up and fling themselves onto the side-
walk point blank from their sacks from their marriage veils
sucking up globules of fat from the damp kitchen floor dressed
up in white lace and with turtleshell shoes seated there in an
easy chair velvety purple silk fabrics a basket heavy with grapes
and with playing cards cups swords coins staves attached to
the cords the silver wires of the hedgehog as he takes the air
by the window cut up in a thousand small pieces by leaps and
by bounds of the wall dense with jasmines fanning the burst
outer crust of the skin of the zambomba drum of the great hairy

tambourine awkward and held in their arms with bones broken
with bleachers stuffed full of sun's marrow and wrapped with a
rasher of bacon a canopy piercing the stone that was pricking
the barb in the eye of the venomous needle that licks it with
strokes from its cockscomb of rockets and bombs

4.8.40

stew of liver and lights of an absolute rigor architectural style of
air rubbing its nakedness over the sweat covered skin of the
terracotta box its guts hanging in shadow in step with the leaves
in hot water over your head with the copperwork tresses the
weights and the balances taking such pleasure between the
moon's sheets the bed rumpled up in the dawn's early light
shoulders lifting the leadweight still green of the rose all ablush
of the crumpled up yellow the violet blue and the rest of the
blues that are lifting their wings the problem resolved in all clar-
ity only the tracks in the air on the brink of the feathers
inscribing the sum of the light the result with slippers embroi-
dered of balconies joyous and swimming through branches and
roots of the bones of the skeleton embalmed of the sky raw
green cucumber wheels that are grinding the wheat and the bar-
ley the harvest a star drill of moths drenched by star showers
opening eyes to the waters the lake that is floating its gangrenes
in cups full and brimming with happiness fistfuls of anise the tip
of the blue banded streamer of two green furrows snagged on a
fish hook a mountain of oranges rising up from the ground and
jumping the barrier rats running in back of the cat in the mirror
through the steel web slaking its scales on the sponge saturated
with vinegar blood that evaporates ribbons and bows of the
sugar mill steadily turning around with its sauce spoon and mak-
ing the mortar ring out on the bell of the sun's rays tooting a
trumpet down in the volcano's funnel eye open and set on the

black veil of the street lamp calling the night watchman out in the middle of the street who is slithering off like a compass with blindfolded eyes in the sand of the hourglass sprouting over their fields the spines on a garment of prickles where tiles stinging forthrightly paint on the patio wall a protuberance thick with fly slime with high pitched neighs of the sun kicked hard on the yellow planks of the clouds nailed on top of the green fat wool compress of sky crumpled up in the bull ring its teeth hammered down on all sides

5.8.40

TAUROMACHIAN EMBLEMS

Bañulos y Salcado (Don Manuel)
resident of Colmenar
blue emblem

Aranda (Don Francisco) resident
of Pérez de la Frontera blue emblem

Barrionuevo (Don Rafael) Córdova
bleu turquoise blanche et rose emblem

Benjumea (Don Diego and Don Pablo)
(Séville) *devise noire*

Cámara (Don José María de la) Séville
black emblem

Concha y Sierra (Exmo Señor Conde de)
Séville
white black and grey leadweight

Espoz y Mina (Ex-Conde de)
(Pamplona) red and green this ranch the same as that known
elsewhere by the name of Carriquiri

Flores (Sra widow and the children of Don Fructuoso)
of Panascosa (Albacete)
orange emblem

Gonzáles Nandín (Don Ángel) Séville
red and yellow emblem

Hernández (Don Antonio) Madrid
violet and white emblem

Ibarra (Don Eduardo) Séville
blue turquoise and straw yellow emblem

López Navarro (Sra widow of Don Carlos)
Colmenar
red and yellow emblem

Martín (Don Anastasio) Séville
devise verte et rouge

Martínez (Don Vicente)
Colmenar Viejo
violet emblem

Mazpule (Don Juan Antonio)
Madrid
white emblem

Miura (Don Antonio) Séville
verte et noire emblem *le 20 avril 1862* a bull *de cette* ranch
Jocinero *tua dans* la plaza de Madrid the torero José Rodríguez
(Pepete)

Orozco y García Ruiz (Illmo Señor Don José)
Séville
rouge blanche et jaune paille emblem
this ranch *est la même que celle nommée de Adalid*

Patilla (Exmo Señor Conde de) Madrid
rouge bleu ciel et blanche

Ripamilán (Don Victoriano)
Egea de los Caballeros
rouge emblem

Saltillo (Exmo Señor Marqués del) Séville
devise bleu ciel et blanche

Solis (Don Augustino)
presbyter *voisin de* Trujillo
rouge emblem

Trespalacios (Don Jacinto) Trujillo
dv rouge et verte

Torres Díez de la Cortina (Don José) Séville
devise bleu céleste et blanche

Veraguas (Exmo Señor Duque de) Madrid
devise rouge et blanche

9.8.40

falls from the sky high blast furnaces wrapped in blood veils of
his wings tree that flings itself out from the window head first to
the sea with candles aflame and unfurled yellow green of an
apple that scratches the cotton its gold coming loose from the
wall daubed with jet blackened aloe with flames of the flange of
the salt blazing up on the blind burro's belly and making the
water wheel turn with his sword he has cut through the mirror

cluster of mouths wreath of ropes smack dab on the water and
scorched by the shadow ass end of the boat like a handful of
snakes typewriting their stories on slices of watermelon licking
their lips the silk eyes of the sword blade

heaven's own skeleton flaunting its bones from the leather bal-
conies heaped up stars rotting spread out each one on his chair
seated waits for the time to settle accounts with the landlord
who's sleeping there sprawled on the beach and naked the wood
from his dreams of the sun drying out in the shade of the
grapevine covered all over with worms

10.8.40

white wing of paper open thrown atop the ashes bolt and chain
of oil emitting light on window panes the crimson vortex of the
little bells disheveled hanks of yellow tinted odor of a heliotrope
that springs up with a bound onto the crystal stone with clothes
an eggplant color shaken by the blows of the green apple cudgel
shirt in shreds of skin torn loose from feathers on that horse hide
melted dribbling wax on faded pink of parapet ropes hanging
from the windows tied to sky wall with their hands so full of
honey nailed betwixt the folds of water yawning there the lumi-
nescence of a little butterfly

a long line in a drawing that dissolves the clarity of image hidden and disguised behind the playfulness its beak extracted from betwixt the fringes of the fissures of its pages silky splinters spinning socks and stockings on a line of redhot coals of frankincense and myrrh with promenades lit up in black that rub their manes down to the ribs of skin of silver paper of the bull ring stiff already bedded on the cream of night

the cotton wheels there on the sugar cart the full moon full of barley water lips set smack against the mirror liquefied betwixt the jasmine cudgels

11.8.40
a tin face playing cymbals there behind the iron gauze the clouds the ox carts flinging stones down from the pile of timber with their claws and from the boat nailed drop by drop onto the silence

velvet wings of leaves of frost that open up their flames with flowers on a crown of lice of stars scratching with milk the wall that hangs down from the wings of cuckoo birds the key and light of oil lamps of an eye that squats in ambush

13.8.40
compass forging on the anvil of the orange flower water of the lemon of the sleeve the milk sword of the lilac cluster from their hands the wheat flag shaken from their arms to drip large honey stains on the potato omelette on the cotton chair the boat its tresses sweaty loaded at the bugle's cry of holy moly on the sword of blue sorbet pearl necklace dinner table set beforehand and dissected in the falling snow a scorcher in the flower painted on the scorecard the medulla oblongata of the book its leaves

astir betwixt the wooden timbers of the coffin of the fringes of
the skyline propped against a wall of maize and yanking from
the ground a vast black triangle its beak stuck high up on a nail
and holding up a thousand thousand gallons of its weight the
door closed with a bar of butter or of silk a spool of blood
removing stitches from his riddled breast a song of nightingales
of death who sits there sopping up the sun betwixt the lips the
wound makes licking at his feet in filigree the drawing so
methodical naively breaking through the labyrinth of leaves
that climb and run disorderly up through the trees asleep there
in a hammock made of papers wrapped around the innards of
the sprig of flowers carried piggy back a dovecote with its wings
ablaze of streamers cleaning out the snot with elbow motions on
the stones brought to a boil above the clouds a greasy sky and
slippery devoid of safeguards a stopped clock with eyelashes
combing the hours' hair rotating on its cheeks past present
future plaything spliced into a thousand pieces trembling its
most dangerous bright colors in a hundred different ways all of
the armor's eyes there on the outside for attack dissimulations of
defense for afterward and well in hand the network of the veins
that must be hurled back at the beast on top and neither gay nor
sad like a most solemn sun the green trumpets of evening per-
fuming the candles holding up the platform with its lights with
black mouths swelling from the flayed skin of the well uprooted
from the depths of wingèd eye and flying like a ball without a
break from sky to earth from earth to sky dried salted tuna flakes
and rayons sausages of laws and tin cans of sardines minus heads
of obligations owed regarding final judgments of a heap of old
rags in a corner of the kitchen garments rank with grunge and
silence with their throats encased in necklaces of pearls of
scarabs in the bull ring wolfing down the satin of the silver half
moon of the milk of the reflected light that's cooing in its nest

the algae fabric rife with branchings green and blue above a purple base a yellow dress and spitting at the arch's face above the doorway orange flavored belches reeling in the goldfish caught on ocher fishhook of the valance as it rubs itself along the center post of the dividing wall the shadow that removes it bit by bit out of the window pane and carries it away wrapped in the powdered sugar of the ax blow of the sun that splits the cloak of cruelty he throws over his shoulders into three parts the angle falling from the dish of lentils overhead to act the judge the freedom of the game left in his hands and separated by the fragment fallen on the ground from his raised arm the bricks that held the vault up now in ruins of the fingerlicking blue bled out that with its paper will dry up the light inserted through the fissures in the planks and swipe sandpaper and a breath of sunlight on the wrinkled skin of sand crushed into powder wearing down the wall the cannonade of sun on horseback there above the lettuce green sky squashed against its rocks

14.8.40

mouthful of scrumptiousness earlobe directed at will toward the pink of her apron black dress with its corals its leaves with a wing attached to grey curtain with violet stripes with her belly swelled up with cojones heavy with bundles of swords of iron rods sprouting from woven hemp fabrics hidden inside the burrow the tumbler of water the fleas of the sun of the tummy to scratch on the door hanging open the armchair the pitcher the buttons they grind into dust on top of the breadcrumbs the faces they paint onto sandgrains deduct from the total sum out in the meadow of solitude mountainside musty with roses the sprig of flowers the blue gone black and then blue that savors the caramel of revenge on the top of the cape soaked through with

egg yolk nougat puff paste dinah's horn of a skyblue color and
shouting their gibberish out of the windows clamping lips on
the bread loaf with its cherries its flies with its putrid bones but-
tery syrupy sweets with breasts of white color smackdab on the
mud plastered wall rind of cheese of the sea and disguised under
feathers while dunking its donuts in cups of hot chocolate closed
doors overturning white wings liquid key of a pigeon the odor of
spikenards of laces of light undoing its bundles with all that
much haste between folds of the clenched fist the purple laid
over the mighty green lace that is carding the hide of the bull
with its sewing machines as complex as it gets for a thousand
good reasons and unseen by the eye stripped down to his balls
from the hunk of skin onward the road blasts a path through the
walls of the city

17.8.40

crab of the dining room of clouds a rounded buffet table with
nine chairs a sideboard packed with spikes and tatters with a mat
made of esparto grass eleven spoons ten forks six knives one sil-
ver ladle a half dozen soup bowls and another twenty-three one
flower vase one tureen three hundred fifty nine butter dishes
two coffee cups one cocoa pot six percolators and ten grinders
twenty goblets two serviettes two tablecloths one bucket full of
water one carafe seventy-three napkin rings three thousand four
hundred twenty one toothpicks one corset and two petticoats ten
quarts of nitric acid three silk stockings one clay whistle in the
image of a bird one broom one change purse and one oil lamp
and three eggs twelve hours by the clock and sixty minutes
hanging loose one poodle and one rabbit one ten-cent coin one
large wool coat without a hem one armchair made of straw
some paintings with wood frames one unstretched canvas one

rendition of an image of the sun asleep and naked on the crest of
some high mountains at his side a basket full of grapes and figs
and covered with a handkerchief with yellow branches on a pur-
ple ground two swords one dagger with a ladder set on wheels
one large blue mantle with embroideries in silver with a pair of
slippers and an inkwell and four pounds of bread one box of salt
and olives lettuces and parsley nuts the window and the grill-
work chained together wringing tresses out above the water as it
grinds them down cries coming from the stack of lilies stuck into
the fire in the kitchen stove the moon's face in the fiesta pried
loose with a yank from in between the safety pin's claws on the
far edge of the roof imprinting songs on threads that weave a
silk cocoon with its machinery the leaves of a small tree seen in
the distance and so very small it stays there on the list the inven-
tory where it says round table ten buffets says thirty-nine chairs
three says sideboards full of spikes and tatters one a mat made of
esparto grass and twenty-five eleven spoons ten forks one hun-
dred fifty-six knives zero and three hundred twenty-three one
ladle 9 half dozen soup bowls two and twenty-three 1227 and
one flower vase 6000 one tureen 20 three hundred fifty-nine but-
ter dishes 1 two cups for coffee fifty and one cocoa pot six
percolators 10 ten grinders 9 twenty goblets 600 two napkins 3
two tablecloths 2 one bucket full of water 33 one carafe 29 sev-
enty-three napkin rings 21 and three thousand four hundred
twenty-one toothpicks 3 one corset 24 two petticoats 50 ten
quarts of nitric acid 32 three silk stockings 6 one clay whistle in
the image of a bird 2 000 000 one broom 60 one change purse
100 one oil lamp 17 and three eggs 4449 twelve hours by the
clock and seventy minutes hanging loose 3479 one poodle 10 one
rabbit 70 one ten-cent coin 1000 one large wool coat without a
hem 102 one armchair made of straw 5 some paintings with

wood frames 10 one unstretched canvas a rendition of the sun
asleep and naked on the crest of some high mountains at his side
a basket full of grapes and figs and covered with a handkerchief
with yellow branches on a purple ground 250 000 and 424 cen-
times two swords 6000 and one dagger 300 with a ladder set on
wheels 7 one blue mantle with embroideries in silver 1 one pair
of slippers 10 one inkwell 40 and four pounds of bread one box
of salt 23 olives 600 lettuces 1 000 000 parsley 15 nuts 80 and the
window and the oven chained together with the water of the
safety pin the moon's face of the fire the cocoon the shouts the
branch that the silk claws weave from the small tree pries it
loose by yanking threads with its machinery nailed down so
hard and harder and more hard the prices in pesetas set at five
reales and the weight is measured in arrobas on this very day the
seventeenth of august in the year of nineteen hundred forty

17 – 19.8.40

Yesterday weather permitting the 18th in fact today the month
of august and a bullfight having taken place tomorrow in the
Cartagena bull ring on a sunday in the year of 1940

[JR]

19.8.40

that if the cotton of the partridge blather that exaggerates and
that enumerates its drawings on the skin of the reflection of the
water from behind the paper wall the cloud unshackled from its
image this one time created by his hands thus to undo the super
complicated knot inevitably evaporates the colors on his ribbons

[JR]

20.8.40

long processional of eyes of walking on the tips of toes above the open fan spread on the bed the lake in shadow of the jasmine forest of the crust of bread only just taken from the oven

[JR]

PARIS 15 SEPTEMBER 40
* SUNDAY *

sparse leaves of the carbon filament suddenly nailing the flesh of the jasmine rafters of the inkwell full of sugar onto the skin of the diamond raising its feathers on the oxen of wheat of the water dripping from the scales of the bark of the sun splattering the snows on the clothing spread out on the brambles

chains of silk from the stones and bricks melting their faces into wax of honey of the tree detached from its roots raining buckets its mane of bread toasted over the arm green apple of three thirty in the afternoon detaching itself from the wall hanging from the rafters

plate full of flies devouring a pile of gold coins that the breath of grapes which rise from the sketches of the tapestry take down from the fastenings of the clouds with lace wiping soot from syrup-smeared lips the moon's reflection trimming its nails inside the mirror

[MW]

17 SEPTEMBER 40

the nails of the roses of the blue that cook on the black violet
awning the open hand of its odors with their cries scare the sug-
ared herd of acanthus leaves away from their tresses

the nails of the roses of the blue that cook on the black violet
awning herd with their cries the acanthus leaves of the skin's
green apple

the grills of the blue of apples herd with their cries the leaves of
the black violet awning the roses that cook in the green skin of
the water quenching their thirst in the soot of their tresses

[MW]

18 SEPTEMBER 40
SEEN IN THE MORNING

I

petrified flames of angora clouds oozing drool on the sky's liquid
bricks stinking up the sheets of the vines * the feet of the table
biting the breast of the sun that wallows at its feet covered in
chains * the canary of the blue's harp sprinkled over the batter
chimes the hour with its little bells

II

cheese crusts tangled hair trees that evaporate on the sky's flag
stone laid on the river's beams the wool oiled by the lamp of his
nostrils butter grass caress of fingers swaddled breath a-tremble

....

III

the window's four corners shred the day that dawns and wham a
rain of dead birds hits the wall and bloodies the room with its
laughter

[PJ]

19 SEPTEMBER 40

∗ ANOTHER MORNING ∗

with all its strength the sky pushes the silk of the sheet stretched
over the emaciated frame of the window and the paleness of its
cheeks makes the pocket full of hair bulge sour sugar green of
roses anemones the blister while sliding its paunch into the room
rips its skin at the butter saw of the plaster's frigid lips drops of
blood flowing from its ripped out feathers turn on the flock of
lanterns heaped in a corner for this feast

[PJ]

5 AND 6 OCTOBER 40

go-between dripping buttery leeches from the maw filled with
the blue of Mother Celestina's powders on the night of the after-
noon's dawn that day the beehive of lights from the sky's
necklace filled with silence cooks its lice in the watercream
toasted on the grill of clothing woven by the spittle of the
palette of the wheat-colored green of the buzzing of the empty
sun its skeleton's spines flour of the lament of the silk of tears
nailing their stone rags onto the metal of the bell of hornets
mouths open of the black pills of the yellow square hanging in
the clouds the wings detached from the tapers strain but don't
work with the usual mathematical precision and the precipitate

drumming of its lights beneath the skirts of the navel the moor-
ish dance of its tongues cauterizing with its swords the waters
of the pins of the cloak blue with the black vomit of yellow
fever of the lead weight of the flock of butterflies of the nudes'
sticky sausages of the sloppy architecture of the hands of the
drapery of mourning and of silver which attach the soot of their
hammer-blows onto the flames of their loges

[MW]

12 OCTOBER 40

* the streets hang from the sky gluing the rapping of its wings
against the half-shaved rose-colored face which melts in the pot
color of lilac of brine that detaches from the skin of the sallow
bread crust color of lime that the leech of the blue sucks from
between the toes of the foot poised at the edge

[MW]

TUESDAY 5 NOVEMBER 40

on the blazing pyre where
the witch was roasting naked
I had fun
paying lip-service
to this afternoon
with my nails
gently flaying
the skin of all
the flames
at five past one
in the morning and later

now ten minutes
to three my fingers still
smelled of warm bread honey
and jasmine

[PJ]

THE PARCHMENT NOTEBOOK

7.11.40

leaps and bounds from in between the legs of cardboard wheels
of day that opens up its leaves in chains a fistful of perfumes a
chicken soup so heavy and the broths of mercury so light the
merry go round milks the wine out of the wings between the
pages of the book it crumbles in between its teeth blood gushing
from the laurel leaf the wounded knife

from in between the lips of the spout of the hemorrhoids of the
leaves of the flint singing litanies for all of these rotten moth
eaten clouds the desperate cries of the marble creases of curtains
of just such a chocolate color of armor the mouth of the rose
bush attending the ear of the box full of rags the paso doble of
its gaze drenched with perfumes and rottenness hooks up its
cooking with chair legs with apricot bones and mechanical
pianos with scales of a leg of lamb of the rabid mouth of a but-
terfly wings of an octopus in raw gold clever caballero on bike
who rotates icy poultices pregnant with veins tears clay whistles
and spouts of a flower vase over the slippery track of the rain-
bow applause and contortions so silly mechanical capitularies
land owners witches and deaf mutes and pain in the guts of the
auto buried and dead in the wall dividing the garden plot and
the orchard set in black light of the long green braided candle of
the linseed flour leek the glove with ermine skins of balls of fire

full of chalk marks and oil drippings from the music that the scraps of toasted bread rain from the broken glass in the wide open window feathers twisted with the smell of peppers and of jasmines with its nude in rags with teeth of steel which pisses from the steam of flowers caught on fish hook from the castor oil the long procession with its oil lamps with the linen cloth with flames of egg of wrinkled wool of alabaster torso this rosette this showy oval hair of cardboard wheels the trumpet of the little car of snow of sun and cooked up on a street lamp full of milk of orange-flower water full of white threads sickly turbid rogues and troublemakers scrawny squalid pumpkin headed very sad and very wormy round and fawning slavish just the color of a quince of half a moon of a whole paint brush of a lake of frogs and beaten black and blue by blows of hammer of a day that opens up a mouth of rose its little ear in fields of spikenards of its toe nails crown of jasmines of a bitter tongue of blue hair of the painted wood of cold so luminous so flashy yellow of its leaves in chains and sinks onto the bed the black escutcheon of a rawhide sun that dangles from the pan pipe of the green suit the night watchman's whistle that sweeps up the nut filled nougat from the court yard of quick silver and the keys and latch of fire bell of the red heels of tips of toes of chicken fat of crouching barges artichokes in flower of the square roots of the merry go round love song of the braying of carnations and of roses and the nibbles out of roof tiles on the silky bed of branches of the scrap of painted paper thick with flies the copper shoe the jumping jack and the adobo of the landscape belly so filled up with shit that it explodes from fat and spits a villa from its guts up and the oil of its convulsions on the meat in the bitumen puddle on the table in the dining room the blue and checkered table cloth usually in time for tea *

* the streets that dangle from a saucy cat stew whimpering and wacky velvet edged with silver carpet collar on the café au lait floor with crumbs from pastry shells a parrot cage with ironed petticoats with clouds with tiny little footsteps silently the fatty moldy faces daubed with sticky musks and rouges the butterflies the bitter absolutely tasty belch of silk steep drop in middle of the navel of the song its long dress decked with bells and chimes in glory on the hill the mountain crushed and powdered in between raw cotton pages of the boss teeth of the rubber mill and very pure and melted virgin wax and jelled and jerked off sweetheart sappy pissing madly going wild the brine of crow's foot and a mortared cockscomb onion-like cucumber-like half opened trumpets of the shrill and sour lemon dripping stubbornly from border of the cooing mauve tiles by the fistful infra pale blue pink and very chubby tasty swanky and soft spoken bridegroom so in love with blue and tender tried and true jammed on all fours into a pool of stifled light into a colored cape of bones well chewed of fishing poles figs very black and filled up to the brim with air of fiddles with invidious color raging green vermilion lover pale and wan with color parceled out so parsimoniously onto the iron scaffolding and velveteen guitars into the open hand of the green bottle drawing measuring with a bare flourish of the cape the snail still wild and smiling forthright festive terrifying very man of pleasure of the orangy green juice and the most faithful servant of the reddish yellow green a very mister green a horrifying green upset by pure clear blue and black blue and by gold of golden silver gilding and the very rascal apple green and almond green which comes unglued from wrinkles in the shrunk and dry skin of the yellowed crust of bread enfeebled color of green lemons that at sound of dinah's horn the strict and necessary blood sucker of dark blue indigo he sucks him off between his toes poised at the edge of

— mouth and eye of arm of cobalt of their nitty manes the bas-
ket full of toothless night time crabs that singe the eye brows in
a nest of rats of playing cards a deck of sprays of flowers yelping
at its caramels and his sighs dangling from the strings of chalk
that sweats along the chimney's width in red that banishes a
flight of french fried anchovies a mustard rag of canvas wrap-
pers and that bottles up the silver cross of pain inside the molar
of the horse hoofs trampling the geraniums in pots of twin pairs
of white oxen cart filled to the bottom of the well of the pot
belly of the bones that strike themselves that blow upon the
fingers of the flute of black veils of the pennant and the plaster
banner of an arm chair full of flowers of a rotten kid and hot
shot tambourine the house key of some rabid bitch and at the
same time dagger dripping blood its makework perking in the
pot-au-feu

and nearsighted bulls are gluing up the shreds of cod the slam-
ming of the doors and rag mops of saliva of toads springing up
their wings against the glass grill of the ribbons on the rattle on
the rebec the zambomba and the double tambourine with torta
looking face all smiles of turtle dove and black bird and the slob-
ber on the beard a fountain like a wart miraculous and soiled
with money and alone here in the world half shaven blind and
stretched out on the terrace of the sky the prison calling out
with shouts of olives of the tower and the curtains blazing blue
and black and burned out pink that melted snuffs the light out
in the oil lamps in the casserole of broken toothless staircases of
braids of garlic and carnations laughter ticklings and a swollen
mess of miseries the green venetians monkey cute and cutest
wild about a sodden soaking piece of pastry and the art of speak-
ing and of saying nothing and a sword plunged in the middle of
the breast and in the wall of ding dongs of the colors blue green

pink and sulfur green and blue pink putrid looking with the
utmost caustic and pale color of the lilacs of the laughter dying
out its frying pans mahogany and tea around the snow ball well
aimed dagger thrust in midst of sun face down and propped up
on a train of toilets snug and happy breaking his cruds to crumbs
over the crazy sum and substance of annoyances of pineapple
sorbets madera ices of the strings on forest looms of chocolates
and feathers a transplanted hill of coal of crowds of shepherds
and of docile frightened sheep of sleights of hand and sleights
of scams of sharpened colored pencils of a head that's painted
and repainted set atop a thimble with a pair of sheep shears of
an agitated sea of reeds

sweets of whitish liquid screech of gauze from plasters moisture
from a wall and pasted to the scabrous scab the reeking ass hole
of the onion seedling sky the perfect fool who cries out loud the
putrid plant exquisite sauce of worms of saffroned plate of
stones of fat of pig meat of the air of chickens and of cinnamon
strung by the gills and cooked and basted on long cane skewers
of the sugar ground to powder of black curtains rings torn loose
by just a jerking of the strings that hang from chicken wings of
colored feathers burning underneath the fragrant breakers
waves of unleashed horses and the arrows prick they prickly
prick you and the hot snow bread that bursts apart so quick
betwixt the fingers his fixed stars a weakness of the drawing on
the bodices of wind swept roses of domestic female smells of
nun's cunt grilled alive so that the song and jabber jabber of the
naked gold finch whips it all at once and like a lecher comes
down on the silver of the chain of teeth and laces in the limpid
water of the wall inside the room in which it screws the silence
churned up so that it hangs there lifeless from the snot around

his hips the stones inside the corner of the grainy cotton eye that
churned the sea up and so tenderly the fish the sharpened knife
rains down on from the tricky funny gussied up and gaudy burst-
ing gut with oily grill work and its nest of lentils set atop the
copper of the aguardiente handkerchiefs of cumin seeds and
pepper scarecrows made of rice of clock against the ear of bed
sheets rooted in the pulp of quinces in the matted hair the pleat-
ed folds the melted odor with the waxy color of its feathered
claws that dead with fear and pasted to the flaky chalk wall in
the painted room within the drawing of the arm stretched out
along the edge of balcony they slip away so calm and clean
amidst the smell of casseroles of lungs and livers of the feast
of june bugs made in middle of a platter of prosciutto of a cage
filled with the fat of holy wafers of its ring they mash the horni-
ness of rope that hangs it like lace work of nails of laurel crown
of crickets' song leaps forth from guillotine hands made of mar-
ble pink and green of broken bands of ice perspiring from its
little bells its crown of fire crowned a crown of lilies set atop the
water seething in the sack of soot of grains of rice of soda pop
and linden tea of purple handkerchiefs

on the door snagged by a belt of cat claws of a feather duster
farting out the fumes of incense of the plain chant of the green
of turned up roasted goats' hoofs of the folds of scarlet tarpaulin
and muffin oil and chocolate with little cakes and myrrh and
bacalao and fox piss with the awful and disgusting taste of soggy
rags a flaming faggot on all fours respectable old fart dolled up
in a garb with grease stains from an ancient lamp of stone oil
gushing forth atop the jet black table cloth alive and kicking in
the mass of lice that shoot off sparks the flowers in the gold
embroidery the itch and scratch that wool makes and the stars in

spines and tendons and the curves of combs replete with cooties
shaggy the cement of sky carnation overblown and smashed to
pieces scabbed and drunk and like a broth of bed bugs itchy big
mouth boaster shaking out blue dandruff from the ink of mus-
sels marzipan of cold soup of the fringes

of the jailhouse of the black patch of the carob tree the blue
shawl gnawed at by the screeches and the melancholy sighs and
cries the candled slashes and the gashes of the swallows the
reflection of a mirror of a pile of bricks a hole that opens the
white mantel of the acid of the bauble of the putrefying metal
of the roof tiles on the sugared couch the mutton's butts and
thrusts that shit on the green sky perched upon the festooned
woods the golden goblets gilded silver cups the outlawed shady
game of leathered ballerinas pigeons all so happy and so floozy
full of fleas the paunch of belly and the gizzards so engorged
with crumb cakes and with clusters of fat grapes the mirrored
cupboard in the dining room jam packed with costumed crows
with spooks and silences and stuffings the pot belly of the purple
false face of the sack of earth worms of the cot and king sized
bed the iron over coat crammed up with syrup of the bunch of
keys of burnt bones of the clouds and of a snail shell staircase
that the tusk of wild boar opens of the whip lash of its high
falutin fan of anchovies inside the rabid mouthful of the tender
crystal charitable charade that yowls down to the bottom of its
furry chains the hazel nut sorbet and the resounding salutation
of the patch and sticky swatch of bitter lozenges of butter fly
with open wings of candle flame inside the clenched fist of the
light that shakes out worms and aloes from the handkerchiefs of
weeping men and pissers of green water melon slices of a sweet
tooth of an egg the hen drops in the skillet and the first born
true legitimate and legal son of a certified and legal marriage a

boy idiot and cousin royal of the royal peacock prism of the
scratch marks royal orangy and lemony with yellow tail and sea
bream roasting on the grill and pissing head down on the blue
cakes if time cockeyed and crippled and yesterday tied to a lop-
sided pole in a mouth full of light were to whimper the flag of
his laughter and exultation of flames and a thread of rice ston-
ing the reflection of silk on the silver and the vine of seesaws of
a certain way set and directed willingly and perpendicularly at
an angle cut by half and only indicated for the inevitably gay
and gray reflection of the inevitable gestures for the wash resist-
ant color of the short sound perceived through the temples of
the broken bellowing from green maize udders of the gilded
wheels of the painting and the day that it made lets it happen
and deposits such minute extravagantes and worm eaten and fas-
tidious fat ointments of mosquitoes of the ivory of its straw mats
on the sea of sand it pulls its hide off covered with pin pricks it
licks and then relicks its wounds eighteen today the month of
august and tomorrow there were accurate black waves of frozen
juice of dark green color of the cries of pain of blue that
overflows disguised as altar boy of orange sulfur of the purple
roses of the saffron vestment of the green so darling so obse-
quious such brightly tinted purple of the violet cape that makes
the sky blue whirl around and barely noticed by the agitated
drippings of the fallen shadows of the spikenard drops the wee
green plaza of the gushy cheeks of closed doors spewing sugar
plums and pine nuts of embroidery of hardened wax of needle
fingers darling hairy dancers of the flower in the almanac the
water in the dish of laces nailed inside the flame inside the
coconut with paleness of a rag left to its fate that dangles from
the foul mouth of the spike plunged through the clasp of trin-
kets of the cock's comb of the crate of raisins buried in between
the jaws of papers written on spillt ink the bulls inside the bull

rings <u>Almondorro</u> ✶ <u>Alchite</u> ✶ <u>Berruena</u> ✶ <u>Cortillo</u> ✶ <u>Pedejero and</u>
<u>100 slashes</u> ✶ <u>Cartagena</u> ✶ <u>Balls of</u> the virgin ✶ <u>Vailfugos</u> ✶
<u>Cagarrera de irizonda and camellias</u> ✶ <u>Tar miracles</u> ✶ <u>Wild olive</u>
<u>tree</u> ✶ and <u>Pitorro</u> tickets in the sun for four pesetas in the shade
eight centimes first rows for five pesetas and the boxes for a flat
thousand reales where a sunday sleeps caught on the keel of the
wide open eye of ribs of almanac fan waving in the wind with
talons of loose hair of sea that rolls the hoop of light bulbs of
the threads that knit the ribboned bow of silken casserole of
witches' stew of detailed drawings of a string of garlics of the
measles that the flowers sting him with there on the sleek and
shiny hairdo of the nacre table cloth the awning drawn and
squeaking at the window that breathes out the soreness of a dish
of fried fish of a shirt torn systematically to shreds a habanera
doleful plaintive faded flower of the shrouded bird magnificent
aggressive blowing from the blue and brown accordion of tripes
of trees of bright stars packed away of taffies of their manes that
get entangled in the thorns of clumps of spear grass of the sum-
mer field of clouds that drag themselves along on belly over
and between the sweaty creases of the agonizing bed sheets of
the colored scrambled eggs set very stiffly in the middle of the
earthen pot of oily-garlic-pepper soups of cock fight and of toad
fight dancing there stark naked for the flag in center of the spree
and clanging in the earthen jar in the nocturnal day break the
guffaws and quavers of the boom bell of the block of tiny bells
the cow bell of the milk of snowy fire of the naked blue ink of
the parchment of the landscape written and confessed just at the
point of giving the last gasps from violin strings from the sighs
and tears of the new patent leather shoe of marble of the
loaded boat the flower belly letting the guitar strings flutter
wilted from the chaff of nests alive with vipers raining scarabs
from its syphilitic rockets on the empty fabric floor embroidery

of orange water painting badly and in black the blue ripe wheat
of yellow of a square a canvas of crushed wheels of delicate and
mournful color lemon hanging in a year of nothing special this
one being 1940 and with crumbs of black bread and of sand and
little pears there on the elm tree for the super lavish third class
burial that dribbles super peacefully along the river's length the
overheated leeches of delightful butter of a craw filled with
the color blue a rainbow in a sack of evil bursting of the pow-
ders of the sorceress our mother and most venerated lady
mother Celestina at the tippy tip of night of day break of that
day in which the wheaten bee hive with the butter fly embroi-
dery the moistened fingers the blind lights of necklace lightly
strung the dishes of fried onions of the sky the casserole
crammed to the neck line of a silence simmering its lice and flies
in orange water cream sauce drawn from the arroyo browned
and moistened on the grill with its fiesta clothes woven and cut
in bits by greetings curtseys genuflections of respectable great
gobs of spit the coughing bouts the olive skinned first cousin col-
ored green wet nurse and executioner of buzz of sun the snoring
from inside its egg shell free of splinters and the bones of its
whole skeleton ground into flour and the flower of the forsaken
silky lamentation from back streets and alleys wringing out their
tears along the body with its dress in tatters nailing down the
ribs of its stone rags above the weeping metal of the hornets'
grumbling of the lace of the brooch of the port wildly wallow-
ing sleepless in the foul smelling bed of the old fashioned pink
of the centipede of the untroubled sea of the wide open mouth

of a bluish white smell of a finely erotic and yellowish drawing
of the weight of some delicate lace of a blue grain of well craft-
ed rice of the hand painted up on the wall that wakes up half
asleep from the roof of the blare of the kettle drum terror of

light that goes starry that's pounded by sticks on the top of the
monstrous stage curtain a mouth with an eye fixed tight on
the crack of the sun that slides into the black purse the green-
ish blue poppy exploding inside of the bottle brimming with
screams with the creakings of broken up canes of the heavy
dense load of the yellowish yellow to be at the limits of yellow
and haughty intensity leap of the spear of fried ham with pota-
toes hanging from clouds giving gluttonous licks of the olives of
spread open wings of Saint Roche's dog tongues of a fan stamp-
ing down on an air of nuts and of raisins of tapers of a goblet of
meat that just sweats and sweats over its dreams the snores and
hiccups of a carton packed with joys which with its street lamps
with loose tresses with not running no but flying with the
imperceptible mad mathematical stock imprecision tapping
heels and quick show of displeasure of delectable caresses comic
tickles of its lights that swim up underneath the tarp of percale
petticoats the coppery resplendent belly button of the shadow
thrown off by the still green cucumber the crowd stopped short
there mid-arroyo to the moorish and the jewish dances of the
goat and the kid the boundings of the jewels carried off from up
his ass hole the pick pocket cat

curandero cauterizing with chorizos from the palm trees from
the water game from spikes of barley fields of the blue gown
embroidered with black vomit from the yellow fever from the
heavy load on shoulder the lead weight of butter flies in flocks of
clammy moons filled up with naked mirrors of the subtle archi-
tecture melted drop by drop from hands with black cloth drapes
of silver sorrow gnawing of the raw oil of its flags and gluing
sweet soot from its jack hammers onto the flames in the box
seats covered with slime on the bags of peanuts of jasmines of
violins the small paper lanterns ignited inside the water jug in

the kiosk of prickly pears as the wheat fights as the pepper cries
out as the blue striped stockings prophesy as the pale cheese
gives forth benedictions as the silk is made to rustle and the per-
cale of the clouds is placed to dry at night there in the window
with the strings undone on the corset placed with the black
dahlias from the coffered ceiling from the bonfire a very special
moorish woman shaggy frisky filling up with kisses and with
jokes the melted lead of flowers the lopsided pitcher with the
curly smiling spangles with the bitter and sweet bouillon with
the furniture smashed like an egg in priestly garb and set down
on the profile of the muddy water of the colored ribbons of the
honeyed garters of the black hair that conceals a shrew a coral
colored squirrel of the trumpets in between their legs and of the
copulative and grotesque gyration of the lathed and gauzy rab-
bits of the grasses of the silver mortar of the forepaw of a
partridge of the scoop of snow that jumps and jumping jumps
out from between thyme mountains of their arms and every
drum beat that dries up with the cockamamies of their grimaces
and graces that brays the color violet that tangles up its skeins of
hemp there on the blue nails of the tangle weeds the gully of
the sparks the painted daisies in the nosegay scratching up the
chasuble the bitter bark in bud the almond wind lyre stripped
clean the body laid out and the waves of the cold bouillon of the
chestnuts of the chairs and of the milk a turkey hen stuffed with
the stars with paper peppermint that draws the curtain back and
the black underwear of axes and of tacks the fried egg with its
peppers its tomatoes and its onions and its taters and the laces on
the cooking pot that's covered up with poppies from the viper's
nest the crystal cart wheels pulling sulfur with rims racing wild-
ly open wide between the threads there in the woof of the good
hearted lanterns chanting teary eyed their dirges in the agitated
bottom of the dancer the blue tambourine of that one out there

in the distance thousand upon thousand times reborn and cutting the time finely chewed in slices lined up on his mantel piece's regal edge and sweeping the bull ring with gold embroidery and with a butter toad that's whistling its song and setting fire to the oil of that old country house the frozen hands dipped in gazpacho of the pleats of the trio of clarinet trumpet and cymbals when the foolish wise death shows its snout for the trauma that's laughing and the smell of fried onions is shaking the braids on the wool of the wings of the sky a strawberry meringue paso doble and frozen blood pudding of a kiosk of lupines of a nude of the skin of an hour that half opens its lips and spits scabs that spring out of the night and roll dice of its caramels over the ashes on top of the kidney adorable face of the water melon that melts it and that it scrapes singeing with fresh broken bread crumbs the hair on the leg of the sun that makes marks on the roof top of the sash of the tongue that licks and compresses with all the characteristic authority its great knowledge gives it the curve of it dutifully waving the silk of the wide open cape of the shot knocking tip toe on the door at extremes of outrageously overdone blue of its power to color things blue and the yellow green traveler whose color fades out in the copious weight of the purplish blue sugar plums with its knuckles on swollen bass drums of a hoarse sounding voice of the green biting into the crazy cicada filled testicle small veil of sand hanging down from the great load of rice and the little face pouting casts smiles at the can of sardines on the balcony bleeding the tangled up ball of the flight of the doves of the scrap of paper that goes through the stones of the wood of the iron of gears of the girders of syrup of fritters of pulleys of feet of canaries of fire of sewing machines and of stitchers for stockings that the mice in the fig bread and bed spreads and singing and leaping for joy with a cluster of flowers from the guts of a horse with wounds

down its back will caress the ear and the ass hole of light that
bursts into stars on the basket of straw of the sun stretched out
sleeping and big footed there on the beach with its sand and its
powder of stars that hangs from the curly hairs of the tile roof
upholding the fig leaf of milk with its hands and kicked in the
head by the she ass of the wall looming up in the wrinkles of sky
glued onto the sun and shaking the coins from its fold on the
tumbler of water of the yellow ensemble of the moist little veil
of the pale blue indigo branches of cream custard cornet of the
half open shutters that makes their accounting and sets up the
sacks and the wheat sacks along with the sacks and the wheat
sacks and counts and recounts their accounts on their fingers to
count out their loneliness dollar by dollar and quarter by quarter
and penny by penny their sorrows and joys grain by grain

[JR]

POEMS AND LITHOGRAPHS

11.2.41

the whole disgusting noisy hodgepodge of blinding lights pro-
jected on the ochre painted on the face full of excrement of the
big drum of the clouds screaming open wound showing its teeth
to the hole of the well flapping its torn wings the glass of the
mirror enclosing the melting flesh of the bones fixed in clay and
the rumpled hair of its tresses raising its arms the pieces of bro-
ken windowpanes stuck to its forehead of the tick-tock of
excited seaweed clocks and sighs and curtains beaten by the lov-
ing blows of perfumes and harrowing wails of flowers crushed
under the wheels of hands separating the water rising on the
table and the crumpled music of the linen ringing at the window
of its greetings — if only from the jumps only from the imper-
ceptible smell of sandalwood of its wet fingers only from the

noise made by its hair beating on the air the pressure of cotton and silk evaporating in the round of dead birds of this afternoon the watch chains of sunlight biting the shoulder of the buffet the sorrow and rage breaking away from the wall covered with gooseshit-blue amaranth branches feather their nest and reap their reward and refusal cups filled to the eyelashes' brim of the golden wine of wrinkles and angles polished by the boredom that creeps in between the folds of the coat hanging on the nails of the color seeping from the basalt rocks of olive green velvet and the dress no sooner put on than torn up flowing on the floor the liquid of its gilded fleeting caresses rubbing garlic on the toasted bread of its form

13.2.41

the juice dripping down from the rotting of the plaster's wing-flap its cries and its tears and the applied itching of its flowers hanging from the satin skin of the bricks lash out at the spectral light of the canvas suspended from the cutting festoons of the clouds and the lace curtains its point-lace and the wild saliva of the music share the half-moon of cotton cutting off the iced chocolate bathroom from its roses and its mallows the arm churning the black butter spitting out the orange peel of pebbles surrounding the window a little more and it's all over but the shouting — the laugh raises its veils and hides behind the oil curtain tearing apart the piano of darkness pointed fishbones of honey suck the milk from the hands of sighs melted sweetness of coal its strong legs stretched out on the sheets picked up at the doors dying from fear dying of thirst dying from hunger laced with anxiety iced the bugle sinking its tooth into the organdy of its bristling feathers splashes the paths of the garden and the long list of regrets of the pearls of the necklace being nailed to the trunks of chopped-down trees — the dance makes its choice

among the dresses hanging on the phantoms — the lines of the
hand watch the exits — the slice of melon licks the lips of the
back of the hand and sneezes — the price is still fixed and fixed
well it's thirty two billion million billion and forty-five centimes
or nothing here's the bill and here's the change from your bank-
note good morning sir good morning sir

14.2.41

first there's the invention of games of real skill in artistic com-
position alas and arrangements of a few bits of sails ripped off
the dreams made with tested materials and learned by heart
haphazardly gathered at the edge of the roads tied to the light-
chains of the lamps of reality which then appeared suddenly
shaken in sleep and waking up with a start in the hollow of the
brambles of light black night of the mirror reflecting it in its
continuous fleeting deformations against the mathematical fire
of waves of perfumes and the raising of swords of magic circles
furiously forcing open the door with her oily teeth and letting
the pearls of chance do what they will on the wheat field pink
with clouds sun grabbed at the neck splashing her open throat
with blood filling with sand the hole made by the weapon ring-
ing for the dead mouths of climbing flowers the smell of
cabbages corroding the neighboring sweetness of the morning
stretched out on the window hanging on the rope all hands
aboard — and let the honey appear more or less at the agreed-
upon time in the middle of the arches of bile being born with a
hairy body freshly clothed perfumed and perfectly clean smiling
drenched with tears the cloak of boards and the sound of her
bed and her hand on the swarming doorknob playing out the
sounds of the bells hanging in enchanted circles for a thousand
leagues around and her cries closed into the burning plate of all
of its blue with whitened leaves of its arms strap hollow belly of

the showy dress and the jewels forever in the ochre pond tram-
pled by the clogs of the day included in the order measures
taken in the act full of precautions a priori — perfumed hot
panpipes painting with the caramel of her hair the hair melting
drop by drop on the naked shoulders of long tangled tresses
filling the vase full of flowers banging her fists on the stone of
the mirror licking the clotted blood reflected in conventional
signs on the slate taking over the scene of her kisses

13.3.41

from more or less the lemony chandeliers of the liquid nails of
evening bursting out into the open ears of the half-open lips of
the windows hanging from the lights covering with their
tongues the slightest jasmine-scented mauve sighs at the bottom
of the sweet pond of lukewarm milk splashing the velvet cloak
hanging on the point of the sword waving its arms in the open
wound of the whitewashed wall dress slashed into rags
uncombed hair twisting her flesh playing a graceful game with
her breasts the folds and the wrinkles of the sales — the saliva of
perfume crowns her with cloves of the bronze-colored blouse of
her eyelashes the black wool of her movements her laugh the
metallic click of cotton the fresh butter of her hands her goat-
like jumps and the length of time oozing out of the sky the
untied strings of her glance mixed into the mulberry-trees sur-
rounding the forgotten field on the chest of drawers the plunge
of the pitch stuck to the wings of the heart hacking its teeth
with all the lead of its body in the bowl of herb tea the flowers
of the bouquet set into irons in the bottom of the hold of the ice-
chest mirror the piece of sheet torn by the sun pouring in
through the sewer of happiness cracking its laugh whip on the
naked back of the ceiling its games of skill its sly wiles its far-out
queenly ways its feet hardly touching water and the heavenly

orchestra stinking of roses with its airs at the corners of the
alcove glowworms dust lamps fleeing the catastrophe the way of
using it remaining hidden behind the canvas — the opening
door runs at the call and throws itself breathlessly into the open
arms waiting for it. The face full of tears grimacing happiness
the hands shaking off the blood of the trip stuck to the sandals
knees as they go up claw the stone at every step the diamond
wears its teeth away on the honey of the silk stretched out in the
morning at nine o'clock on the shivering naked zephyr the bed
opens its leaves flees the future the long complicated arabesques
glued to the silences held back by the tails of their dresses of
thorns of curtains burning incense myrrh and benzene with
locked doors gleaming with windowpanes — a white horse goes
from window to window

21.3.41

tulle curtains ripping through the heart on the blue silk of the
armchairs stifling the cries of tears in the depths of the round
bosoms

30.4.41

the pot full of figs overflowing with snails and fireworks spat out
in both hands splashing with all its spurts the rounded stones
tapping at the door — and the hammer blows of such gentle
whites of the feathers and silks of the dish of shellfish of flowers
and cries stretched out on the ropes and the open mouths flying
to the windows hanging on the twisted branches of the tulips
dyed with green and red bitten at the angles with the bottle
green of the mud of the marsh dipping its well-sharpened
knives into the mercury of the sauce stewing in the palm of the
hands of wools of the rug singing on the leaves violently
squeezed into a crowd thick in the four corners of the white-

washed wall and torn so angrily on its dress perfumed by its involuntary incense accuses it pushes it into confessions tortures it castrates it and throws it all ground up onto the sky behind the acidic clouds and the onions of the wilted roses of the nails driven into the back of the various four walls of the room completely forced and slapped onto the air of this music raining infinitely more agreeably mixed into the colors of the bouquet through its uncombed hair and its laughter than by its jumps its nervous fits its tears its blood flowing drop by drop and the little bells of its shaking spangles fireproofing the bits of straw of the curtain sleeping in front of the cerise color swimming at its fingertips the honey oozing from the white paper waving around between the fingers of the darkness and the light tightly squeezed dying of fear in the most wretched corner

1.5.41

the window scratches the mantilla its screams chalked on the slate monsieur monsieur come come quickly I must spank the spanks of the chambermaid before noon monsieur monsieur everything is ready the bedroom is set the table is above all ready the children have already returned from school and Madame is already emptied of her whole bag of tricks and freezing in her dress the guy next door saw her this morning and finds her stunning monsieur come on up quickly it is time to go to bed to untie such heavy wings from the feet it is dark and it isn't safe to let yourself go too far from the port borne away by the velvet of the bricks hanging on the balconies of the lit torches it is irresistibly too late the skin coming off the bunch of grapes of the green horse of linen surrounding it gnaws the tongue hanging from its eye while swallowing the drooling flames dancing inside the vase full of milk — the four legs of the table soak in the melted ice of the wardrobe and look at themselves inside it — the hand

of the door leaning on the arm of the armchair held up by the
pearls of the curtains and the amethyst velvet of the burning
venetian blinds of the bells waking up howling and cauterizing
the wounds of the sun sprinkling the rock cotton with false gold
and tying it to waves of wood foam from the frame courageously
holding up the weight of the marble columns — the fruit opens
its doors to all comers its needles moving with unbelievable
slowness in the middle of the frying-pan where the potatoes are
jumping butterfly wings frying souls in the blood of grilled
blood-sausage in the middle of the onions and snapdragon of the
sheet stamped at its throat with broad silver epaulettes of the
initial bread soaked in the urine of the head of the beer wetting
the shoulders of the porters of cellars packed with flowers and
gold that in clear language and sayings as we often say things
without making an unnecessary fuss simply in good figures well
counted make some without the others wholesale more than the
predicted sum over that expenses pay them already for fines
more or less fine commissions proofs in hand charges chagrin
and rents of calmness but the retail sum the price the revenues
the fortune happiness and imagined or real caresses the risks the
Japanese lanterns lit in the daytime set aside the chandeliers the
long greyhound races from one star to the other the training of
the packs his life life hot chestnuts here let's go back with our
feet close together over the long list a bucket full of black olives
a bucket full of green olives two liters of oil a velvet olive
armchair a used rug a wardrobe a chest a few chairs a pair of
sandals two clogs a cot a writing-desk a bathtub two basins four
pillowcases at the bottom of a saucepan some leftover apple-and-
orange-sauce a bunch of radishes four knives a flute and various
other musical instruments — in the dovecote two hundred pairs
of doves mice and rats straw bird droppings for a price of one or
two thousand five hundred francs — in a bag next to the escape

window in two seed chests for six months — in the kitchen the
three burners of the stoves the lamp full of oil a pack of candles
a wicker basket full of charcoal a book of matches a big clay pot
full of melted butter — fresh butter in a plate — a few potatoes
under the sink and a few leeks and onions — the woman's arm
slicing in half the green window of budding leaves of the square
handkerchief of the landscape breaking the lukewarm mirror of
the hole sneezing the little window hanging on the other one —
the bleeding of the sun infecting the wound made exactly on
time the big late breakfast brought steaming hot to bed on the
wall dancing on the ground over three quarters of the room
revolt in the heart of the piece of sideboard roughly lit up at the
elbow by the slap of the door violently opened a pond of cream
flooding the clogs of the characters sitting between the furniture
infested by darkness the face of the tablecloth flooded with
sweat shitting out its bowels the white covering the dress of
whitewash of the wall with such pale bronzed pink of the rose
dying in the glass — the cigar color goes out enveloping the dark
corner driven like a nail behind the door with its smell grating
its solar hairs around the reaper cradling it in its sleep and regu-
lating its tears and laughter in colored numbers of paintbrushes
of plumes planted in the ceiling reflecting the pond full of the
cries of ducks and copper filet gathered at the harps of the reeds
of the sewing machines and reading the lines of the hand on the
right knee of the door frame held half open by the saber of the
rainbow sticking in its nose

3.5.41

the 1 pulling his pipe from between his teeth — the 2 sitting on
the floor covered in ashes — a naked woman taking her body out
of her flesh — two children playing in the water of a stream

flowing along the wall cut by the axe blow of the blackness coming down from the sun taken out of the written page — a thousand birds one thousand five hundred twenty four mice — the line of the drawing-pen of the arrow crossing the sky covered with swallows placed over the arch of the bridge — the arch of the entry door — the arch of a big window to the left and ten others on the right hand side — the aromatic plants growing on the windows of the roof hidden by the scaffolding of the tour — sweat combing the hair of the mill wheel playing solitaire with the wheels of the cart full of hay — the huge amphorae spread out on the sand — the wine spilled on the tablecloths covering the folds of the blouse cutting the bread set voluntarily straight on the hollow mattress of the whistle flooded with the molten metal of the bees the crust bristling with nails and pins the 1 puts his pipe back in the pocket of his mouth blows his nose scandalously and belches the 2 lying on the ground snores asleep — the children who have come back on the grass drying their clothes in the shade — drop after drop the stones swell and vomit on the piece of sea one can make out hidden behind the chants and music of the lilacs on the furniture the clock strikes against the clouds opening like a flower at the door rounded off by the voice of the sun which unloads the mash of bones and fish bones of its overcoats and fancy dresses. The fourteen hundred francs given to the friend who came this morning are already flowering ripe between the sheets — children come and see the prints left on the flour covering the blue dress of the bride burning on the fire the black lace shirt her stockings and jewels are full of the feast of her body and animate with the convulvulus of her graces and stretching out her leg to the end of her foot with a big kick of her boot in the ribs she wakes up the 2 — two you're a pig one lost for a foundling a corpse a swallow a slipper a camel a drawer of a chest a cucumber a tomato would you tell me the time and time I need not another time clear limpid transparent and fresh iced coming out totally dry from the spring stand up shake a leg dance and make me laugh

13.5.41

chasuble of blood thrown over the naked shoulders of the green wheat shivering between the wet sheets symphonic orchestra of hacked-up flesh hanging from the flowering trees of the wall painted in ochre flapping its big apple-green mauve-white wings tearing its beak against the panes fatty architectural forms stuck on the waves of perfumes of earth of music and birds shopping-basket full of food surrounded by climbing roses shot through with a swarm of bees in the uncombed hair of the landscape spread out under the sun of the four paws of the mountain of rice of the rocks placed on the stones sunk into the mud of the sky up to the ankles the hanging tongue of the plough stuck to plowing sweating the lead of the weight of the effort committed to the center of the bouquet twisted by the chains of flowers surprised in the middle of the rough skin of their eyes staring up and down of the dress its broken folds its rips the worn fabric covered with sots the thousand and one rips its filth its vermin the golden arches of the stones in a peacock fan and the windows closed far off on the houses encrusted with the fine sand of the trees of the woods and the yawning white feathers flying out of the glass of water. The high burning candles of the big rowboats waiting for the raised neck of the raindrops of the blowing flageolet in the fresh air the green olives of the fingers the jar of rosemary neck raised the high burning candles of the big rowboats lying at the edge of the well listen to the perfume of the rain blowing into the flute of the fingers of the green olives

14.5.41

the party began much later around five o'clock the children
already in bed the maids having put on their evening dresses and
combed their braids. Wearing egg white. Their limbs ringed
with leaves laughing like beasts grazed their gestures and their
graces with soap bubbles which flew out of the mirrors of the
silk arrows which hung down from their dances and the wails of
nails driven into their body blindly by spots of fire of the sink
which were excessively controlling the anxiety hanging on the
corners of the oriental rug rolled up into a ball on the bed — the
bitterness polishing the evening was spreading out its oil spot
on the sheets — the shadow coming up from the starry sky was
cutting the smell of cinnamon into round slices of the least ges-
ture coming out of the box and the knitted eyebrows of the
oranges were draping their nudes of the invisible music of colors
hidden behind the curtains basket full of totally naked girls
embroidered with silver and gold their foreheads their breasts
their hands their hips when the chest of the door knocks its two
feet on the night

16.9.41

at exactly a quarter to four in the sunshine the 1's child and the
other one out on the windowsill playing with his fingernails and
his dark and light spots in the trumpets of the ringing which
sticks to his mauve cheeks in the stickiness of fly-legs of the soap
bubbles of its cries melting the pink dress with red polka-dots
into the burning white of the perfumed lozenges of her hair the
sugar dissolved at the bottom of the cup and the whole landscape
included inside the closed fists of the sun — the fringes of the
curtain covered with thumbtacks decorating it decoratively with
blue and Veronese green oozing methodically hidden and pru-
dently put away under a bell jar the music the fireworks and the

perfumes of the flying hands of a few flowers standing up their pikes picking on the pile of the ink-covered bread waving madly around in the rules of the game and the ceremonies the caresses the threats the blows all their claws bared timidly imitating the orchestra of desires and the brass band of disgusts moving their torn underwear around in the soup their mother five foot five two arms two legs two hands two feet a head two eyes two ears a nose a mouth a stomach hair guts two teats a bellybutton an asshole and the cunt of veins of blood of farts of urine of meat of fat of tendons and the belly full of bones — her mother her mom looked at the child of the 1 and the other one she loved her gave her the broth of her breasts washed her morning and evening combed her and went to the movies and the theater and the seaside with her and gave her slaps mommy mommy I'm through mommy I'm thirsty mommy I'm hungry mommy I'm sleepy do you want me to wipe your nose are you hot are you cold potty peepee beddy-bye — oh how heavy the wings of the horse are to carry said the 1 putting the package down on the sink — neither rain nor fine weather nor the snow and still less the vines in autumn and the fields of oats and wheat in summer and the spring and winter all together in one bouquet of thousands of millions of lamps burning on the chest of drawers. The contracted sofa rises to the ceiling the chair creaks its ropes and the varnished wood of the skirts the marbles tied to the curtains go slowly down the stairs — the clock covers its mouth on the windowpane and hides the plaque of the time still breathing behind the feather curtain — the rolled-up rug purrs in the ear of the unnailed door standing in the middle of the kitchen it bleeds white as wax made by the moon bees the fat surrounding its linen dress holds it up with its jasmine and perfumes it the long train of the knife cuts the light in two and separates it with its claws from the glued paper squeezing it.

The night coming out of the coat botanizes its stench on the
open book of the window — a heavy extract of melissa balm
flies chained up through the room.

[DB]

TUESDAY 24.11.41

drop of water hanging on the rampart of flames of the bunch of
flowers waving around at the fingertips of the burning lips of
the sound of the reeds scratch the night the cries the curses and
the bursts of laughter the ribbons of mixed colors exalting the
stench of the crabs rotting on the beach of the wing rising from
the body abandoned to the will of the waves

[DB]

23.2.42

distinctly naked hidden on the daub of the wheels come off the
immobile golden chariot and ice cold feet glued to the fire of
painted perfumes screaming attached to the irons planted in
live flesh a talking amphora muse of a thousand disguises huge
one-woman orchestra blowing her sea-shell illuminations and
hoar-frosts on the landscape's taut skin stuck to the window
panes one hand detaches itself from the arms lays its lips on the
bottom of the arcs of ribbons with thousands of irritated colors
he takes the ice cold breast of the taut wings the liquid castles
sparkling with playing cards cutting out the oiled shadow coat-
ing the torn evening gown of the shutters the divine finger that
threatens the apple-green stain with its nail the mouse-gray
painting and the unstitched blues of the cup whip the waning
roses the bronze feathers and the bisters and the smiles of chants
dances and calligraphies so complicated and odorous the crazy
orgy imprinted on the tiles' ochre tubes a drop of flakes decants

on the folds of the corsage opened by the weapon the willed
cadence closed flowers of the clock thinned in the aquatint of
the tambourine's gestures its beak hitting the marble the
calmness' precipitation arrives throw anguish and complaints
overboard grilled poppy seed and the noise of fat coins bouncing
on stripped brick tolling the hour at each wing beat the attacks
of the leaves dying on every floor and the marks of fire inscribed
on the skin of scales suffering the moon-powdered vine-shoots
and the obstacle races lost or won in circuses spread between the
hairs of heaven accord the victims the sighs and indulgences of
the wall hanging on the mirrors' mirages one single hope beats
the tambourine standing on water that shoots up a cataract the
harvest over the corn brought in snowed as a rain of gold and
silver on the open belly of time's fan developing its graces and
caresses the starch that will cover the whole page props up
chance which depends on the tree its dried fruits and jars of
blackberries the bile stuck to the finger sings and whistles in the
gilded feather that advances dragging its naked legs neither a
grain of rice nor a firefly nor a pin the rough drawing of a worm
throttles the sheep's grass' slate-gray and comes to eat its soup
from the hollowed hand of the lilac scarf that tears more visibly
on the brambles than by ear a child is weeping

[PJ]

11.3.42

gloved with flowers ironically burnt stretched painted stoically
with golden nails naked in her crumpled dress set fire by a thou-
sand lamps column of marble open to the blows of the fan bent
on beams of jasmine crystal iced with flames of bugles rattling
furiously their silks on the open hands of bells wood stuffed with
springtime and with amphoras full of milk smoked stiff chocks

on the paralyzed wagon wheels dragged by the songs evaporated
from so many solitary aromas the folds and the drawings of folds
and the lacework shaped by wasp bites of the luminous rings of
the park enribboned with the stream of musical instruments
bathed by the sun the cup the immense necessary space and
infinity clenched by the golden pincers of dances the blond
willed illumination scratching her scabies itch on the beams her
consequences unveiled combing her tresses on each star stabbed
in the water of the full glass of water set on the marble table its
attributes its laws its customs the quantity of salt or pepper of oil
and vinegar the panic-stricken colors that speak and the amorous
needments and the joy inscribed on the tablet of honor solar
pastille open to thirty six thousand candles trembling in the
windows the rose pinks the mallow mauves the apple greens and
the bronze milk of calcium the blue fingernails of the pale yel-
lows plate full of figs and grapes moved to tears the pond of
reeds stretches its thick cloth waxed with blue and tan squares
its beard full of cream on the white wood of the pregnant belly
of the table hidden in the panel of light suspended from the ice

[RK]

18 MARCH 42

the portrait is drawn in high tongues of fire on the plaited straw
of the deck of cards of pieces of crystal [   ] of the prism
stripped of its leaves — the hatchet blows so barely fallen
caramelize the uprisen incense — a sudden desire to strangle
intensifies the aquatint transfixing the flowers of her turned-on
fans — the unfastened dress of her ice turns its wings around
the cake of amber — arranged so careful of her person so proper
and polished with all her neighbors the eighteen year old adult
appeared to have rung on the metal at least thirty five times —

her wax furniture polished with palm oil her dresses and her
knives of fresh air gleaming and wise smelled good the verbena
the birdlime and the cigar with acrobats — the angel demon her
aunt and the concierge frequently interrogated by the mailman
of printed matter had no illusions and were eternally losing
interest in her anguishes — incalculably telling lies rats and
mice in the wind and she is flattering like somebody else the
golden crust of her words and her laughter contracted the leafed
paste clotted between her long desires and made it turn around
at the corners of the dial — every third Friday of the month
seated at her curtain she cut off urgently and coarsely the inter-
minable shrub of stones the long necklaces of gathered stars
crushed below the wheels — the first time that she was aware of
the golden stream rained on the hard silk of the cheaply counted
numbers of the sticky guests the dress of the garden painted in
colors so fresh was spattered with shame and suspicion — the
arrival at the inspection station the unloading of steamer trunks
and the transportation of bicycles fooled nobody — one single
livid tone come from the carriage moistened the drawing of the
flight of pigeons stetching out of the thin strip of clay earth
with its bells on the slippery ramp — all the black spread in
sooty snow over the sharp ridges of the sun drowned with cries
blinds with its wet sheets the streams enribboned with transpar-
ent feathers glued to the backs of huge mud oxen singing in the
courtyard — the lantern of her hands fixed to the devouring
banquet broken with all its branches the epidermis gets torn on
the meshes — the fringe of the carpet drinks all the water from
the pitcher imbibed from music — under the table the azure
surface glued to the boards tears the letter into a thousand pieces
— the living calcium of heaven is devoured slowly by the cater-
pillars

[RK]

2.4.42

it was not useless to three bodies made of mud and of light to
stay enveloped with shadow and with sadness a quarter century
overtaken to reconstitute them with all the pieces the wings
trailing too full of azure prickling from all its flowers built on
the granite of the rocks harshly at each stage of the window is lit
up like a night-light obscuring the gnawed rim of the dish the
interminable chain of peplums stirred silently by the moon the
smell so violent of the deep violet tone spread over the apple
green and the dew moistening with rose the lemon calming
until completely stifled the bitter orange music thrusting its hot
sighs into the indulgent open ear of the yellow ocher abruptly
awakened by the tough and tender words of the excessive white
perfume bronzed in the square reflecting her entirely naked mis-
erable wedding dinner inaugurated so noisily so shamefully in
full solitude says the 2 the morning separating itself from the
lake risen gently the skin sustaining the little boat attached to
the sweating branch a bowl of milk the witchcraft working
directly on her destiny englobes it in polished ivory dripping
from will o' the wisps kindled abruptly on each leaf which stirs a
finger of air the oil of her lips walks on the whole reach of her
arm sketched by the grass

[RK]

24 DECEMBER 1942

on the egg laid at long last the address shaped by the rain risen
so early squeaks with the regal azureal whites of her moans the
aroma of the lunar one lying with her bouquets stretched out in
indian file — the necessity made into a target and the order of

departure and detached judge of each thing and naked descends
silently rose by rose the creeping steps deliciously embellished
with perfumes and musics

[RK]

22.1.43

aureole aureolated with mashed stars long swan's neck harle-
quined with great claws with sulfured wine braided from the
corsage uncoiled as river with pebbles jumping yelling at the
mouths of festoons of grilled bees step by step of the sung cou-
plet the bitter olives loosened the cascade of flowers bitten into
with great joy precipitation and acrobatics spread out avidly
thrown by the handful to the clear and resounding reflections
fixed on every fish-bone stuck to every light that sticks out above
the stone struck lemon of the fife detached violently from the
silk stretched flushed crimson on the bronze spikes waving about
moon to moon with naked breasts and dances tearing long and
crackling veils in pink and periwinkle thrown over hill and dale
of so many imprisoned Bengal lights round number of cloud
hunkered down in degrading grandiloquent posture firm and
sweating come to the specific dislocated point irremediably
stripped of all baggage of perfume and wings shaken into a
golden broth at the doors and balconies figured in great detail
deposited mile by mile at each open branch the insinuating
moon the raw and devoted repasts warmly dished up to the nests
swarming between the pressed leaves appease pearl by pearl and
bacon scrap by bacon scrap the egg positioned totally uselessly
each silence emptied each burning truss dissolved each bowl
torn from the drawing that ferments oils the flame of day twist-
ed into a fan in capricious and demonstrative itching of tears
and sighs but to each pity its croissant and brioche and anise seed

to each soup its cream its butter its salt its cloves of garlic its pep-
per its onions its potatoes and its thousand masks and masks all
around and a round

[PJ]

10.3.43

white blue white yellow and rose white of an apple green turned
pale in the sweet flames of the quarter hour pinned to every
flower followed so closely at each step by her fingers oiling the
deck of cards at each discarded word such sweet aubades the
child's silk dress with pink spangles the bronzed pink of its star
gardens painted with the white flock of turquoises discreetly
adjusted to the silver balls of the feathers of such a delicate lilac
plaited ovals of the festoon of orange flowers and rope ladders
great floods of crimson ribbons heavy woolen curtains pulled by
six pairs of terracotta oxen decorated with so much laughter and
fruit filling the basket in large bubbles point- and pillow-lace
of the melted butter of the overflowing broth her grace and
games with both feet savvily detached and decoratively removed
from the sauce the unmeasured measure of the raised curtains
the dexterity of her leaps and contortions in the water of the
squalling pool the star points back to flowers of sulfur her
sweeping flights through the silk paper framed in flames one toe
of the left foot barely touching the cheek her unique and heart-
breaking song and pearls love made kind discreetly veils with its
rays the immaculate image having appeared shining and pure
fiction drawn inside every grain of rice boiled rice fat rice mea-
ger rice rice pudding sprinkled with cinnamon the way of
making it of cooking it dry it take it taste it love it nothing but
the rice soup just put on the fire slow the aroma and the bite and
horribly torn sad and alone painted room faded a feast of ennui

neck sliced by the ax blows of the sticky hands of the sun com-
ing in drunk plumb in the middle of overflowing village fair
torn by his banquet rags hermetically riding his donkey

[PJ]

20.3.43

an azure table covered with sugar a file a screw-driver a map
foxy errands to be run in embroideries in silks the most comi-
cal colors an old dressing-gown come down from heaven and
transparent its one thousand and a hundred of stained glass win-
dows bristling with all its feathers set alight at each offering
tossed into the soup pot all day long silently resigned to all and
any serenade the list increases the distress and signs it on the
breast with a claw of incense and with her songs rimes dances
and with complaints reconciled to the corners holding up the
whole edifice with her pitiful history to hand back without pity
to the tears cutting thread by thread the woof of the impossible
love revealed with so many precautions and sorrow asleep and
naked with each gathered and so roughly autopsied flower with
each shadow licked by any oar raised from the foam sprinkled
pearl to pink of each of the incommensurable stretched linens of
the complicated unsewing machines in the shadows of the stars
hung out to dry the thirsty musics of the melancholy passages of
her hair come undone the forceful initiative painting suiting her
charms shaken at each window that gives on spring snowballing
all responsibility thought to be good catch and put into chains all
said and done and said secretly into the ear of the landscape the
fat exploded belly of the sun kneaded and set out in the moon-
shine on the slate curtain with violin strings...

[PJ]

26 APRIL 43

TO THE SALMON-PINK CARESSES OF THE LEAF a thousand times half-opened and fixed detached offered as music to the fires and long trains of spangles waved and crazy so said and splashed in glory and rockets screamed and painted to the pearly distinct braids to the solitudes seen all mixed up with the caressing burned distillations to the branches and to the raised hangings to the sordid little secrets and to the unfortunate discoveries in digestions and prayers vomited from a point into far enamored sumptuous arabesques and ritornellos of the decompositions and tears to the spattered and festooned arcs labors torn in perfumes and in crowns and diabolic sated processions to the tendernesses prepared disappeared and undone so late of each long trajectory revolted enveloped stretched in the woods to hooked and shredded trances in meat and bone unfolded into veils and vellums oars smack raised in flames and good-byes rigorously projected as bait to the crowd of mirrors aping the drained apparition at the bottom of the raised lakes of the sun with large brush strokes painting three quarters of the sideboard buried in the mess of hairs of the fur caulking with cotton waste the belly open to the light with large strokes of the icy roof of the stretched sheet of the water armor screamed at the window with all the strength of the gay bouquet in plucked apparel to all chance and risk imagined.

[PJ]

[16 – 30 MAY 1943]

16.5.43

the flute the grapes the umbrella the armor the tree and the accordion the butterfly wings of the sugar of the blue fan of the lake and the azure waves of the silks of the strings hanging from the bouquets of roses of the ladders one and incalculable outsized flood of doves released drunk on the cutting festoons of prisms fixed to the bells decomposing with its thousand lit candles the green flocks of wool illuminated by the gentle acrobatics of the lanterns hanging from each arc string and the definitive dawn

30 MAY 1943

intervention at each blood drop spattered in iridescent sheaves and in silent mirrors on fire and festivities put off developed in music and songs rolled up as fields and silks parsimoniously distilled detailed descriptions on each page on each line on each crushed sun...

[PJ]

4 – 9 FEBRUARY 1944

from between the fingers of the gentle caravans of oriflammes of steeled sheaves in dead leaf shedding petals gropingly immense stoppered vessels the dances and screams imposed horizontally in good order and details at the lively pink of the oh so laughing points of the stars of the fan of the honey jar tolling the bells varied in numbers and musics at 5 o'clock hooked to the table of white wood toughly painted with whip lashes in celestial blue with the tender colors of the fringes splattered in torrents of panes in sweet and large lemons wild plighting of troths and vine leaves as well suspended in the middle of soups of acids as dead with fright and full of indulgence

[PJ]

8 – 9 NOVEMBER 1944

on the shrubs of ink fresh butter lace fans open in sated scattered divinities the incandescent crystal that sings on the wing on the bee's wax of the rose-bush gathers with delicate and supple spoonfuls the airy houses of cards of the perfumed male voices of feathers oiling the road

the miraculous rainbow festoons of the jars full of milk drinking with loud yells the azureal blue jumping with both feet on the tropics of the mirror hanging with all hands at the window

[PJ]

27 JULY 47. ANTIBES

the boreal dawn of the closed fan of her mane of hair the nails jammed into the curtains of sweat of the clenched screams at the spear-head of the scared flocks of bronze moons beating their wings kneeling around giant amphorae dragged by the white lemon of the sheets dirtied by the couple's horizontal blue orange of the oxen acidulating the gold of the jasmine of the ogival frames of the glasses filled with wine hidden under the teeth lace enveloping with his arms in fountains itchings and games deploying its arabesques above the bugle bands of the rainbow flags so carefully codifying the steel of accidental bites marshmallow grapes and festoon of honey waving their paws in the pond and the stinking regrets unctuously folded and ironed on the marble receive and respectfully greet the faraway acquisition and farandole of artifice shaken out over the cinders of the kitchen garden.

The children blaze torn from the quicklime of the leaves of quicksilver that grills at the bottom of the twisted blade of the knife scratching the wound.

the caressing ugliness of the paper sown with rose and amaranth continues its purring at the exact hour when the clock wilts and melts its wax lip to lip between the folds of the lake stretched out on the strings pinning the window to the cast shadow relieving itself exactly at the foot of the gallows painted green.

And the so unexpected manner of presenting doles and condolences uncountable archipelago lost with all hands dissolved in the good ice-cold soup fried with both feet on the scarf of regrets of so many convolutions. But physically perfect.

[PJ]

Françoise's Album*

VALLAURIS 1 JANUARY 1951

Yan minou and the others and the turtle and the doves and the fire of the stove that's working well and *las torrijas* brought this morning by Arias and the hazelnuts and grapes that Agard brought us before going to lunch at his brother-in-law's and mr.

---

*SOME NOTES FOR THE FOLLOWING: Yan minou = Picasso's dog. *Las torrijas* = French toast. Arias = Picasso's hairdresser. Agard = potter at the Madoura pottery works. Tonin = M. Michel, the gardener. Valsuani = Picasso's foundryman. Paloma = Picasso's daughter. A. Castel = an organizer of bullfights.

and mrs. Ramié with her box of cakes from chez Rohr in Cannes so welcome and the husband of the dentist of Vallauris brings his best wishes and an invitation to have coffee at his house and the false exit to go to work in the factory and returning before enjoying the road preferring to stay home with my three great loves

P.S. I had forgotten Tonin's after lunch visit bringing us as present a bottle of wine from our grapes from la Galloise and with my opinel pocket knife scratched Valsuani's botched bronze this first day of the year 1951 here in Vallauris

VALLAURIS THURSDAY 7 JUNE 1951

we're in the sun

I hear Paloma crying in the garden

I see the tip of my foot stretched out on the bed and the fireplace the little radio the books the newspapers the letters Rousseau's portraits of his wife and himself this afternoon at twenty past 4

and I see the armchair and the white jersey that I wear at night and the blue jersey bought in Paris at Old England and on the wall Goya's engraving: *lluvia de toros* (a rain of bulls)

and in the mirror the upside down world of the landscape and the room

and on the bed the plywood board the sketchbook the Zola novel *Abbé Mouret's Lapse* the box of color crayons the slip-cover binding with pencil of Françoise's book in which I draw and the miniature sword offered by A. Castel last year in Nîmes on a day of bullfights

and the sun coming in already tiring leaning on the door stretch-
ing its legs toward the fire-place

Paloma's voice very soft and the noise of wooden toys on the
sand bruising the wheels whose scream? tearing the stretched
canvas of the screen and that drawing on the same day at ¼ past
10 in the evening for whom?

[PJ]

18 JULY 1951 VALLAURIS

organdy forget-me-not tree gone haywire palm torn from the
immeasurable blue frozen by the sun detached from its course
the stretched out fingers of dawn receiving right on her breast
the shower of stars bronzing with all its teeth the enamored
songs of the frogs in two Bengal fires the swarming of aromas
the flags and lace nailed to the strips of amaranth cloth of her
gazes the dry grass grazing the rope of the gallows waiting on
knees the quick sword cutting the throat of the wound left half
open

[PJ]

VALLAURIS 20 JULY 1951

playing card hidden in the middle of the flood of silence played
between the sheets stretched from the eolian harp marbles
scratched at the knees by the oil of the amphorae set down on
top of them

the habit the risks the dances and capers lining the procession of
the graces carrying in their hair the light torn from the taut
strings of the alcove

the arms of the armchair catching the charge straight in the
chest

drop by drop evening undoes its ribbons on the dress of melted
butter of the blue square perfectly imitating the night hitting its
lips against the mirror

a butterfly undoes its wings in hiding and hangs its clogs from
the trembling crystal of the moon

acid candy mint lozenge blue and pink packet of pralines
the acid screen of the mauve cutting the green leaves of the
packet of pralines with the candy-pink of the fifes

three francs ninety three the marshmallow the iced coffee three
hundred ninety five the mint lozenges and the total the sum of
the sum of the sum

what a may evening what a racket what a samba the wanton ape
sets the alarm-clock to the hour of happiness and signs the regis-
ter with its tail

the blue house slipper with Chinese drawings sighs pleasure
dragging its guts through the arena a bouquet of gladiolas
nailed to the granite tears its chains in the honey

the moon plays it close to the vest and softly sets the clouds on
fire

(a donkey brays far away)

[PJ]

St-Tropez 23 July 1951

the wedding dress of the little flower hooked to the strings of the virgin crucified on the grill purrs at the edge of the last drop that makes the cup of eau de vie overflow

[PJ]

Vallauris 26 – 28 September 1951

And what does it matter if the wheels and the cart and the screams the grimaces of the sighs of the dying moon overflow in fifes and lacunae the fields of jasmine braiding her bronzed hair into sheaves of swords if on waking brooks on the amaranth sky the sickles of the bed sheets dragging its guts over the bricks the spattered stains of the stars germinate the blue cocoons of night the purity of the drawing on the cobalt violet stirring up the salt of the wings hatching the boiling pearls sleeping in separate rooms reaping graces loves and sweetness in the architecture of her back her buttocks illuminating the grand eloquent discourse sung with both arms at the window her arm dismantles drop by drop cascading the source of happiness down upon the crumpled marble of the periwinkle blue sheets night covers the buckram of her face with the flight of birds wrinkling the mirror with sticky fingers covered with the honey of the hives scraped at the stars' satin the bridge's arch rears under the harp's strings

the capital letter of her name tears the canvas and uncovers in the painting the source a rain of almonds sugars the bottom of the lake with the make-up oiling her body over the bites' lattice a veil of ashes chokes the screams of the sun grabbed with both arms by absence a star-fish creakingly clambers up its cries the amphora full of kisses at the end of the rope

the goat is in full swing and chases the wolf from the arena

love betrays its weapons and bites the dust by beating its wings against the window panes

one can hear the hour that sits at the edge of the waterfall

one madman two madmen three madmen a thousand madmen ten madmen thirty madmen madmen and madmen the orchestra plays a rumba

the shoemaker's daughter the baker's daughter the pigeons' daughter the godson's daughter papa's daughter mama's daughter the daughter of her daughter and the minor daughter and the father's daughter and the mother's daughter the forefather's daughter and the papa's daughter and the giant's daughter the dwarf's daughter all and every daughter and all the illegitimate daughters late in the season of the country of the people of pleasure daughter of the streets sitting laying down standing up kneeling

on a chair asleep awake fat skinny silent talkative dirty filthy clean intelligent stupid organized caressing cantankerous and all the boys local dancers son of a whore son of a priest winged pumpkins box of thumbtacks starry blue sky pink sky bronzed lemon almond green the first to laugh will...

and the magic numbers to count them the X and the Z the 24 first demons of the month the salt box the lettuces the melon the aromatic herbs and the bag of tricks from the bottom of the bottom of the story and the good mornings good evenings and thank you thank you from everyone all things considered

here finish this serial novel to start with the beginning of the next one historically put into the vulgar tongue with meticulous and jealous care by the holy author may keep me drawbridge of her naked body capricious itch of the heap of stars drinking from the hollow of her hands puddles of forget-me-nots the brief moments of hidden happiness immobilizing the source of joists

wax tablecloth spread over the full moon jimmying the door of the dungeon rigodoon murmured into the lock plugged with the wax impression calculating the size of the disaster legs fan-like opened the chair kneeling holding tight between her fingers against her breast the nylon shirt offering her oat fields to the jets of the fountain attached to the gallows propping up the night the slice of melon biting lustily the barbed rain of the peonies' excessive flight

evening gets there at the right time pale and spattered with pins to establish the facts and save the day

[PJ]

21.10.51 Vallauris

"Suicide in hell"

"to save everyone you had yourself killed that's all very well and a success my friend and I thank you but the life of one must not be sacrificed for anybody nor the life of all for one now and for this specific occurrence we condemn you to live forever and each day a word to the wise that's all"

the phony smart aleck immediately put his nose to the hole of the toilets and smelling the bouquet of overripe roses something rummaged around his brain and belched forth a few sublime thoughts... disturbed by the music of the light beating iron-hard on the copper of the sauce pans the slice-of-brie sun stuck to the linens stretched to breaking point on the broken rays of the inverted reflections of morning ringing the bells on the collar around the neck of the beast the birth of the nude who appeared in the sleeping water of the open knife legs spread on the bed raised up the frayed corner of the curtain hanging from the ceiling the sheet of flames falling heavily on the wall of the room and the bed her caramel candies and oils draping the alcove in fine arabesques and careful devilries faggots made in haste from vine shoots roasting days and nights fixed to the window wine flowing freely and the black aloe flour emptying pockets in the heart the smallest fault shedding light on the stupidity revealed at such high cost scraping the bottom of the pot and pulling the worms worm after worm from the nose

[PJ]

PARIS 28.3.52

If not discreetly secluded and stupidly collected surrounded by aromas and girandoles nearly alone and terribly wrapped up in numbers the gong stroke hitting the ray of such sweet light hanging from the folds of the cloth spread out so scandalously on the sheet's whiteness lets its silk threads loose over the whole oat field holds back drop by drop claws unsheathed and laughs toothily the inverse image of its happiness.

The large lilac puddle of the nude dispersed over the tepid milk spilled on the almond green cotton tripped up by the pulled curtains sets fire to the straw in soap bubbles and sagely knits its mathematics.

The sauerkraut was good the hair of the beast smelled of jonquils the saintly mishmash laid low the sleeping dawn.

A smell of lavender scraped his nose on the rancid butter of the sun nailing his luck to the joists.

[PJ]

PARIS 31 MARCH 1952
for Beloyannis

the glimmer of the lanterns' oil lighting up the night of a Madrid may evening the noble faces of the people shot down by the rapacious stranger in Goya's painting is the same seed of horror sewn by the fistful of projectors on the open chest of Greece by governments sweating with fear and hate. A huge white dove dusts the anger of its mourning over the earth

[PJ]

[JULY] 1952

I

books torn and burned
marbles broken Venus head of Minerva.
horses harnessed with mourning dragging the cart.
wheat fields waving sheaves of flames.
pigeons flying through the bodies of the ruined dead

II

Pegasus ploughman attached with traces of flowers.
swims in ring-around-the-rosy surrounding the cart boat
    vine-shoots.

[PJ]

VALLAURIS 23 DECEMBER 1952
For Mr. Edouard Pignon

"The flabby ogre stretched out in full drunkenness on the solar dial filching on the screen the remains of the evening soup frozen with fright but in the distance exactly on the line of the horizon the cast shadow of the invisible castle shredded the orange skin of the sun already gone to bed"

[PJ]

FOURNAS WORKSHOP VALLAURIS 18.10.1954

Why cry so so much over the flowering almond trees? raised around the arch of honey of the ogive hanging from the blazing ridges unearthed today so gallantly displayed at the window. The hands full of salt encircling the curve of music tolling the bell on the flags flying at half-mast. The hour up so early biting into stale bread — dragging its guts under the sink. The rage accompanying the procession and the fanfare. The children cooked to a turn watering the sheaf with cries and laughter. The far-sighted council twisting its sheets on the grass. The hunt cutting corners casting off its linens on the roof of all its grandeur. And the congealed sugar and the thousand and one hundred flowers of the azure oozing breath on the point-lace pompons hanging from the branches. Necessity shaped into lozenges and triangles breaks in its acquired dimension at the joists. Love telling their fortune to the swallows' nests lying broken on the slabs of the terrace. An absolute position extremely difficult to hold lying straight up at the edge of an emerald boat. The necessity of doing the numbers and the dishes before evening. To stuff the peelings thrown down the passing days the vases of marble holding all the blood spilled gushes drop by drop into the nettles. Total decadence made queen and *chevaux de frise* of all accomplished facts. The aurora borealis comically disguised as a lender grasshopper.

Period.

[PJ]

FOURNAS WORKSHOP VALLAURIS — 19.10.54
LANDSCAPE WITH LAMP

A white azure rainbowy bronzed sudden desire of sheaves of palms irised by thorns twisting dawn from the claws folded back in a circle and throbbing curves the shaft of the column of forget-me-nots planted on the cloth of the lake spread out at his feet.

The music branch sliding its fingers along the veil floating in the branches. And the wet cottons of her gaze gathering the last drop of perfume distilled from the slow herds of stars.

One hand caressing the back of the goat of the hour marking the tempos to be held.

The useless pink of the violet lost with all hands not using the page. And the grimace of the mirror inserting the image between the crumpled sheets of the unmade bed of the sky. And the anguish of having arrived too late at the brilliance of the bouquet tensed with a thousand spangles grilling its horses in oil. The great amphorae poured out over the clouds roaring its tears on the open sea of the road. Screams and harrowing laments. The chain in the middle of the room relieving itself on the matting.

Drop by drop night undoes its braids at the edge of the roof and drips on the brasero.

The chaperon waits behind the door. At each knock the curtain rises and the great thirst shows its teeth to the public facing it. A round of partridges takes its bearing on the edge of the string hanging from the ribbons of the dish of beans offered so generously by the alms. One douses the sky in honey one nails the flyer for the party over it. The regiment extends its *sardanes** and shoots blanks at the winning number.

[PJ]

---

*Catalan dance.

TODAY THE 23RD OF FEBRUARY 1955
OJO
Songs of Summer dedicated to Don Jaime Sabartés y Gual

I

this little colored girl
has balls as green as grass
her rolly-polly bishop
grows beans in his moustache

II

the balls of little Eulalia
show not a shred of chaff
while the nuts of Sabartés
have the down of a golden calf

III

the friars with bulging guts
are painting pictures that
would make a sweet young thing
squeal like an alley cat

*

for Don Jaime Sabartés on his Saint's Day

I

my grandmother's big balls
are shining midst the thistles
and where the young girls roam
the grindstones whet their whistles

II

the sausage that you shove
up the ass of your señora
feels like a passion fruit
and the chokes of estremadura

III

the cardinal of cock
and the archbishop of gash
are a couple of well hung boys
with an eye for garlic and cash

IV

from the chairs on which the nuns
and the sacristan dropped their pants
hot honey sizzles their buns
till they cross themselves and dance

[JR]

5.11.57

PORTRAIT OF HÉLÈNE PARMELIN

Sitting nearly in heap of harvested grasses laughing intent
nailed to the clouds and magnificently swept by the waves. The
silver tray of her gaze bedevils the card played in tears on the
crystal that scrapes its luxury at the window.

An inoperative inopportune thirst for azure overhangs the bun-
ker of the sinner woman on the seashore.

Ah ! the seagulls ! plus the letters received and to be answered
dirt with dirt in the so gently awakened quietude.

Portrait that would be done in a rush without erasures without eraser or bread crumbs through the soft bark of a sun.

[PJ]

12.9.58

for Don Rodrigo Díaz de Vivar de Silva y Velázquez

Carpenter in rinkytinky metal
an alms box for the cuts of baby beef
anxieties of rosemary and thyme
timekeeper of scrambled eggs and sausage
a cloud split equally from side to side
fandango sounds sent forth across the wheat fields
knocked off their pins so easily atop
the cricket cages for the sun to soak his
feet in egg whites of the moon

[JR]

HUNK OF SKIN

8.1.59

on the new lush
grass at the
well-rim   a
careless young man
was sleeping all
most nude   wearing
skins of lamb or bear
next to the two or three
predetermined cardinal points
frog and partridge outside and in
side crumbs set to soak

next the oven
their muletas and silken
fabrics on top and
their table d'hôte dinners.
of metal and hard boiled
egg and faster and running
made hot coals and close
enuf to shoot a chicken and
a seam of split watermelon
hanging from every
crow.
nothing more
waiting for the tambourine and
the wing of a pine grove and
the fringes of candlelight
making their calculations on
the taut fabric
of stone woods   huddled
among the groves of fig
trees casting their
reckonings under
the belly-button of the mortar hoarse
with cries and mending
slid under the door
writ out with fat brush above
the fragment of syrupy sky
posted as
sentinel   edge of the crib
sparkling out

crumbs and wolf-whistles
over the house

pitched into the sea   the house
fly in the land
scape   fried in the pan
freezing his hands
on the water-faucet
      spigot.

9.1.59

I

the boxes of
shoeblacking
tot up their reckonings
shins open and out
stretched   smelling of mallows
nailed to the gate of the
corral   painted in bands
of ochre for the fiesta   torn
to shreds and covered with combed out
pimples in the flour of eyes
dangling from strings
of Estremadura chorizos
playing violin in the middle of
the plaza of tears and
anxieties over clusters of sar
dines dusted with rice and fandangos
at the hour of fire
in the pine grove tangling
the tablecloth with crabs
of flint   with soup
set in the window
sparkling

II

then the mailman came and
the collector of handclapping and olés
and the parish blindman
and the blackbird
Ramon's daughters and doña Paquita's also
the oldest daughter   the old maid
and the priest standing coldly apart painted
saffron and green
loaded with noodles and black
grapes of cotton and aloes   fat and
very erect   become radishes and
fryingpan full of eggs
and home fries   fried
cracklings covered with fleas
and cattle bells and the question
carried on the shoulder   poor
and rich swept off by the rainstorm
above the burning wheat   soaking
his shirt with
hail   the dirty linen

III

Phyllis
the oldest one
her fleas itching already
got stupid and threw herself
into bed dressed
in what she was wearing   the
tears
and sighs

and threw herself down
on top of the mattress
and the porcelain dog so as to
pass for Messalina   which
she is not   as the mayor's son
and the innkeeper believed   who went
crazy with happiness
one banging the tambourine   the other
the rebec   splashing music
over the suit and the laces
hanging between the legs of
the Venetian
blinds half-open into
the room making
stairways of SUN for
flies taking afternoon walks
and gold in a dustcloud of water
orange blossom and Celestina's
mother   sheer magic
powders

IV

when the mailman figured
out what the little girl was doing
on the brownish velvet cloth blue
from the flock of toads praying under
neath the black/and/blue turquoise the
piece of cloak stained coral from the rag
the ball of jasmine
to whistle up their
amphoras and their oxen
he did his silly acrobatics again

and ran afoul of the plot—
Nothing missing but the
arrival of the queen mother colonel
and her daughters
so that the function blew up in the hand
the girl got all tangled up in her calculations
and a seed jumped out and up her rump, not
to order or
by ordinance
as God ordains
nor by pharmaceutical recognition
certainly not
just to be pleasant

                              V

nor ought it be
thought a joke
nor wisecrack
nor sugar-sweet nor
goblin if not for
having seized the passing
hour limping along the top of its lungs
swallowing the fish's tongue
and tickling the boy and his grandfather
climbing onto the burro
seen very far off to the far
reaches of the road
scratching in the dust
stomping
for no one would have
said or done
or undone

nailed down or
pulled out
the porcupine's quills since
at the slightest noise
at the first drop of rain
the flour sack would have soaked her
tresses in the kettle
would have
made the mountain
a tinkle bell
and to crunch the rosebush
upon the sea of
the table set
with the soup
the *porron*
the bread the
spoons
the knife the
tomatoes and
her face

                              VI

Every silver
lining has its
dark cloud said
the cobbler and
you don't skin your
mother in the open
window
the splinters and splices of sun
licking the chair rungs   crying
the whole rockinghorse afternoon in

an austere corner the
light
harrowed by mules
with a clean peal of laughter
the dawn's brass
band cauterizes the wound
the fingers made in the skin
of afternoon
in the mustard-colored
sky painted cobalt
trampling underfoot
the green bread
of the poppy sand
twisting its dances.
At 4 in the afternoon
not at 5 the
lightning-swift arrival of
the merry-go-round
's daughter
fixes the colors in the tureen
the light grows
indifferent and
suddenly
it went sour the
dance with the merry-go-
uncle

VII

Sesame
drenched to the ears and
drunk as a skunk and balling
of the first water

and of the second and
of the third throwing
off sparks and plenty of action
cursing and coughing
peeing on top of the
piano farting   into the cornet
his wife
Ruby
she-ass and saint
was weeping
pulling at the rough edges of
the wrinkled rag paper that was
swathing her crab's legs under
her skirts   tiny oysters
and legitimate sons from legitimate matrimony
Johnny   Henry   and
Baldomero
So that would have been okay
if the dirty brushes were
not scraping hopes and hates
off the palette   the
whole filing cabinet full of
belches that a father and
mother boil over
and over again in
the pot of joy
the ebullience of a fiesta day
on the point of   becoming
caramel candy

VIII

One cheese shoe
one boot of rice
pair of eggs a
nest of snails
one brush and
one chicken
a canary
one quail
a flowerpot
an inkpot   a
plugged nickel
a blackbird
a story
a pencil
a jug   one
Walloon one
blind hen the
history of mother Celestina
and a cuadrilla of kids from Sevilla
bullfighters
uncle Parrakeet
the others and the rest there
San Roque's dog three four one-half and
one-quarter
the sea and the waves and the fish
the countryside and the lambs
the cows
and the bulls
Lagartijo the matador and the
lady lizards
Ecija's   4   kids, almonds

chestnuts   walnuts   hazelnuts
and raisins
partridges
quail
linnets
basil
thyme   rosemary
lavender

                                         IX

smoke of dried herbs
merry-go-round
wires
stone
wood and whitewash
red wine
lees
hard liquor rabbit
olives table
chair bottle glass
brick
sand
black pepper and salt lemon
orange shirt
undershirt
under drawers stockings
and socks stones
and stones and more
stones and such and such and so and such
and so and such and such and so and so
and such and 1 and 2.   and 3.   and 4 and 5 and 6
and 7 and 8 and 9 and 10 and 11 and 12 and 13 and

14 and 15 and 16 and 17 and 18 and 19
and 20 and 21 and 22 and 23 and 24 and 25
and 26 and 27 and 28 and 29 and 30 and 31 and 32 and 33
and 34 and 35 and 36 and 37 and 38 and 39 and 40 and 41
and 42 and 43 and 44 and 45 and...

[PB]

THE BURIAL OF THE COUNT OF ORGAZ

6.1.57. CANNES A.M.

1   here there's nothing but some oil and shredded beef.

2   son of a bitch bitch wise guy double wise guy gash rheu-
    matic wolf and ragtag owl

0   flower child with eyelids fluttering and yakking on the top
    of makeup box bent nail pried open with a knife point.

2   mickey rat dressed like a priest who sheds the skin from
    rags of darkness.

1   so having gotten the open envelope without a stamp it could
    have been eaten by the mailman or his grandmother and
    not responsible to anybody happy days.

2   but just hold on there! seeing what must be done is to un-
    wind and bind the bundle to the ball and pluck the wind
    out of our sails.

1   old itch and cravings to break doors and windows down in
    heat or cold to start in taking shots and partridges and lions

0   skyhigh fringes.

2   the two thieves.

1   and so the hustle bustle of a binge.

2   with broken pots to make a soup of pinks and roses in
    gazpacho trembling points of light to take a count of every-
    thing and make a chain of every egg they lay.

0   and nothing more than any evening at the bull ring seeing

nothing more is lacking not so much as thanks but no thanks.

2 i don't say that what i don't say i don't say by saying i don't say it.

1 a mess of i-say and a mess of say-it-to-me and a mess of say of don't-say like a mess of castanets all praying with their torches and their fried eggs lightly lightly.

2 most likely things here aren't meant for nudes and showcases not in museums nor the larger fashionable boutiques — because that's the way it is.

0 nothing more than a glowworm hanging from the ceiling lighting up the dance inside the chandelier.

2 dog with so many heads so skinny and so paunchy.

0 anyone would say that you have never seen him fighting bulls and seen the peoples come up heads or tails so that you don't know where you're going or where you're coming from while clipping coupons and vignettes all made into a lottery and all the starry engine into a game of ball.

1 because you're already such a joker what with all those faces that you carry you painted one atop the other melted and already dry and framed and hung on every leaf and feather duster.

0 no don Juan either

1 don't tell me that you're not not telling me that yes it all will be explained to you by Minuni and Paco Reina.

2 hard harder than a stone and fresh like lettuce.

0 chapter 31 by order of the king and times long gone between a rock and hard place settled and unruly full of wind and from the other side a crackling sound of lightnings tripes and snails and blood puddings not in the least pissed off at having left the sack of calamares at the station in the middle of the river curdling up.

2   thanks a lot and give a ribbon to the goat and to the kid and
     to the pigeons seeing how the wheat is shooting up.
1   so don't tell me any more go scratch
2   if what i'm waiting for is you to sing so that you take the
     scales off of the sun.
1   don't get dressed up in gold or sequins if you're cold put on
     the garb of nakedness with grape leaves and begin to dance
     because today is Sunday.
0   i'm not saying anything you know already what i'm saying
     i'm not saying any more you know already what i've said.
1   one knows what one knows one knows what is known the
     known what isn't known already is what's known and then
     forgotten what is known and isn't lived what's seen and
     barely seen what isn't ever seen and wanted both to see and
     to be seen within a wine stain on a table top beneath the
     empty glass beside a knife and little scraps of bread.
2   i have believed it to be so again the light is fading out if you
     should light the light would not need light to see light
     clearly.
1   don't you be talking nonsense dance and sing you big
     capuchin monk and don't you tell me any stories.

12.1.57

the most complete gap on the stage
the cast of $0 - 0 -$

the most important matters totally outside the question of pre-
scriptive signs picky picky and a sweet jelly roll.

27.1.57

apparition of old cunt and research into garbage cans for a little
or too much reality *du quain quain*

national holiday with fireworks balls military marches and ec-
clesiastical illuminations

14.8.57

the burial of the Count of Orgaz continues

Don Diego Firm and Steady Don Ramon Don Pedro Don
Gonzalo Don the Judge and Don the Pilgrim Don the Flavio and
Don Gustavo Don the Rich and Don the Flower Don the
Sausage Don the Instant Don Ricardo Don the Rumble Don the
Joyboy Don the Blond and Don the Brunet Don the Greybeard
at the open circle's edge they eat the silk the water pipe rains
down the golden wires of a party of small owls crying sucking
needled fringes planted head down on the table top spread full of
silver coins just to the left of the electric soda fan placed in the
window facing on the port adorned with jasmines bits of wood
of chasubles and cocks' feet an entire flock they sausagize the
keys of the oil feather duster of the chants and chirps that cook
between the digits of the she-goat's wings. The cunning that can
strip the nets and bundles of the stars and lode stars of their foot
can pull the azure's skin off and can bleed it drop by drop onto
the curtain's open palm amid the smell of tripes the bugle calls
announcing the arrival of the Magi still more drunk than some-
one's loony aunt big footed loose and snoring and can sew the
lightning's trousseau by machine the trousseau in a summer
dream that brings some girl out to the dance this night if run-
ning quick and fast she doesn't tumble down for joy between the
busted arms of some plush chair some christmas morn some
fourteenth of july some married off and childless overcoat and
fancy cape a shroud of lights and caramels jug water soft arroyo
covered o'er with blazing banderillas noon time singing dancing
flames from alcohol mint garments cock and bull who scratch

their lice under the splash board of the rosy colored kitchen wall.

And here the story and the celebration end. And whatever has already happened even a madman wouldn't know.

The mailman's wife and her cousin went down to the bull fights, the mailman made off with his sister-in-law's sister Amalia and as for the nephew nobody knows what he did that whole afternoon and what time he got back to the house. It wasn't that night or the following day when the trouble got started but on Aunt Regueldo's saint's day in the midst of her party that the shit hit the fan. Perdaguino's daughter let a fart off from under her blouse and pulling her tits from her blouse she lifted her skirts up and showed us her pussy. Just picture the face of the priest and the fussing around of the nephew the goat herder's daughters the bimbos over the way and the nuns who were crossing themselves and choking with laughter from all of that thunder and lightning.

Carmen   tralala la la la......
            toreador toreador toreador

the four young girls in their beds who bury the Count of Orgaz

the child playing the piano suspended hung by the neck on horseback dressed like a chef with a (underline)funeral(/underline) bonnet his left hand is holding a frying pan for a shield — (the saddle cloth silver and black) this has nothing to do with Las Meninas

hanging from two hooks on the ceiling one ham and some chorizos

Modesto Castilla the natural son of D. Ramon Pérez Cortales

D. de S. y V. [Diego de Silva y Velázquez] sets his <u>palette-mirror</u> up facing the mirror that's nailed on the wall in the depths of his chamber

the figure in the doorway is Goya who's painting making himself a self-portrait who wears a chef's hat sombrero a pair of striped pants like Courbet and me — and is using a frying pan as a palette

the fourth girl from the left is on horseback the horse has a black saddle blanket with spangles of silver

spiffed up like a picador

on top of the picture an owl that came here one night to kill the doves in the room in which I am painting

every last dove

on the keys of the piano a cigarette butt still aglow
and two guardia civiles positioned behind las Meninas

in the sky where they bury the C. of Orgaz Pepeillo — Gallito and Manolete

in their beds las Meninas act out the burial of the Count of Orgaz

2.12.57

the whole room busted up and thrown around chopped into pieces sprawled out face up fell asleep there early strewn with lice and goldfinches. The young boys shivering were jerking off screaming and the girls downstairs were shedding their white hair by handfuls wringing out the palm trees loaded with fried figs.

The mailman's wife was clambering and racing hiking up her skirts in midst of all those flare-ups of the keys and bells. Her aunt the wife of the night watchman followed her a mile or so half dead with cold and her kid like a hot cinder was eating his supper perched on a cordon of clouds from the feather duster. Sons of a whore and son-in-law of a fire marshal their four bits squirreled away and blinded were rotting their curtains and backdrops at three and a half past her pussy

Olés and the clapping of palms were response to the tears cater-wauled by the lizard at that hour the very most blackbird discovered the pleasure of singing its masses what joy and what laughs that were spooking the priest when hearing the sound of the flute that was running and jumping on top of the table.

Not the screams nor the scratches and kicks made the day go away to lie down on its flower bed next to the girl in the shop-keeper's shirt from downstairs. Much later on and still later the mess got itself straightened out when the summertime aunts and the wintertime aunts all got here and settled accounts got rid of the ducks come hell or high water to temper the nails and the bedbugs with fritters reconsecrated set right side up.

The letters and the prayers didn't make things sweet and peachy
they sat down in a corner no one said amen or let a peep out and
they fell asleep.

Why look for causes and for snailshells through the starry heav-
ens

a big fat smile is spreading out behind the venetians painted
there in green. The sun with knife jabs murders her in yellow
and squeezes out the blue between his fingers.

What doggedness and what a big fat asshole that the clouds this
evening have the color of an eyelash and the color of a fire and
what a bunch of buggers they all are. Their sugar veils are mois-
tening the tresses on the ocean's neck their screaming flooding
the forgotten dish of lentils

the ram with crows feet slams his crane's foot on the envelope of
onion skin the letters opened one by one the other following the
rivulet the road and the arroyo washing out and hanging out
their memories to dry them on the rosemary they are the little
angels who are crying and the others angels flying with the cur-
rent laughing sleep sleep little babe because the bogeyman is
coming he will snatch away the babes who aren't sleeping

16.1.58

the girls from downstairs slipped themselves into an envelope
they slapped a stamp on it and stuck it in the mail box and
unseen and unclean from there they go off to the strip joint and
see where *les girls* "The Heehaws" strut their *streepchips* asleep
in their cradles and sheltered from sun and from moon and so

happy and spewing forth chitchat from any old shit. And no riot
got kicked off that night in the theater. The guards had to ask
for the key to the crapper for hours on end before nabbing that
ratpack. Naked like worms in a pear and shaking with cold.

17.1.58
the butterflies were going from flower to flower laying fried eggs
on the branches and the blue sheep du jour were rending their
feathers in the puddles of syrup.

8.6.58
chanoine fait du poil des roues de l'arc-en-ciel
[canon law made of rainbow wheel hair]

19.6.58
sun squatting down makes its own Don Rodrigo Díaz de Vivar on
the edge of the cistern surrounded by poppies in the midst of
bent wheat stalks and in front of the sea.

Watermelon slices soaking their nuns and their monks on the
terraces

the pigeon shoot shakes its old rags in the syrup

and the marzipan houses with sparks shooting off between bam-
boo grilles on the carousel grinding their griefs down to fronds
and festoons on the blue percale cape

the clarion calls and they toss out the key in the river and a cop-
per pipe pisses all over the salt works fandango and laugh of a
night like the one the moon painted with spit from its horns

unfurls little by little its sugary guiles on the walls and its grappling hooks piercing the lips of a bell as it shakes off the dust from St. John's night.

Old gold and fritters of water small sugar cubes aguardiente a night of tin leaves and of lettuce

21.7.58

verdigris toro and lamp tripes and son of a bitch bitch and tailor for priests with the eyes of a partridge in silver and gold the nose of a rat and an Alcaniz millstone and unripened fruit when his mother-in-law's letter smashed the cashbox to bits hallelujah. The three daughters of the bridegroom the weaver of shoes got dressed in fine clothes and set out from home around five in the morning. They grabbed hold of a buggy and all in a turmoil they got to the farm by 9:30 that day there was nobody waiting for them which if there wasn't they would have polished the world off would have plucked some old rag from its innards and buckled it on for the banquet but all they could do was rip out its guts and show off the chitlins low laughs and high masses in summer would head off to sing for those sugary skies and those spice cakes and bunches of jasmines got up on their feet by dint of the clouds and the fistfuls of roses stripped down to their shorthairs and with their bare fists they grabbed hold of the three glass panes on the wardrobe sans hangings of damask sans funeral dirges and step after step got soaked to the marrow. Uncle John at that hour was hanging around the café sprawled out on the benches and waiting for lunchtime.

The smallest of all the three sisters next stuck out her cock and pissed in the porridge then put on her night cap and wiped her ass clean and started to pray like a saint.

And through the eye of a needle more and more lanterns and lights were beginning to burst into bunches of stars left to dry somewhere over the ocean. Scouring brushes fried bacon candied almonds and smells of <u>sweet basil</u> and their curls hanging loose belly up on the cushions their legs fanning the sheets with ivory screams and with screaming of lilies and kisses with fingers like scissors painting the stage curtain up in the alcove dissolved in a sauce of gum arabic of the brush stroke of hot living lime falling down silently drop after drop on the bull ring.

And afterwards or a little before underneath or on top of the roof the candlesticks lit of the razors of swallows crisscrossing in flight the blue of their wounds right over their heads or their tails phosphorescing the wheat they are smoking the cheese rinds and kidneys of fleas of flags turning gold on the beach one more time it was worse still the judge and the priest cut a deal they would dandle the babe in his cradle would sing him a death song with no sense of shame with the skin tanned down to the bone with so many scratches and kisses and pulling off yard after yard of the jack fishes' scales with their mouths hanging open and the owls scratching away belly button of binges and crooked guitars their feet getting soaked in the spurt of blood cascading down from the neck of the silver fleeced lamb from the silken cockades from the lines tangled shredded and set in a milk dish and propped on the window sill in the night air and not even one butterfly more would gather its harvest from the slices of melon and the watermelons that the three young girls lugged on their shoulders.

How ashamed it all made them to see themselves painted like rabbits dying of laughter and fright changed into sausages scratching their tummies and tits waking up early and dreaming

all day and painting by night in the night air if only their auntie
could see them Aunt Clara the gravedigger's bride that jerk
Nicodemus the far biggest asshole in town and still just the
sweetest and neatest he is yes but also the poorest so what will
we do with him what do you want us to do with him yes it's all
done now and there's nothing more we can say it's all done now
the three girls are like that and not either God or the devil will
turn them around they each have their graces their angel their
duende and if they should fuck it's because they like fucking it
makes them feel good and after they do they can sleep and not
dream because dreaming so much they are always awake when
they dream and thus did he say it the man who knows who the
town idiot is who was passing his time throwing stones at the
church bells or singing away in the plaza perched somewhere
over the ax blade the thrust of the guillotine shadow with its
thousands of quintals of sun of the mattress of light kicked
apart by the hoofs of the ages

5.8.58

thoroughbred from head to toe and compass point for shaving
tales and proverbs out among the skyhigh prickly pears the great
typewriter lies for pimps and crystal wine glasses in flames the
primal image solitary hooked by the lapel paints its game on top
of the tile roof abuses grape leaf placed in grieving eye its jet
black ink and tears cascading from the table marinade the sea
bream with its problems so improbable the cracks in which the
sun can thrust its fingers every chair in place and every dirty rag
erected facing face to face the crust of burlap skin thrust up her
buttocks in a sauce that rings alarm bells in the cauldron volume
one and chapter something of the chunk of rye bread opened
wide the caterwauling oompahpah band kneeling at the altar
frying pan a miracle and spell of tailor and of hangman covered

o'er with oil stains grease spots green blood of the backdrop half
constructed of the big blue landscape on the easel drying out its
lemon juice and onion juice mixed all together in the yellow
puddle of the sheets on the blue peasants cap black bonnet and
red fan and loads of tripe feet stomping pomegranate flower
wreath of gold threads silver jasmine and dry bread filled up
with tomatoes beans and onions oil and salt and peppers incogni-
to lunches dressed up as a madman priest dragged off in bulky
cruet holders of poured concrete bridges o'er the dreck of clouds
red hot the azure broken down that sleeps it off at trace of old
ape's pointed nose with howdydoos and thanks and genuflections
in square roots and round ones too to your most worthy lord not
mine shit weddings so refined and shiny like the silk from bal-
conies aflutter on the sugar nougat palace makes you smack your
lips both thick and thin this summer afternoon collector of a
pack of lies and black yolk of the hundred year old egg laid by
the brooding hen of that drunk carrousel that fires off its old
wives tales and laughter for those very heavens like a child

8.8.58

but by then at that time from the girls down below to their aunt
Tia Juana they all were dead drunk and scratching their cunts
and naked like at a fiesta with nothing to do but to look at the
clock and to fan their wet pussies so eager they were to be fucked
by the first available postman who gets to the town hall his burro
slung over his back and his wife in his tummy and gets in a
godawful fight with the boys from the port and there was no
other way out but to make the hot into cold or the cold into hot
and to light up the lamps and the bengali whizbangs and fry the
fritters and churros up on the skillet the tears rolling down from
their sugar canes over the wheat field and was that not the
brouhaha that broke out when Philomel got to her feet up on

the table and pissed in the ciborium and tied the mournful ban-
derilla noodles into knots the ugliest and richest counting and
recounting all her troubles sang the copla of her fingers under-
neath the table with her cousin but her oh so pesky uncle
Gumersindo acting like he didn't see him climbed up in a flash
and running to the mountain put his nets out in the bushes and
not with decoy nor with linnet launched his pigeon call and sly
maneuvers and right there was the heaviest and best part of the
story nor were shots heard nor were sighs the girl was in no
mood for tragedies or comedies the never ending story was
already dry and stale the spume that glazed it smacked of jas-
mines and carnations also spikenards as the cold that cracked the
naked body of the saint did also gnash and smash the flesh of
goatskin full of water and perambulating down the ogive of the
rear end of the heap of broken roof tiles scattered at the rocky
seaside with its cliffs of charcoal blue its look so very roguish
that it was in this way that the priest draws pleasure from his
fried eggs and potatoes

chapter one raw owl's eye here follows and links up the novel but
this time is neither wise nor foolish and not such a good example
since the letter that they got and dropped into the box the same
day with no stamp nor trumpet made the sprig of olive and the
dove like someone swallowing a bone and sucking on the bottom
of his foot just like a sea bream such a shame that after all those
cries and those fandangos the young girls of the reverend priest
should still be showing off their charms and tricks in a small cot
that crawls with bed bugs when the hole was split in half so that
not even the most wise could patch it up in spite of any spite
back in the bed — a poster of a bullfight night by night the
green corn and the gilding of the blue frame scheme behind the
veil of the venetian blinds the door ajar her dark eyes shutting

tight but long before the light that fouls the velvet white that
eats away the razor blade starts shaking and rolls out the oil
lamp flame in middle of the hand placed helter skelter on the
carpet scrap of silk along her arm extended for the length of
the arroyo of the nib he draws with from the color of her
memory her rainbow voice and scent of fried suns and the smell
of fish and watermelons and the air of pure havanas and of
clams and basil later at 2:30 or at 3:00 that morning by the sea-
side Barcelona on Barceloneta beach some Saint Johns Night
and wrapped in scraps of paper made of silk

PART THE SECOND

9.8.58

here ends the letter and the signature follows and sets forth the
day month and year and next comes the list of the witnesses —
Don Juan Don Pedro Don Rodrigo Don the Clever Don the Firm
and Steady and Don Jaime and Don Gonzalo Don Felipe and
the whole gang of Dons and next there comes the list of the
expenses and arrears what had been paid long years ago and
what will have to be paid what the children wear and what
clothes still were at the laundry woman's house and furthermore
the oompahs and the flags propped at the corners and the cross-
ings of this loveliest of city streets surrounded by its wonder
working fountains and the freshest of all wells with sky high
heaps of watermelons and of cantaloupes with head hair free at
last from clinging grape vines coffee puddle of blue snow
whistling its choruses right at the necks of swans stuck on a
shoal of dark green ice a wagon load of tar borne by two blond
wingèd burros thick with flies who bray their donkey serenades
and their venetian lanterns on the stretched skin of the velvet
drum the violet in window frame yanked loose so violently from

box of seething quicklime up to its nostrils in the horse corral
and blown to pieces on the olive tree congealed at head of a large
hunk of bed suspended in a gush of moonlight measuring a dose
of pepper for the salsa that can make the river spin around at
bottom of the mirrored cupboard closet carried on its shoulders
by the night that gnaws a bone and sprinkles bread crumbs in
the bouillon with the light of rockets and with sweetnesses upon
the face clean shaven and rice powdered by the zephyred polecat
pussy flower gilded candied almond hurdygurdy with a crank a
garden bench in yellow with a bell that tolls a clock atop the
convent tower sugar water on the chestnut colored ocean of the
field of wheat with cobalt blue and black just on the verge of
turning sour with a lilac with the olive tree's trunk grinding
teeth against the green and silver garment with feet moistened
by a slice of juicy lemon with the dry grass of a mill its loose
hair trickling down on the crossed arms of fig trees shrubs
beyond all reason in the water wheel that thwarts the urge to
sleep

at the ambush of a day that climbs the stairway on its knees that
faces on the courtyard where its unripe almonds make a ring
around the firefly the coldness of the nightingale's chanson
aglow in the cold tufts of light a milky pellet letting down its
fringes on the blue ultramarine bedspread hanging from the
largest flag pole with white plaster daubed onto a spot of wall
splotchy with peppered ochre so that it scrapes the rind of night
already woken and discovered in an unmade bed a fallen leg left
dangling almost to the floor and with the other stretched out to
the wall and pointing up and swollen by a shower from the
moon where the four slits in the blinds suck up its white light
painted white on white and blue and dusky white and white of a
pure white and clean and white and silver

and a white that paints the wall in white blue indigo a slice and splice of gold white melon and of cacti stuck into the topknot of the lime roof of the blue crow of the open door set upright on the side of the caramel pink red wine owl of the flight of pigeons squawking on their snare drums and their brushes in the fried oil of the wings of stars that fell against the paving stones and shattered stamping on the hoofs that lead the dance up in the topmost fig tree wrapped up in a cloak with smells of sea and shellfish mouths wide open like at mass

after that the boss's and the priest's girls got on well and all together went off walking on the beach. The cousins bought them anchovies and smelts and took them out behind the pilings to catch a breath of air that at that time of night black life a wolf's maw with more light inside a pepper green like any night possessed a face more like a pear or like a handrolled cigarette than like a lily — the oldest one more wacky than a nanny goat set off a bunch of fire crackers down among the rushes and wore out Enrique's patience over swings and not quite perfect orange waters but as for the youngest and the shrewdest not the sharpest of the cousins ever saw her but later on we knew she'd run off with a guy who'd gone to hunt for crickets and who stole Enrique's watch alas Enrique poor Enrique not on his return nor even one month later did he know about the way his cock itched when he pissed from which the joke got back to him and La Rosita oh so pretty with her mare's behind and boobs like globes of gouda and so graceful did no more than wiggle her zambomba at the grandson of Perico uncle doctor underneath his cape for whom the bell tolls for a fire showing off his tricks and what he knows so he won't lose the land and touch the ground with his cojones and take aim smack at her neck for while that little girl already knew that old proverb by heart she acted dumb and

choked on the fishbone out there where she'd placed the small
red warning light along the edge of the wide-open trenchworks

this is the little missive that the bride received after three days
when opening the window tossing out the deep fried little night
birds just to juice them up

and next we come to things that really matter

350,339	loads of ordinary cock and bull shit
237,421	loads of super deluxe cock and bull shit
1,223	hundredweights of brebis cheeses
253	more hundredweights of dried figs
1,473	kilos of raisins and
2,749	tons of goose quills used for writing
7	hundredweights of ribbons in all colors
12	dozen toothless combs for bald men
2	dozen ornamental combs
one	crock in metal filled with bedbugs
	and another filled with lice
one	lamb
one	he-goat
one	pair of mules with muleteer

BY
ORDER OF
THE AUTHORITIES

the music of a village band
the girls from upstairs and from downstairs
and the mothers and the grandmothers and aunts
all in their bathing outfits with bikinis riding in an ox drawn
cart.
at three o'clock p.m. and all the lotteries past present and to
come are being drawn — the shreds of dirty kitchen rags in all
the windows

20.8.59

there leave two trucks to hose the bull ring down and slap bang
in the middle a roustabout comes on a butterfly stuck with a pin
on a wine cork on strands of electrical wiring they have hung by
the neck whole rows of spectators sticking them up on a sky full
of clouds torn apart by thunder and lightning — it's beginning
to rain and turn cold. They are stripping the women and cutting
up like confetti the monks lashed to the strings of raw sausages
puffing away on a bag pipe out in the wheat field already mowed
down and with pieces of gummy paper are affixing the postage
stamps needed to pay off the costs of the bull fight — the little
school girls are rushing in whistling and lashed to the wheels of
the truck — Consuelito the oldest climbs up on a horse and
swallows it whole — the school marm flays a half yard of her
skin then sits down on a chair in front of the bull pen where she
implants her banderillas unafraid and unpraying. The bull
comes out or it doesn't come out it's the mailman who strikes up
the band and sets off on a march with all of his family grand-
mother mother and sisters-in-law with the kiddies in tow the
youngest in strollers the big ones going on foot in their large
woolen coats and their slickers some made of leather and others
cut out of oil skin — the waves start to pummel the door and to
drop the bar right on the back of the ocean wide open and
whistling its guts out its slices of melon soiled linens a kettle of
laurel leaves corpus christi processions bathing suits footlights
covered with flies frogs in concert and bitter adhesives to flavor
the soup and the crumbs of the late starting train and the lunar
and lunatic rabbit placed in front of the poster sewn onto the
hem of the green velvet skirt like a bed full of lizards the little
boy lizards with their little girl lizards their fishing poles and
their silky gold horns their swords and their hourless watches

their ditches with hair up in buns and toupees so briny and bitter with sugar and mint with their flesh like a quince's their ears springing locks in their ropings.

THIRD SEGMENT

there did finally arrive the card announcing the festivities on monday night and next morning at dawn there were fires and worms up every ass hole and sugar palms appeared in every window the stars with pink and green cockades showed off their black hair to the sun down on their knees beside the well and touched and then retouched their makeup looking at the half moons on their fingernails and on the tiles with verdant clusters of black grapes in profile on the swarming blues the blue striped t-shirt and the greenish blue the sugared blue slapped on the pink the purple diaper of the lilac bunched up in the nest of the celestial purple of the blue omphalos of the camp bed straightened up with sunny smells of she goats and of he goats on the bank of some old mountain stream with such good spirits and no laughs or cries — at six began the dance of all the old retainers of the houses castles railroad stations taverns bakeries and tailor shops and priests and barbers serving girls for fancy ladies nursemaids road gangs — all the girls from two weeks old to forty-something years decked out with roses and carnations jasmines spikenards handed out the ritzy french toast to the young guys and the higher ups — the sister of old Montserrat and La Pamela hit the jackpot and took off beaming to the olive grove. Then Don Augusto Manuel the shameless got soused up and sopping wet out on the Andalusian's veranda. Thanks be to the presence of the Mayor's spirit nothing came to pass but things were ugly for the next six weeks not counting holidays and sundays.

Here there was no one more in charge than me said Señor Rumansos pegbox de oficio and oldest brother of his kith and kin Juan Pedro and Gonzalo de la Merced and Julia and Rufina. Left without a father from the age of two days and a half good form and cleaved from head to toe they totaled up a million hundredweights and then the knackers lugged them down there on their backs — the baby of the bunch got married at age eighty something and gave birth at month's end to a burro the other one got married to a crippled sandal weaver and she gave her husband ten blind rabbits and a partridge. The humungus woman stayed a widow well before she had the pair of water-melons that her husband owner of the flea ranch got for her one night back at the saint's fair in the plaza hidden in the little boat — the children — Pedro little Pedro we won't speak of him no more seeing how he acted flashy Manolete-like and wound up down and out tough shit and no one in his family would say hello to him he ended like a doorman in a whore house in china-town — Janete was a half a cretin but was very shrewd he acted like a jerk when he would play the lottery and won the big one — he got married with some babe the bastard daughter of the priest they said who cheated on him and gave birth from a young dimwitted bull who in the Siguenza bull ring was knocked off by El Pelao on February 13th 107 and they had to deck him out with twenty-nine pairs of fire shooting banderillas — Gonzalo went to war in Africa he went and nothing more was heard from him he didn't marry and he had no children. This family is like a paragon even today a lot of things are told about them true or false we have to factor in to our account of the corrida of this primitive humanity recorded on a post card.

The melon slices and the scraps of blotting paper upside down and snookering the surf that licks its chops over a half a water-

melon its wheel barrow rattles in the whitish foam of someone's
linen laid out on the roof — the smooth silk of her body lunges
at the nacre and the sword hilt thrust into the honey bun of
where she dances — the refrain that makes the jasmine twinkle
on the vine sings of a light that blows in from the garden warm
with love and with a pinch of blue that dangles from the grapes
— the rosy evening flavor whistles up its snail shells in its arms
it rocks a drop of dew erupting in the lambkin's fleece

an onion unwinds its strings inside the caramel awakening of
the moon — the silver lace the pigeons raise up making light of
their sad plight

[JR]

AFTERWORD

MICHEL LEIRIS

PICASSO THE WRITER,

OR

POETRY UNHINGED

...I'm already worn down by the miracle of knowing nothing in this world, not having ever learned a thing but loving lots of things to eat them up alive...

Thus speaks Picasso in a Spanish language poem, a poem that appears to be an inaugural work, no other poetic text having been found to precede it.

Free of euphonic or rhythmic constraints, and even of the constraint of rational meaning, and in a vein closer (on the whole) to Dadaist nihilism than to Surrealism, Picasso played the truant, advancing where he would, drifting with the flow of words as with that of ideas (the latter being unable to exist without the former, which are in a sense their substance, and not just their vehicle). So appear, in their abrupt singularity, most of Picasso's numerous poems, the first known to us dating from April 18, 1935, and the most recent from August 20, 1959 (fourteen years before death brought an end to a period illustrated solely by sumptuously captivating works). This last date is mentioned — as if to properly situate a diary entry — at the start of the final section of his last written work: *El Entierro del Conde de Orgaz [The Burial of the Count of Orgaz],* a theatrical sketch veering quickly towards pure poetry. This work seems to mark — in Spanish, as if the maternal language had imposed itself for these final pages as for the initial ones — the end of a literary activity covering a period of twenty-five years, over a quarter of the life of this artist, ever the friend of poets, who painted the portraits of many of those of today, of yesterday (Mallarmé), and of yesteryear (Góngora), and who included Apollinaire, then Eluard, in his most intimate circle.

A free-flowing stream that never takes on a discursive form, and which, upon its route, proves richly electric, so seems to me Picasso's writing. This writing becomes only slightly organized in his major works: his two plays — one satirical, the protagonist of which, Gros Pied, seems to incarnate a caricature of the author, and which uses as its sordid backdrop the Parisian shortages of the early forties caused by the German occupation; the other essentially lyrical and situated in a dreamlike vegetable garden in which adolescents frolic day and night, a garden haunted by fantastic apparitions including a highly tragic Pegasus, disemboweled like the horse of a picador. These two plays, *Le Désir attrapé par la queue [Desire Trapped by the Tail]* and *Les Quatre Petites Filles [The Four Little Girls],* were written over a sustained period and are more structured than the usual poems, if only due to the exchange of dialogue and to the insertion of scenic indications, which introduce an entirely different register, thus breaking the continuity of the accent. These texts, which we may presume were created with no immediate dramaturgical aim in mind, were nonetheless brought to the stage, a feat to which *El Entierro* would not normally have lent itself.... This large Spanish fresco, teeming with characters in true picaresque style, takes its title from a famous painting by El Greco. The initial dialogue form is soon cast off, as if the author, obeying only his fancy, had strayed from his initial project without canceling its early results. But, given that in the first two of these masterworks (those that did indeed see stage lights) the dialogue appears noticeably more restrained, how can we define a Picasso poem, a poem that need not be signed "Picasso" to be identified, and which runs as small a risk of error as a plastic work born of the complicity of his eye and hand acting together to create a concrete, or at least a visible object?

In moderato, disparate elements are uttered in the manner of learned truths, jumbled in Spanish or in French, sometimes simply enumerated like inventory, neither unified in statements nor resulting from metaphor, elements that may be supremely valuable or trivial, a soliloquy with no logical consequence. An eternal tense prevails (sometimes relieved by the imperative or the infinitive common to product instructions or kitchen recipes): the present indicative. The thing is here, right here, or is happening at this very moment. Profits and losses. The daily progress of a prodigious artist who, next to his work as an absolute *displayer*, kept a kind of date book, in which pell-mell are written, not what really happened but what occurred to him. Systole and diastole, diurnal and nocturnal, highs and lows, good luck and bad. As the title of the pamphlet *Trozo de piel [Hunk of Skin]*, a collection of a few of the late poems, plainly states, it is a "hunk of skin." Life itself — this "life of life" that, with death as its counterpart, is named in a reading in which the four little girls in *Les Quatre Petites Filles* participate at the beginning of act VI — life is to be drunk and eaten, with its upbeats and downbeats. A poetry at ground level, never rising above the sea, though adopting its waves and swirls.

A wave that never tires of foaming at the surface, like color or like a rainbow of colors with names (it seems) spoken almost lovingly. A risky procession of disparate objects designated by words, but which, despite the intensity of their presence, are only words, billiard balls that roll and bump, launched regularly into absurd adventures, free reining only at the level of utterance, which seems to vouch for and refer to a reality, one that eventually becomes confusingly inane. A kind of psalmody in which the impossible is often signified, in which only the clusters of vocables count, brought into play and calling to each other, occasionally to the point of attack. To virtually make happen that which reasonably could not, but which takes form thanks to an assertion that must, one might say, be believed at its word; such is the astounding power with which we find this type of writing, at each instant, to be gifted. *"Fiat lux,"* "Open Sesame": a wave of the magic wand. Let it be said, and so it is!

Sometimes — as in new versions — the same thread of text is taken up several times, creating from one version to the next a new combination of elements in new order, as if manipulating them offered a gamut of possibilities, all of which had to be tried. Elsewhere, nothing more than a shattering litany in which the word "sky" is repeated indefinitely; soon it is spiced with images, after having been so with adjectives indicating its colors to the exclusion of blue, which, tardy but not absent, appears last, thrice reinforced, a simple, perfectly secular coronation. In the end it is a dance of language rather than of the things to which the words allude, a dance not unlike a waltz of emotions, since we encounter — in parts and among other things — the affirmation of love, in passages whose savor and freshness speak by themselves and suffice to translate in the most tactile way this emotion that engulfs the entire being. A barometer of the reigning climate as well as of moods, a kaleidoscope whose elements the poet, season after season, stalking the wonder that will one day bring saturation and fulfillment, never tires of

ruminating, a devourer of reality or pseudo-realities by interme-
diary of the words that evoke them.

An adherent of the waking dream, a superplayer of ambient
sounds allowing his fingers to sleepwalk upon the keys, system-
atically forgetting his astonishing powers of construction each
time he held a pen, Picasso always found a startling equilibrium,
be it the most acrobatic, and gave in willingly — even in his
plays, poems with several voices — to fabulous interior mono-
logues hindered neither by rhetorical protocol nor by a defined
subject, sprinkled here and there with echoes of bullfights and
other memories of Spain. Picasso was an insatiable player of
words as others, obeying only their impulses, play a musical
instrument. Among the modern authors to whom we can if we
must compare him, despite his fierce singularity, in order to try
to situate him on the literary map — a man who already at the
height of his fame was overjoyed to see *Les Quatre Petites Filles*
published in Gallimard's *Serie blanche,* for this seemed to fully
consecrate him as a writer — I see only James Joyce. Joyce, in his
Finnegans Wake (here a wake, just as we have a funeral in *El
Entierro del Conde de Orgaz,* this other final work with the epic
tone of a Last Judgment), displayed an equal capacity to pro-
mote language as a real thing (one might say) — a language
that eats or drinks heartily — and to use it with as much daz-
zling liberty. This is a trait that is both common to and
distinguishes the two, as distant from one another as proved to
be, in word and in spirit, the two prestigious products of our
century: the great writer, ever Dublinese despite his exile, and
the great artist originally from a sun-filled Andalusian city.
One never hesitating to create new words, seeking to make
their meaning flourish below the surface; the other in whose
writing, suggested as well by the many calm affirmations of the

burlesquely absurd content as by the empty passages, in which
the machine mashes nothing even seemingly solid — as in the
casual tralalalala of a series of musical notes each named by
its name or else, another flash of irony, in the telling of a
rosary of numbers with no relation to the context — the *nada* of
non-sense culminates, like a black sun, in the glaucous sky of
humor.

— MICHEL LEIRIS
translated from French by Carol Volk

SELECTED EXACT CHANGE TITLES

GUILLAUME APOLLINAIRE
* THE HERESIARCH & CO.
* THE POET ASSASSINATED

LOUIS ARAGON
* PARIS PEASANT
* THE ADVENTURES OF
  TELEMACHUS

ANTONIN ARTAUD
* WATCHFIENDS & RACK SCREAMS

LEONORA CARRINGTON
* THE HEARING TRUMPET

GIORGIO DE CHIRICO
* HEBDOMEROS

SALVADOR DALÍ
* OUI

ALICE JAMES
* THE DEATH AND LETTERS OF
  ALICE JAMES

ALFRED JARRY
* EXPLOITS & OPINIONS OF
  DR. FAUSTROLL, PATAPHYSICIAN
* THE SUPERMALE

FRANZ KAFKA
* THE BLUE OCTAVO NOTEBOOKS

LAUTRÉAMONT
* MALDOROR

CHRIS MARKER
* IMMEMORY

GÉRARD DE NERVAL
* AURÉLIA

FERNANDO PESSOA
* THE BOOK OF DISQUIET

JEROME ROTHENBERG (ED.)
* REVOLUTION OF THE WORD

RAYMOND ROUSSEL
* HOW I WROTE CERTAIN OF
  MY BOOKS

KURT SCHWITTERS
* PPPPPP

PHILIPPE SOUPAULT
* LAST NIGHTS OF PARIS

GERTRUDE STEIN
* EVERYBODY'S AUTOBIOGRAPHY

STEFAN THEMERSON
* BAYAMUS & CARDINAL PÖLÄTÜO

DENTON WELCH
* IN YOUTH IS PLEASURE
* VOICE THROUGH A CLOUD
* MAIDEN VOYAGE

UNICA ZÜRN
* DARK SPRING

EXACT CHANGE 5 BREWSTER STREET, CAMBRIDGE, MA 02138
WWW.EXACTCHANGE.COM